ADVANCES IN
LIBRARY ADMINISTRATION
AND ORGANIZATION

Volume 14 • 1996

ADVANCES IN LIBRARY ADMINISTRATION AND ORGANIZATION

Editors: DELMUS E. WILLIAMS
Dean, University Libraries
University of Akron

EDWARD D. GARTEN
Dean of Libraries and Information Technologies
University of Dayton

VOLUME 14 • 1996

 JAI PRESS INC.

Greenwich, Connecticut   *London, England*

CONTENTS

INTRODUCTION

When many of us now managing academic libraries first entered the profession, "the times they are a' changing" seemed to apply to others in other organizational contexts. Academic life appeared to change gradually and libraries seemed as constants within that environment. Most certainly we refocused our organizations to meet the challenges of outreach, the challenges of first, then second generation automated systems, as well as the challenges presented by the need to heighten interlibrary and networked cooperation. Fundamentally, however, we always believed that, because libraries were conservative organizations, change would be incremental and digested with relative ease and that we would be provided with the same relatively secure future we had known in the past. But as I write this Introduction, I clearly remember *The New York Times'* early March 1996 series that provided a candid, disturbing look at the "downsizing of America."

For many in academia there is still little resonance with the millions of casualties of organizational restructuring, corporate downsizing, and mergers. Still it's hard not to feel the twitch of anxiety when we read articles like those in the *Times'* series, articles which describe in excruciating detail the pain, suffering, and uncertainty which attends much of our present organizational life. We wonder just when our own college or university will be caught up by external forces and be forced to radically restructure as governments have. It would be folly to assume that higher education, especially private higher education, can somehow remain unaffected by the forces that are shaping business and government. And yet there is precious little evidence to date that more than a handful of institutions of higher education have reinvented themselves or begun the difficult task of fully analyzing their internal processes.

Nonetheless, in halting and typically conservative fashion, most academic library administrators have kept pace in the implementation or adaptation of organizational currents including the emphasis on teams, the viewing of the library as a learning organization, the renewed emphasis on customer orientation and total quality management, and the practice of business process reengineering. New ways of cooperation across organizational lines are being explored, new approaches (at least for libraries) toward investing in human resources are being proposed and implemented. And new means for harnessing technology are being capitalized upon to make our work more efficient and responsive to changing expectations.

Perhaps I am especially sensitive to the difficulty and challenge associated with organizational renewal, having recently led an extensive restructuring of the libraries and academic technology services with which I'm associated. What has been most apparent to me (as if I shouldn't have known it all along) was the tremendous anxiety experienced by nearly all of my staff as we embarked on a lengthy organizational reinvention process, one that likely will have no end. Certainly, the anxiety was apparent among those who feared that their roles and jobs might be changed appreciably—and some were—following the reorganization; but anxiety was apparent, also, among those I had initially thought of as change-leaders. Even when accomplished with energy, insight, and caution, transforming a library today can be fraught with land mines, nearly always hidden. Some staff that seemed so eager for change surprised me with the depth of their resistance while others that I had supposed would raise fierce roadblocks have pleasantly surprised me. Perhaps it is only that I am a poor judge of people, which I will not dismiss. It is true that nine months into the change process, while the changes so far have been implemented with care, there appears only one constant: We are all *very* tired at the end of the day. Attending to change requires massive amounts of physical and emotional energies.

In this volume of *ALAO* you will *not* find contributions from library administrators who have had to radically downsize their libraries as a result of parent university restructuring and downsizing. And yet we know that this has happened and likely will continue to happen in the future. Perhaps such selected experiences might form the basis for a future volume. Del Williams and I share the opinion that the contributors which form this volume of *ALAO* have been thinking about practical and solid, if not always novel or comprehensive, ways of changing the way we use human resources and technology. Many have been engaged with the development of collaborative approaches to the creation of more responsive client-focused libraries. All have participated in the creation of library organizations that truly learn from their opportunities, both missed and grasped. The contributions of Geri Bunker and Barbara Horgan and that of James Marcum make use of the organizational learning concepts suggested by Peter Senge in *The Fifth Discipline: The Art and Practice of the Learning Organization*. Erik de Bruijn and Margaret Friesen of the University of British Columbia present a comprehensive and thoughtfully developed approach to library staff training based on some of the best practices now emergent in academic libraries, while Linda Marie Golian and Michael Galbraith offer a fresh look at mentoring programs and their value to the change-receptive library. Providing two slants on the transformed roles of reference librarians, Robert Burkhardt and Marilyn Lary suggest means through which libraries can reinvent front-line information services that are, at once, client-sensitive and continually adaptive. The volume concludes with Onadell Bly's overview of the literature concerned with the rapidly converging paths of academic libraries and computing centers and Rashelle Karp's extensive review of the literature of joint use libraries.

Kierkegaard once told a story about a man who, upon getting paid, walked to town and spent his money on a pair of new shoes and stockings, good times and much drink. Trying in his drunken state to get home that evening, he lay down in the middle of the highway and fell asleep. Then along came a wagon, and the driver shouted to him to move or he would run over the man's legs. The drunken peasant awoke then, looked at his legs but did not recognize them because of the new shoes and stockings. So he told the wagon driver:

"Drive on, they're not my legs." It seems to me that our chief challenges today and for the foreseeable future relate to our capacity to sustain agile libraries while remembering that changes in what we put on our "legs" makes them no less ours. To accomplish this we must select and keep self-aware professional and support staff, people who recognize and appreciate the traditions that have anchored us deeply within a historically-rich profession. These traditions , at least in their finer moments, have met new challenges with healthy measures of self-criticism and self-awareness, and the successful library will be the one that is prepared to change while remaining aware of that which has always made libraries valuable. Workplace transformation taking place around us will be crucial to our continued health as a profession, but it will not be sufficient without an eye to what it is that we do well.

Edward D. Garten
Co-editor

STRATEGIC COLLABORATIVE MODELS:
INFORMATION TECHNOLOGY AND THE LIBRARY

Geri R. Bunker and Barbara Horgan

The past two decades have been characterized by a plethora of new management theories which claim to have solutions to difficulties facing organizations in the information age. These include the learning organization, the use of teams, Total Quality Management (TQM) and Business Process Reengineering (BPR). In this paper we suggest that while none of these theories is a panacea, there are elements in each which can promote collaboration between libraries and information technology (IT) organizations and can foster their continued growth as "learning organizations."

None of these theories is truly new. One of the most popular, TQM, was initiated in the 1950s by W. Edwards Deming and adopted first by the Japanese. Interest in the learning organization started in the early 1970s with Don Michael's book *On Learning to Plan–and Planning to Learn* (Senge, 1990, p. xii). BPR is a more recent phenomenon of the early 1990s, whereas the use of teams is as old

Advances in Library Administration and Organization,
Volume 14, pages 1-38.
Copyright © 1996 by JAI Press Inc.
All rights of reproduction in any form reserved.
ISBN: 0-7623-0098-1

as athletic competition. While each of the management fads or strategies we describe has kernels of insight, we contend that the concept of the learning organization as described in Peter Senge's *The Fifth Discipline: The Art & Practice of the Learning Organization* integrates many of the other strategies' insights, embodies the most comprehensive approach for organizations adapting to change and outlines techniques and theories that can help library and IT staff work together more effectively.

The fall 1994 issue of *Cause/Effect*, a publication of CAUSE (the association for managing and using information resources in higher education), was dedicated to information technology and library relationships. In that issue, collaboration is variously defined as "working together toward shared group goals" and "the process of shared creation" (Kiesler, 1994, p. 8). In both of these senses, collaboration between librarians and information technologists is seen as valuable, even necessary. The need for these two groups to collaborate arises from convergence of their missions, user demands for coordinated services, competition for resources, and advances in electronic storage, retrieval and sharing of information. Moreover, the pace of technology requires rapid yet flexible responses, not protracted haggling over territories, roles and responsibilities. What's needed are strategies to accelerate the collaborative process; strategies adaptable enough to deal with change yet creative enough to foster both internal and external cooperative efforts. Furthermore, these strategies should be seen as a means to the end of satisfying client needs for integrated information services as well as methods to sustain continuing dialogue, innovation and organizational growth.

Moving from separateness to synergy can be facilitated by the selective use of certain management methods. These techniques include the use of teams, changes in reporting structures, integration, outsourcing, commitment to a shared vision, cross-pollination, as well as elements of some popular external-stimulus approaches such as the learning organization, TQM and BPR. The success of these strategies in the collaborative setting depends upon library and computing leaders' willingness and ability to embrace a common vision, articulate a clear direction, share risks, accept new responsibilities and ensure commitment of their staffs to the shared vision.

These partnerships imply long-term commitment to working on the relationships among collaborating entities. Rosabeth Kanter described eight conditions for successful collaboration (Kanter, 1994, p. 100). She argues persuasively that truly advantageous partnerships require real commitment to the relationships themselves and not mere attention to the benefits of any one specific deal. Like good marriages, relationships between libraries and IT organizations need to meet certain criteria for ensured success. Among these, Kanter lists:

- individual excellence of each of the partners independently
- long-term goals of each organization which include the relationship itself as an important strategy
- the partners' complementary skills and assets
- investment of resources
- open flow of information
- integration developed through working linkages and connections
- the relationship's formal status within the institution
- integrity as displayed by mutual respect between the partners.

Whichever management methods are selected, collaborating organizations must explicitly commit to promoting the health of the long-term relationship through learning together and maintaining meaningful dialogue.

STRATEGIES—THE LEARNING ORGANIZATION, TEAMS, TQM, AND BPR

Some of the strategies we will discuss began, quite predictably, in the business world. It is perhaps somewhat ironic that "the learning organization" was first embraced in business and not in higher education. Nevertheless, each of the four popular strategies that we review has promise for dealing effectively with some of the problems facing higher education today: shrinking budgets, retraining the workforce, demands for accountability and lack of coordinated services. Peter Ewell contends in *Total Quality and Academic Practice* that not only are times difficult for colleges and universities; there are also different things happening which cannot be dealt with by the usual belt tightening alone. Taxpayers are unwilling to support further increases, no matter how worthy the cause. Increasingly demanding consumers are asking for quality service delivered at lower cost, "a linkage that for higher education has been virtually unimaginable" (Ewell, 1993, pp. 50-52). Ewell argues that times are in fact different and therefore require a new way of managing, which he believes the Total Quality approach offers.

Although many schools and businesses are adopting Total Quality approaches and other popular strategies as panaceas, there are present significant difficulties which can sabotage their wholesale introduction and success. First, these solutions are very resource-intensive, requiring additional staff and money for training and consultants at a time when most institutions are strapped for resources. Second, they take a long time to achieve results when the crisis in higher education demands rapid response. Third, maintaining current operations and services while undertaking organizational change of the magnitude suggested by TQM and BPR is very difficult. Fourth, using consultants to introduce these new programs may become an addiction. Also, consultants often present packaged training plans not suited to the organization or its culture.

In addition, much of the literature and research focuses on business models of the adaptation of these techniques. There are significantly different variables to consider in an academic setting. Faculty autonomy, for instance, can preclude the "total" adoption of a strategy throughout the organization—the approach advocated by management gurus and more easily achieved in corporations. The reluctance of leaders in higher education to play an aggressive and creative role, as many corporate chief executive officers have done, is another barrier to implementing these new management strategies in higher education. Although it is common to speak of the education process, educators do not often think of teaching as a "process" to be analyzed and measured the way business processes are.

Many leaders in higher education, however, recognize the need to respond to the serious problems they face with new strategies; the traditional methods are no longer working in a rapidly changing environment. These leaders are deciding to direct or redirect resources toward strategies with long-term results, encouraging the synergistic efforts of teams and promoting organizations that can learn and grow. Nowhere are changes more rapid and dramatic than in information technology and libraries. Therefore, these two organizations are ideally poised to take advantage of new management strategies, both for their own organizational improvement and for the promotion of collaborative efforts between them. Rather than adopting any one approach entirely, librarians and IT professionals may find portions of these techniques promote improved client service, synergy, adaptation to change, and reorganization of outmoded structures.

The Learning Organization

All these strategies have been labeled as management fads, to be supplanted by the next generation of "new" ideas. Peter Senge describes this succession in the introduction to *The Fifth Discipline: The Art and Practice of the Learning Organization* when he explains how he "suddenly became aware that 'the learning organization' would likely become a new management fad." Senge also recognized that besides being a fad, the work being done "represented a unique perspective and body of knowledge that could contribute to organization learning." He wanted "to put a stake in the ground" at the beginning of the fad cycle in hopes of having a more long-term impact, so that the fad cycle did not end before the capabilities of the perspective were realized (Senge, 1990, p. ix).

The Fifth Discipline represents Senge's "stake in the ground" by describing five disciplines that contribute to organizational learning: systems thinking (the "fifth" or integrating one), personal mastery, mental models, shared vision and team learning. Senge defines discipline as a "body of theory and technique that must be studied and mastered to be put into practice" (p. 10). The five disciplines of the learning organization provide "theory and techniques" that can also promote effective working relationships between libraries and IT groups. The focus of the disciplines on developing "an organization that is continually expanding its capacity to create its future" (p. 14) is ideally suited to the task that lies ahead for these two entities. The changes in technology occurring now that necessitate collaborative efforts will be followed by other changes to which libraries and IT organizations must adapt through continued growth, openness and dialogue. The disciplines also provide mechanisms for recognizing and letting go of outmoded or untested assumptions as well as for recognizing interrelationships and processes of change rather than mere events.

One of the most powerful of Senge's five disciplines, the concept of mental models—"deeply ingrained assumptions and generalizations... that influence how we understand the world and how we take action" (p. 8)—helps explain why many ideas or insights into outmoded organizational practice fail to be realized. The reason for this failure may be that these new ideas conflict with powerful, tacit mental models that people are unwilling to give up. The mental models held by librarians and information technology staff are, no doubt, often in conflict. Descriptions of the differences in their cultures are too numerous to cite. Not only do these conflicting views exist; they are often not explicitly stated, questioned and discussed in dialogue to generate creative solutions for working together productively.

At Gettysburg College, for example, different questions asked about these two groups' cultures produced different results in terms of their ability to work together. When a survey of organizational culture was first done of library and computing services' staff, the two groups appeared to be 180 degrees apart in their openness to change, proactivity, and flexible work environment. When the two groups were queried about their desired future (as opposed to present) environment, the descriptions were remarkably similar. This similarity convinced college leadership that these two groups could be merged successfully (Aebersold and Haaland, 1994).

Some of the tools used to uncover and deal with mental models are "advocacy," or making your own views explicit, and "inquiry," asking others to make their views clear. Senge points out that managers are adept as advocates and usually less successful with inquiry, but balancing both skills is essential for dialogue, a form of discourse which attempts to go beyond any one individual's understanding. For Peter Boehm, a contemporary physicist interested in systems thinking, the results of dialogue are described this way: "People are no longer primarily in opposition, nor can they be said to be interacting, rather they are participating in the pool of common meaning, which is capable of constant development and change" (Senge, 1990, p. 241). "Dialogue is different from discussion in which the subject of common interest may be analyzed and dissected from many points of view" (p. 240).

Although not all discourse can rise to the level of dialogue, both Senge and Boehm suggest that it is at this level where team learning, shared vision, and organizational growth can be achieved. In *The Fifth Discipline* and *The Fifth Discipline Fieldbook* (1994), Senge and others provide exercises and guidelines for mastering the discipline of balancing inquiry and advocacy. These guidelines cover how to advocate one's own views, how to inquire into others' views and how to overcome hesitancy to express views or experiment with alternative ideas[1] (Senge, 1990, pp. 200-201).

Uncovering mental models, encouraging dialogue, building shared vision and team learning have obvious applicability to collaborative efforts. The concepts of systems thinking and leveraged action are less obvious but no less powerful as techniques for promoting library and information technology partnerships. The essence of systems thinking is "seeing interrelationships rather than linear cause-effect chains and seeing processes of change rather than snapshots (events)" (Senge, 1990, p. 73). Systems thinking emphasizes feedback loops, recognition of recurring structures (archetypes), and circles of causality. As we diagram the reinforcing and balancing feedback loops of systems thinking, where one action influences another, we come to recognize certain "systems archetypes, structures that recur in our work and personal lives again and again" (p. 92).

By diagramming and recognizing these repeating patterns of behavior, we see opportunities for "leveraged action," a term Senge uses to connote "a change which—with a minimum of effort—would lead to lasting significant improvement" (Senge, 1990, p. 64). Clearly the discipline of systems thinking, when learned and practiced by IT and library managers and staff, can increase understanding of the dilemmas they jointly face and the leveraged actions they can employ to effect solutions or improve processes. The graphical nature of the feedback loops makes them an effective tool for team or work group discussion and dialogue.

Systems Thinking In Action

An extremely important collaboration, one which is emblematic of the systems approach to problem solving, is bearing fruit at the University of Washington today in the form of the Integrated Advanced Information Management Systems (IAIMS) Project, funded by the National Library of Medicine. This work reflects profound commitment to improving delivery of health care through the promotion of "efficient, rapid access to information essential to progress in administration, patient care, education, and research ... in our nation's academic health centers" (Association of Academic Health Centers Study Group on Information Sciences, 1991). The multiphase, multimillion dollar effort is one of several funded across the nation and proposes to "enrich and extend our integrated information systems infrastructure through the development of intelligent systems interface(s), networks, availability of databases and other information resources, training of faculty, staff and students to use the technology and by creation of tools to empower the users in our increasingly electronic environment" (Fuller, 1993, p. 1).

Participants and driving forces at the UW include the Director of the Health Sciences Library and Information Center, who also serves as Coordinator, Health Sciences Information Systems Integration; the Associate Vice-President for Computing & Communications; the deans of the six medical schools and the directors of two medical centers as well as the Medical Centers Information Systems. This high-level commitment is realized and nurtured by ongoing collaboration of "researchers, educators, clinicians, librarians, policy makers, information technology experts and administrative staff" who use the best practices of other institutions engaged in like development, and who "focus on people instead of technology" (AAAHC, 1991, p. 1).

This type of planning and implementation simply is not possible without a profound understanding of the complex matrix which defines health and patient care information. A systems approach is prerequisite to solving the problems inherent in integrating health information in a meaningful way for health care providers. This collaboration is an example of the mastery Senge speaks of when he describes systems thinking. "The art of systems thinking lies in being able to recognize increasingly (dynamically) complex and subtle structures...amid the wealth of details, pressures, and cross currents that attend all real management settings. In fact, the essence of mastering systems thinking...lies in seeing patterns where others see only events and forces to react to" (Senge, 1990, p. 126).

Seeing Change as a Constant within the System

It is critical to an organization's stability that the inevitable forces of change be seen in the context of the long-term learning process. From top management on down, openness to changing traditional patterns and structures must be encouraged and seen as a positive and inevitable force. Change should be expected and even anticipated as a source of opportunities. Library and IT managers should, both separately and jointly, review evolving roles in their organizations. Rather than encouraging competing for niches, a systems approach implies the adoption of an inclusive attitude which views library and information technology positions as all part of the same "job family" (Woodsworth and Maylone, 1993).

In an organization which has the capacity to learn, managers create the environment and provide resources needed to adjust to change; staff identify opportunities for improvement and implement change. Listening to clients and to each other is an important part of this process. Regular time together—in joint meetings, shared working spaces, collaborative projects—encourages communication and questioning of current practices in IT organizations and libraries. Used appropriately, job sharing spreads expertise and responsibility for operational functions across units and organizations.

Peter Senge uses an analysis technique he calls the "left hand column" to encourage open dialogue and dealing with the type of hidden assumptions which can block real communication among librarians and IT professionals and consequently their ability to collaborate and respond to changing conditions. The process begins by choosing an exchange between two speakers, recording what was said in the right-hand column, and adding what was being thought in the left-hand column. Not only does this exercise expose hidden agendas and assumptions, if undertaken in the proper spirit, it can show "how we undermine opportunities for learning in conflictive situations" (Senge, 1990, pp. 195-197).

Four of the five disciplines of the learning organization—mental models, shared vision, team learning and systems thinking—appear to be valuable strategies for advancing collaboration between libraries and information technology organizations. Personal mastery, another of the disciplines, depends more on an individual's willingness to articulate his or her vision and commit to achieving it. In organizations, the leadership's clarity and strength of vision is often a critical factor in the success of its endeavors. Only when management and staff both feel that they have the power to set personal and shared goals and achieve them will chances for success be maximized. Emphasizing personal mastery when setting goals for collaboration, therefore, enhances the opportunities for effective working relationships.

Certain other techniques which are part of the practice of the disciplines—advocacy and inquiry and leveraged action, for example—provide tools for improved communication, an essential component of collaboration, as well as new ways of looking at shared problems and solutions. Other management fads have elements that foster learning organizations as well. We look at those elements they possess that promote organizational growth, adaptation to change, understanding of processes and cycles, and opportunity for enhancing collaborative efforts between IT organizations and libraries.

Teams

The use of teams is central to all of the new management theories. It is seen as a positive force for worker empowerment, client satisfaction, coping with change, the breaking down of organizational barriers and creating opportunities for synergy or "team learning" as Senge defines it. According to Jon Katzenbach, a team may be defined as "... a small group (less than 20 persons) with complementary skills, committed to a common purpose and set of specific performance goals. Members are committed to working together to achieve the team's purpose and hold each other jointly and fully accountable for the team's results" (Katzenbach, 1993, p. 24).

Teams, when working effectively, feature certain strengths and offer powerful benefits. Among these are the following.

- Teams offer an optimal management method for performance-driven initiatives (i.e., they work best under pressure—they get results).
- Combining the skills and experience of many people almost always creates a synergy which exceeds any individual's skills and experience.
- Joint development of goals and methods fosters communication skills necessary to real-time problem solving (i.e., as conditions change and new problems and opportunities arise, communication enables flexibility and responsiveness).
- Teams provide a unique social dimension that enhances the work and makes performance its own reward. Being part of something larger than oneself is a strong motivator.

If team members are trained, their skill sets are broadened; employees increase their value to the organization by cross-training, gaining a wider perspective and embracing the mission of the whole organization.

- If empowered with decision-making authority, teams can adapt quickly to change. This is critical given the rapid rate of change in the technology-driven environment of the knowledge industry.

Conversely, the use of teams also implies some risks, challenges and constraints.

- A team will eventually fail if the organization is not performance-driven.
- When teams fail, morale sinks and cynicism soars.
- Politics constantly fight with performance drivers.
- Reward systems need overhauling in most organizations today. All too often, it does not "pay to play" (instead, workloads are increased).

Teams, when trained, trusted and supported, can offer win/win solutions for libraries and IT organizations facing performance challenges. Because teams are highly adaptive, the team approach is an enduring strategy; skills learned by one team are transferable to new tasks and changing situations. But using teams to promote synergy will only be successful under certain conditions. Across and within the organizations, teams only thrive where there is excellent verbal and written communication, a high level of interpersonal trust and authority residing in the team for decision-making.

What is typically missing, both within an organizational unit and across the organization generally, is a clearly articulated and commonly embraced understanding of:

- the mission of the parent and constituent organizations
- specific team purposes and objectives
- service level agreements between the partners
- reward structures for team participation.

The importance of successful team play is underscored in the popular work, *Reinventing Government*:

If we are to tap the skills and commitment of development specialists, teachers, and environmental protection officers, we cannot treat them like industrial workers on an assembly line. Employers of all kinds have learned the same thing: to make effective use of knowledge workers, they must give them authority to make decisions. Management fads come and go, as all public employees know. But participation is not a fad; it is all around us, in virtually every industry (Osborne and Gaebler, 1992, p. 30).

At Oregon State University, a team-based organization was developed by integrating the university library and computing services. Through a combination of team-based and leader-based decision making, the stresses inherent in this change were managed. The leader focussed the attention of cross-organizational teams on various "hot issues" and held a retreat where the teams gave their reports. The leader then offered some proposals to manage the changes needed and the teams responded to her proposals. Through a process of soliciting feedback from the entire staff, revising the proposals according to this input and forming new teams to manage the transition, the information services division managed tremendous change for the benefit of all. Barriers between the library and the computing staff were bridged, and new teams were able to design a new building to house the team-based service organization (Hughes, 1994).

Gettysburg College also used a teams approach to manage the transition to a new organization, Strategic Information Resources, that combined computing services and the library. A core and an extended team were set up to undertake the creation of project deliverables and manage communication about the process of Business Process Renewal or BPR. After further work with all staff to identify departmental activities and cycles, three more BPR teams were created—Planning, Response, and Training. Three more teams are planned for the near future—New Initiatives, Operations and Selections; all of these are intended to be cross-functional and will have both library and computing representatives (Aebersold and Haaland, 1994).

Where there is no clear performance initiative, working groups, which focus on individual performance, are sometimes more appropriate than teams. In higher-management situations or in areas where the organization's large size and/or entrenched bureaucracy prevents the formation of a performance-driven team, a working group may be effectively employed. An organization which is capable of examining its assumptions and learning new strategies will use teams and working groups in appropriate circumstances. De Paul University, for example, restructured its Information Technology Division entirely in eighteen months during 1993-1994, resulting in a lean, flattened and cross-functional organization with seven work groups based upon function, new job responsibilities and new job skill sets. A teams approach was emphasized throughout the division within and across work groups, and cross-functional teams are now responsible for most division projects.

Even within the sphere of team work, however, many organizations suffer from learning disabilities and need help exposing and overcoming their faulty assumptions. Organizations must be able to examine their practices and culture to ferret out attitudes that prevent learning and the effective use of collaborative teams (Senge, 1990, pp. 18-25). Senge identifies seven conditions which are familiar to all of us:

1. "I am my position"—employees over-identify with their own tasks and functions, leading to an inability to take responsibility for the work of the whole organization. Workers become inflexible and excessively focussed on the importance of just part of the whole.
2. "The Enemy is Out There"—actually flows from the first disability, in that there is no systemic understanding of the work of the organization and its place within its environment. Failures are blamed on "external" circumstances rather than being understood as failures to adjust internally to some shift in the environment.
3. "The Illusion of Taking Charge"—or becoming "proactive" is seductive. All too often, instead of initiating an action based on introspection and an understanding of our place in the system, we disguise a defensive move as proactive.
4. "The Fixation on Events"—especially current events, as causative, leads to a short-range perception of our threats and challenges. Ironically, it is the gradual processes which tend to destroy organizations and societies, for example "the arms race, environmental decay, the erosion of a society's public education system, increasingly obsolete physical capital..." (p. 22).

5. "The Parable of the Boiled Frog"—wherein the frog is warmed slowly but steadily, from grogginess to death, even though he is unrestrained in the hot water. Organizations lose their ability to sense threats to their survival as a result of their fixation on recent events, when that fixation obscures the pattern unfolding over time.

6. "The Delusion of Learning from Experience"—for instance, we are not truly able to directly experience the consequences of our decisions. This is true because critical decisions have system-wide results, many of which are not felt for decades. We do not get to benefit from trial and error in important arenas, and therefore we cannot practice and reinforce good decision-making skills. We split large organizations up into units in order to better understand the subsystems, then get lost in the turf-wars which result.

7. "The Myth of the Management Team"—the same managers who assumed responsibility for the subsystem soon become the defender of the turf. When placed on teams in these circumstances, managers spend their time posing in an attitude of cohesion. Disagreements are not aired, so learning is stifled. Collective inquiry is threatening to most people educated in America (we must individually come up with all the answers).

To make a teams approach really work requires significant commitment by the parent organizations and a willingness to overcome these learning disabilities and work together. Creating learning organizations requires commitment of tangible resources as well as dedication. To embark half-heartedly upon teams-building, such as, without proper allocation of resources for training and planning, is to court disaster. Performance is further hampered when teams are allowed to stagnate or are not supported enthusiastically by upper management. Teams can be successful only if properly planned and adequately supported in an environment where learning is a commonly embraced value and open inquiry is the order of the day.

Total Quality Management

Another popular management strategy for improving service operations is Total Quality Management. While TQM evolved with

Edward Deming in the 1950s, it was not until the mid-to late 1980s that it became popular in this country. For Deming, TQM consisted of fourteen points or steps[2], which had to be embraced by the entire organization, including "create constancy of purpose toward improvement of product and service" and "break down barriers between departments" (Butterfield, 1991, pp. 50-59; Deming, 1982). More recent definitions of TQM, such as Philip Crosby's "conformance to requirements" (Crosby, 1979, p. 15) and the American Society for Quality Control's (ASQC) "systematic approach to the search for excellence," are briefer.

The Malcolm Baldrige National Quality Award, established in 1987 as a private/public partnership to encourage quality in American companies, elaborates on several aspects of quality and requires extensive documentation by those who apply for the award in these categories: Leadership, Information and Analysis, Strategic Quality Planning, Human Resource Utilization, Quality Assurance of Products and Services, Quality Results, and Customer Satisfaction (the last being the most heavily weighted) (Brown, 1992). Most quality approaches, though, have the following elements: client focus, empowerment of all employees, strong emphases on training, teams, benchmarking and continuous process improvement.

Although TQM began in business, higher education has adopted it as a strategy more recently, in some cases under the sponsorship of a corporation (Robinson, Akers, Artzt, Poling, Galvin, and Allaire, 1991). *Change, the Magazine of Higher Learning*, published an entire issue dedicated to TQM on campus in May-June, 1993, which included articles from many institutions which have jumped on the TQM bandwagon: Georgia Tech, Penn State, the University of Maryland, Maricopa Community Colleges and the University of Wisconsin (Seymour, 1993). Most institutions began their TQM efforts by focusing on improvement of administrative operations and processes. More recently academic productivity and "quality" are seen as areas for improvement, and many business schools have implemented quality techniques in their programs (Benke and Hermanson, 1992).

In the earlier cited example of Oregon State University, team learning was successful because all staff had been trained in team process and functioning as part of a university-wide TQM effort sponsored by the IBM corporation. The library was one of the first areas on campus to participate in the TQM effort. Karyle Butcher

describes the early reluctance and later acceptance of the techniques
in "TQM: the OSU Library's Experience" (Butcher, 1993, pp. 45-56).
Adoption of TQM approaches, in fact, led to the eventual decision
to place library and computing under one administration in a move
to improve processes and provide greater coordination of services.
Because of TQM and team training, this merger is becoming more
than just an umbrella organization for the two groups. Instead, a
shared understanding of how similar operations can be combined for
the benefit of the institution, its mission and its community, is arising
from the cross-functional teams.

The Maricopa Community College System has been a leader in
TQM initiatives in both administrative and academic areas. More
recently, their TQM efforts have been combined with initiatives for
the learning organization. On the academic side, faculty have been
reexamining the learning paradigm through round table discussions,
applying continuous quality improvement to the classroom and
exploring the use of systems thinking for the improvement of
instruction. Current activities in enabling change that have been
initiated by IT at the Maricopa Community Colleges include:

- the new strategic planning methodology called "the learning
  action plan" (Balzer, 1994);
- the personal action plan for each individual;
- the reengineering and system development of major new
  systems efforts;
- executive leadership with the Board of Trustees and college
  presidents; and
- use of cross-functional teams that include students.

As with the OSU example, Maricopa is selecting strategies from
among the different management fads: TQM, the learning
organization, teams and Business Process Re-Engineering (BPR).
Before we describe this last-mentioned strategy and its links to the
others, it may be helpful to summarize the benefits of TQM, its pitfalls
and how it can promote the learning organization and the
collaborative efforts of libraries and IT.

The strengths of TQM are that it focuses on the client, can lower
costs while providing better, more timely service and that it brings
strength and depth to organizations by empowering employees. It

also provides a structured method for improving processes and measuring results.

Like the disciplines of the learning organization, the TQM approach uses teams to examine processes and challenge assumptions. The danger in this strategy is that the process can become an end in itself, rather than a means to improve client satisfaction, business processes and synergistic learning. An excessive proliferation of teams without addressing client needs and institutional goals can sometimes result. Senge also feels that TQM is not always an effective tool for dealing with the dynamic complexity facing most organizations today, and certainly libraries and IT departments (Senge, 1990, p. 267). Instead, he thinks that understanding systems archetypes and leveraged action will uncover underlying causes that might be glossed over using the quality approach.

As the Maricopa Community Colleges example demonstrates, some higher education institutions are using TQM in combination with systems thinking to create a learning organization, viewing the strategies as complementary rather than exclusive. Understanding the systems archetypes (recurring organizational structures that can inhibit growth) and mental models, for instance, can reveal why TQM efforts are not always successful and suggest leveraged actions to improve the success rate. At OSU, because of an understanding of TQM concepts, the staff were able to achieve the synergy Senge describes as "team learning" to effect a transition to a new organizational structure using library and IT staff on cross-functional teams.

Benchmarking, an important component of the TQM approach, is an assessment tool which can be employed as a leveraged action. The term can connote constant statistical monitoring of processes; but more broadly defined, benchmarking means measuring one's own organization's performance in qualitative or quantitative ways against other similar organizations which are models of successful or efficient operation. Both types of benchmarking can be used to improve client services. In addition, if librarians and information technologists learn from each other, observing and implementing each others' best practices, collaboration increases and products and services shared between organizations improve.

For example, at Seattle University, the library liaison program, which pairs librarians with departments and colleges for collection planning and development, served as a model for a "client service representative" in Information Services (the information technology department at SU). Computing staff designated as service representatives are paired with a liaison in each college or administrative area for communication about technical needs and changes as well as for planning new information technology services and training programs. This example represents a particularly relevant adoption of "best practices"—that is, the services are germane to the missions of both organizations. In *The Fifth Discipline*, Senge warns against merely "emulating a model," a practice which some businesses try to pass off as "learning from the best practices of so-called leading firms" (Senge, 1990, p. 11). Benchmarking is not an end in itself but a leveraged action to be appropriately employed within the systems thinking approach.

Another practice which has been employed in the business world and adopted by some libraries and computing organizations can also be used as a leveraged action when dealing with changing needs. This practice is outsourcing—using external resources to offer services that have traditionally been provided internally. Outsourcing can provide expertise that would be difficult if not impossible to provide in-house. Small computing organizations, for instance, often cannot afford the staffing resources required to plan and implement a campus network and must outsource wiring and even installation of network cards and software to contractors for a limited period of time. In this way, leveraging resources obviates the need to fundamentally alter staffing within an otherwise thriving organization.

Outsourcing has its dangers, however. Top financial managers can be persuaded by vendors that it is a panacea, sometimes without careful consideration of the potential consequences. When not used selectively, outsourcing can lead to dependency upon external resources. When goals, deliverables and time lines are not clearly established by the contracting organization, a lack of control can result. Just as with teams, well developed service level agreements between the parties are critical to its success but not easily developed or monitored. Rather than employing outsourcing indiscriminately, managers need to employ systems thinking to uncover where it is the most effective leveraged action to deal with a problem or reverse a downward cycle of client satisfaction with services.

Outsourcing training to introduce new concepts and techniques— including teams, TQM and BPR—is often more cost effective than using internal resources. Trainers who have expertise in these techniques are brought in to train staff, train the trainers, and/or recommend a course of action to improve service delivery and collaboration. It might be impossible to have these people on staff, and difficult to train existing staff on all the management strategies without outsourcing help. There are also dangers in employing outside help, however. Many consultants recommend standardized "packaged" approaches that are not customized to the local environment. If the techniques do not suit the local culture, there is likely to be resistance to their adoption.

At the University of Washington Libraries, creative use of outsourcing has been found to provide significant benefits. The Cataloging Division enjoys the contract services of the bibliographic utility, OCLC, for original cataloging of certain foreign language titles, Thai in particular. In addition, approval book contracts now come with options for cataloging copy included, which facilitates the Libraries' ability to collect a wide scope of materials without having to employ specialty catalogers. The same is true for U.S. Government Documents, in that vendors of bibliographic records for these documents become the producers of the original classification work. The UW also shares in a collaborative cataloging arrangement with other universities' cataloging divisions—trading local cataloging work in Arabic, for example, for work done at the University of Minnesota for Scandinavian language materials.

Business Process Reengineering (BPR)

The most recent management trend is Business Process Reengineering. According to Michael Hammer, the guru of BPR, this strategy involves a fundamental rethinking and radical redesign of business process to achieve dramatic improvements in critical contemporary measures of performance: cost, quality, service and speed (Hammer and Champy, 1993, p. 11). BPR is broader in scope and takes longer to implement than most quality programs. It is touted as a technique far more revolutionary than TQM, requiring reinventing, making sweeping changes in management and organizational structure. Jobs change from simple tasks to multidimensional work, so that workers achieve a greater sense of completion, closure and accomplishment. As with the learning organization, BPR emphasizes a need to change outdated rules and assumptions.

In BPR, the typical departmental functional divisions are discarded in favor of process-oriented teams. At the University of Idaho, for example, hierarchical and functional structures in the IT organization were disbanded to create a flat organization, with no staff member reporting to anyone but the top management team. This radical reorganization facilitated equal and open team recruitment. Now employees see themselves as team members rather than as aligned with a particular functional area. Teams are created to deal with problems or improve processes and are disbanded after the issues are resolved.

Some useful attributes of BPR are that it is client driven and it facilitates worker empowerment, giving workers authority to implement tasks which have been made their responsibility. It also forces a holistic rather than a piecemeal examination of processes. But problems occur when organizations adopt programs such as BPR without regard to local conditions and values. Unlike TQM, BPR is radical—it requires, by definition, the changing of a process rather than its improvement. It should only be embarked upon if there is commitment from the top to pursuing a radical solution; resources to facilitate that change—consultant support, money and time for training—and recognition of how BPR will impact operations.

The principle of leveraged action in systems thinking—which involves implementing action to change a cycle, an action often nonobvious and seemingly minor—is antithetical to the broad scope of BPR. In BPR, change must be sweeping and all-encompassing. For Senge, the solution to an organization dilemma lies not in the obvious "fix" of throwing out the old organization or change for the sake of change, but in looking for underlying causes of failure and a "lever" to do much with little. With the wholesale change advocated by BPR, it would seem impossible to analyze the effects of any one action.

Senge argues that the learning organization is more radical than most so-called radical approaches like BPR because the learning organization aims to change, not the way things are done, but the way we think and interact, a more basic and personal shift that allows organization to really change, learn, and grow. Two institutions which have embarked upon BPR efforts (DePaul and Gettysburg) made dramatic, fundamental changes in policy, process and practice. The human resource issues they encountered, which are often given less attention in descriptions of BPR, point to the difficulties of changing the way things are done before changing the way people think and interact.

DePaul University's restructuring of its IT division eliminated several reporting lines and consolidated units of vastly different culture and organizational structure: Information Services, Academic Computing Services, Telecommunications, and the Office of Institutional Planning and Research. Several peripheral support functions were eliminated, and duplications in functions were consolidated to achieve a single direction. Full-time headcount was reduced by 15 percent, and Business Process Reengineering was added as an ongoing function. The new division adopted a team-based horizontal structure to achieve shared values, responsiveness to institutional needs, and significantly improved performance. The design principles included using a holistic approach for the change process, employing a flat, cross-functional structure and services.

Unlike Oregon State University, however, where teams themselves developed the new organizational structures, each staff member at De Paul went through a job analysis process, all directors positions were opened for applications and the restructuring was imposed from above. Describing the lessons learned, the Vice-President for University Planning and Information Technology emphasized the importance of constant refocusing on strategic goals, training, executive sponsorship and an effective management team. Once the organization is redesigned, she indicated, further restructuring is likely. In addition, there were high human costs with restructuring and "the pace of change an IT organization undertakes depends largely on its willingness to endure pain and stress" (Chan, 1994).

Gettysburg College merged the computing services division and the library into a single division using Business Process Renewal (Gettysburg's use of the acronym BPR) and process innovation. These approaches mandated that designers of a new process ask themselves "Regardless of how we have accomplished the objective in the past, what is the best possible way to do it now?" Gettysburg started with strategic and tactical goals and developed a three-phase plan to move from initiation through direction-setting to innovation. The entire staff was involved in matching knowledge, skill abilities and personal characteristics with 45 departmental activities identified by management teams. The personnel problems encountered were anxiety about identity in the new organization and resistance to change. According to the Vice-President for Strategic Information

Resources, communication was key in reducing these problems, but "not everyone will be happy with the new arrangements, and we expect some fallout" (Aebersold and Haaland, 1994). The price that Gettysburg and De Paul paid for rapid change without prior training or involvement of the staff is increased stress and strife, the reluctance of staff to accept the change and a possible lack of shared vision.

MANAGEMENT SUPPORT AND STRATEGIES

Often organizations become so embroiled in the minutiae of their operations that they become unable to adjust their perspectives to allow innovative solutions and are blinded to new opportunities. Leadership is required, therefore, for successful implementation of any new organizational model or strategy. It is the manager, particularly the top manager, who can see the big picture most clearly, who can allocate or reallocate resources to provide training and job restructuring and who can facilitate the development of a shared vision. The manager, however, cannot dictate or mandate a shared vision. True commitment among the staff must be built through the use of the strategies we have described: uncovering and dealing with hidden assumptions as well as promoting dialogue through advocacy and inquiry skills. Other factors to consider in developing a shared vision are managing the creative tension between vision and reality, focusing on positive rather than negative visions, and understanding how the limits to growth structure can arrest the building of momentum behind a shared vision (Senge, 1990, pp. 225-230).

The New Role of Leadership

One key to success with a collaborative approach is top management's support for the strategy. Not only must the leaders believe in the collaborative effort, they must articulate that belief in terms of a shared mission, vision and goals—in meetings, jointly published statements and other visible indicators. For the concepts of the learning organization to take hold, the management teams of the library and IT organizations need to understand and embrace them first, then work with their staff to help them understand and apply the disciplines. The leader in the learning organization does not control; he or she becomes a designer, steward, teacher and manager of the creative tension between the reality and the vision of the organization.

Commitment and Enrollment

According to Senge, there are three ways in which staff can embrace an idea, mission or vision. They may comply, enroll or commit. Managers seek the last kind of support because only then do staff want the vision, feel dedicated to making it happen and allow themselves to be creative in making it a reality. With enrollment, staff may want a vision but feel that it is management's vision, not their own, and are not willing to take risks to see that it is achieved. With compliance staff may see the benefits of the vision but will only do what is expected and no more. In fact, with grudging compliance, staff do not see the benefits but do not want to lose their jobs and therefore comply. To foster enrollment and commitment to a shared vision, Senge suggests that managers follow certain guidelines: be enrolled yourself; be on the level and describe the vision as simply and honestly as you can; let the other person choose. It is a hard lesson for many managers to face, Senge asserts, that "ultimately there is nothing you can do to get another person to enroll or commit" (Senge, 1990, p. 223).

Besides building a shared vision for collaboration, management must anchor this in the governing ideas of each organization, emphasizing the similar missions and core values without ignoring the reality of differences. While it is critical to build a vision of the future, making clear the purpose or mission of the organization gives a sense of that organization's contribution to a greater whole. Core values, such as honesty, integrity, openness, equal opportunity, guide the organizations on a day-to-day basis. As Gettysburg College discovered in surveying library and computing staff, their visions of the future were similar despite different values. Discussing where the values and missions differ can provide a fruitful topic for dialogue and improved relationships. Understanding each other is key to working effectively together.

Resource Allocation

Statements of collaboration must be backed by resource allocation by top management. Allowing mid-level managers to control their budgets is a clear indicator of high-level support. Risk-taking and innovation should be promoted and supported through reward and recognition. Another consideration in resource allocation is the development of service level agreements—who will do what, provide what, in what time frame, with what response time. Anita Lowry's article "The Information Arcade at the University of Iowa," gives a recipe for success which includes "Documented agreements regarding the respective responsibilities for and contributions to the project, with specific commitments in terms of personnel, funds, and other resources" (Lowry, 1994, p. 44).

At the University of Washington, the University Advisory Committee on Academic Technology, beginning in 1988, recommended the building of strategic relationships between Computing & Communications and the University Libraries (Watts, 1990, p. 1). They also recommended increased use of centrally maintained hardware and advocated 100 percent building connectivity by 1997 using tcp/ip protocols. Many projects have come to completion through the joint work of the Computing & Communications and Libraries organizations. In all cases, resources were allocated within all participating groups, and university funding was made available as well.

At Seattle University, the Associate Vice-President for Information Services initiated a Campus-Wide Information System (CWIS) team to include not only a programmer, Help Desk Manager and a public services librarian, but also the university publications officer, the Business School computing coordinator and a representative from the student body, the largest end-user community. Team members are given a budget to accomplish tasks that require additional resources.

The Importance of Training

An important component of resource allocation for the manager is ensuring adequate time and funding for staff and management training: in the concept, structure, and effective functioning of teams; in process design and redesign; in dialogue, advocacy, inquiry; and in all the disciplines of the learning organization. These concepts all require significant practice; they are not instantly learned and commitment to them is not easily achieved. Often the first line item to be cut in the budget in times of tight funding is training when in fact it should be one of the last. The ability to deal with change effectively is critical in these times; staff need the tools to cope and even flourish in an uncertain environment. Management's commitment to staff in the form of training programs that address difficulties and promote solutions can have an enormous impact on morale and productivity.

In addition, team skills are more challenging to develop than individual skills (Senge, 1990, p. 258). Developing team learning among management team members is even more difficult, but must precede developing team learning among the staff. The problem for managers is that their environment is virtually devoid of opportunities for regular simulated practice. Management teams are most often deciding about specific situations under great pressure, with the resulting decision final as soon as it is made. Senge argues that we need more opportunities for practice, using dialogue sessions that are structured with the following guidelines: (1) Have all members of the "team" (those who need one another to act) together; (2) Explain the ground rules of dialogue; (3) Enforce the ground rules so that if anyone finds himself unable to "suspend" his assumptions, the team acknowledges that it is now "discussing" not "dialoguing"; (4) Make possible and encourage team members to raise the most difficult, subtle, and conflictive issues essential to the team's work (Senge, 1990, pp. 259-260). Such sessions also obviously have potential for combined library/IT management teams to dialogue on "the most difficult, subtle, and conflictual issues."

LESSONS LEARNED

In the following two examples, the University of Washington and Seattle University, libraries and IT organizations achieved synergistic effects through collaboration in situations where resources were scarce. Although many organizations use teams to collaborate across organizations, if some of the fundamental concepts which define the learning organization are not employed, especially the art and practice of dialogue, these collaborative efforts are often self-limiting. Groups left to struggle together without outside assistance in challenging their assumptions are often caught in dead-end discussions. The management training being offered at Seattle

University is a good example of directors making a commitment to the success of the collaboration.

The University of Washington Experience

As we have discussed, leveraging resources within an organization can often make the difference between success and failure, as some situations need but little adjustment to be rectified. Leveraging resources can also be accomplished with cross-organizational teams, which share staff, pool dollars, and provide cross-training opportunities. In 1992 the University of Washington undertook to replace its automated library management system and to build a campus-wide information system. The campus was (and is) dedicated to open networking, a uniform interface to information resources, and a collaborative approach to campus-wide computing.

In accord with the University Advisory Committee on Academic Technology's directive (Watts, 1990, p. 1), the Libraries and Computing & Communications (C&C) have jointly built an information system for the campus which includes administrative information, computing technology policies, procedures and events, the libraries' online catalog, locally mounted abstracting and indexing databases, and Internet searching tools.

They pooled funding and secured a matching amount from the university in order to replace the existing proprietary (Geac) library management system (ILS) with one which could be snugly integrated with the campus tcp/ip network. C&C's Information Systems and the University Libraries jointly negotiated a contract with Innovative Interfaces, Inc. for their unix-based ILS. This was all part of the manifestation of a well-articulated vision for networking, workstation deployment and information technology across the campus. That vision is an essential element of collaborative change in any complex environment. Public access to information and bibliographic data had been provided by the joint development of both a graphical and a character-based user interface (Willow and UWIN/Wilco). The Health Sciences Library and Information Center, in conjunction with Computing & Communications' Information Systems (IS), had earlier developed the X11/Motif based GUI (Willow, a general purpose information retrieval tool) for use with MEDLINE. With librarians and faculty guiding the functional design, and the IS programming staff using up-to-date development tools, the mix of expertise proved very successful. Willow functionality was then adapted for the lowest-common denominator interface, producing the character-oriented analogue, Wilco.[4]

Because the Innovative database is maintained in the libraries, using the Innovative Interfaces "off the shelf" system, librarians and programmers worked on small development teams, one of which produced a MARC format loader for the BRS Onsite system (which Willow and Wilco query). Librarians provided the MARC expertise, and helped the programmers to map appropriate tagged fields to BRS paragraph structures. Outsourcing was used again to preprocess the library catalog by a service provider. The libraries now regularly send their data out incrementally, to be "massaged" by authorities preprocessors. In this way, a careful mix of outsourcing and local, joint development was used in order to meet the common goals in a timely fashion, and with the resources available. By fall 1994, most of the teams had disbanded, having achieved their charges. The new services were absorbed into the operational stream, and cross-divisional advisory groups were appointed to oversee the services. Remaining interorganizational groups include the Innovative Operations Group and the Interfaces Working Group. These continue to add functionality to the base system and to enhance the users' interface to bibliographic resources.

In addition, a new set of teams has sprung up in both the libraries and within the C&C. The advent of the World Wide Web and its many browsers has spurred the need for cross-organizational planning and implementation of campus information resources. The "home team" from the C&C was given the mandate to produce a prototype Home Page for the University of Washington. Four programmers and graphics experts set to work to frame the early system. Simultaneously, the libraries prepared their own Home Page using a combination of skilled staff from throughout the system, collectively known as the Web Services Team. A Libraries Home Page was designed and built in anticipation of an early fall, 1994 release of the University Home Page, but that deployment was delayed until second semester as the "home team" attempted to incorporate the existing CWIS resources into the graphical world of the Web. It became apparent almost immediately that some overarching design decisions were needed. In order to facilitate a coherent structure, the C&C set about surveying colleges' and departments' local area administrators to assess Web usage and growth. UW Libraries was solicited to partner in the effort to fashion a taxonomy useful to any end-user. An official institutional environment, easy to navigate and easily extended, is the goal sought. Most important is the design objective of ease-of-use for the novice and professional searcher alike. A major milestone will be the agreement on a semantic schema useful to many types of information seekers. All of this collaboration is still in the very early stages. Extremely delicate handling of the issue of sphere of expertise seems to be needed. Although there is more than tacit agreement on the need for and benefits of collaboration in this project, much work is yet to be done to encourage real dialogue among the parties. The culture in both domains is rather one of "discussion" rather than one of open "dialogue," as Senge defines the terms. Both organizations will be challenged to suspend their assumptions about each others' grasp of epistemology, graphical design and information-seeking behaviors. In order for the group work to be successful, both organizations will have to take risks not lightly undertaken in such large, slow-moving bureaucracies.

The UWired project is another example of collaboration initiated by the UW Libraries, the Office of Undergraduate Education, and C&C, and then extended to faculty and Apple Computer during the 1994-1995 academic year. "The primary goal of the UWired project is to integrate electronic communication and information navigation skills into teaching and learning at the University of Washington." Focusing on sustained instruction, the project has been successful in "Bringing together librarians, computing experts, faculty, staff, and students, its purpose is to create an electronic community in which communication, collaboration, and information technology become ongoing, integral parts of teaching and learning at the University of Washington" (UWired, 1994). Students were instructed in bibliographic finding and analysis techniques, Internet navigation, and coached to develop needed information literacy skills. Sixty-five students in six "Freshman Interest Groups" (FIGs) were served over the academic year, divided into areas of academic interest in which the students lived in the same dorm and were loaned Macintosh PowerBooks with ethernet connectivity built in. The program and its Librarian sponsor received an ACRL award. Currently, expansion to triple the number of FIGs, streamline the curriculum development phase and utilize desktop rather than laptop technology is being planned (UWired, 1994).

Seattle University's Experience

Seattle University (SU), a private, Jesuit university comprising about 6,000 students, also located in Seattle, Washington, offers many contrasts to the University of Washington, a large public research institution. Because resources are scarcer at this smaller institution and there is less bureaucracy, collaborative technology projects between the library and Information Services (IS) were necessary if projects were to move forward. The library alone did not have the resources or expertise to even begin the library automation effort. After a library automation system was installed, joint projects have continued. In addition, Information Services has designed a strategic planning process for technology that includes the library as a partner, and IS has begun training to understand and implement concepts of the learning organization which it hopes to extend to improving library/IT relationships.

The first major cooperative effort, the library development project, used collaborative teams, resource sharing, top management support, and flexible boundaries to achieve the goal of meeting client needs for an automated catalog available anywhere on and off campus. When a new Associate Vice-President for Information Services (AVP) arrived at Seattle University in the fall of 1991, funds had been set aside for a library project, but the Library Director did not have access to them. Because of her recent experience in implementing an automated library system and a campus-wide network elsewhere, the associate VP was charged by the Provost to lead the automation project with the Library Director and was given funding for the project.

Before the project was initiated at several meetings between the library director and the AVP, it was decided that a white paper outlining the changing roles of the library and the similarities between its mission and that of the IT organization would be developed for discussion among the staff of each organization. Although this white paper could be considered a shared vision statement, it was developed entirely by the two managers without staff consultation, and there was no attempt to enroll or commit the staff beyond circulating the paper. Discussion of the white paper, in fact, brought out many of the conflicting "mental models" that had been causing conflict. Some librarians felt that they had been involved in information technology for longer than the IS staff recognized and that now IS was trying to take over the library. Because no mechanisms were employed, such as those described by Senge in *The Fifth Discipline*, to deal with these often untested beliefs, many of the disagreements among the staff persist. Nonetheless, at the management level there was agreement to collaborate and cooperate.

Examining the technology resources of the library, the AVP decided to ask the University Cabinet for additional funds to acquire microcomputers and to begin to network within the Library. Simultaneously, a campus-wide network project was being proposed, with future access to the library holdings from anywhere on and off campus as one of the primary benefits. The cabinet request for additional funding was accepted, and IS staff trained library staff in office automation tools and networking.

The automation team used in this effort was composed of equal numbers of IS and library professionals. Information Services contributed an under-utilized RISC machine to run the library system. They also agreed to manage hardware and provide network maintenance, to prepare and monitor the overall project plan and to perform financial and technical analyses of alternatives. The librarians developed evaluation tools and scenarios for examining functionality and setting priorities. A champagne toast ended the planning phase of the project.

Relationships, however, were sometimes strained. Librarians disliked the name "information services" being given to a computing organization and were still suspicious that IS was trying to take them over. After the selection, an implementation team including IS personnel focused on technical details, but another team, LISP (Library-IS Partnership), undertook the task of building bridges and identifying projects "beyond OPAC." The Associate Vice-President served on the Search Committee for a new Library Director, who now chairs the group. Because of the monthly meetings of LISP, the library became a key partner in developing SU's CWIS, and the library and IS now offer Internet courses jointly developed and taught.

After several months of LISP meetings, the library director and AVP decided on a new approach to dealing with their shared issues and concerns. They decided to meet biweekly to address issues and strategies and then form cross-functional teams to work on implementing proposals and solving problems. Because Information

Services has space in the library which the library would like to acquire, a discussion of how to use the space jointly has begun. The proposal of a training room, designed by IS staff with input from the library, jointly funded by IS and the library, and used by each of the groups, has been put forth. The library would own the room, schedule its use, and make available certain hours to IS for general university training purposes. Another proposal was to have the IS training materials and even the trainer housed in the room, so that it could be open for drop-in, self-paced training on software. The proposal has taken many twists and turns, but it is likely that whatever emerges will be of benefit to both parties.

What the library/IT partnership at SU has lacked so far are tools for the cross-functional teams to facilitate the collaboration and improve processes. A new initiative in IS may provide some techniques for dealing more effectively with the undercurrents of conflict and unspoken, unchallenged assumptions about each other's goals, purposes and motives. This new initiative may also promote improvement in the processes of client service delivery. Over the past few months, using outside consultants, the IS organization began training in understanding the concepts and disciplines of the learning organization. At first, all staff were given some introduction to systems thinking and leveraged action and provided with opportunities in a group setting to diagram the down-spiraling cycle of client satisfaction. The leveraged actions identified to change the cycle were translated into action plans, and cross-functional staff teams developed timetables to implement these plans. At the same time, the IS management team began more intensive training in the disciplines of the learning organization so that they could function more effectively as a team and begin to train their staff in these disciplines.

The potential benefit of this training is that the techniques can also be used to improve the library/IT relationship. By jointly exploring mental models, learning to inquire, understand and challenge each others' faulty beliefs and assumptions, the reasons for conflict can be discussed and common solutions proposed. When inaccurate mental models are removed, opportunities for real shared vision and team learning are possible. Teams can use the concepts of systems thinking, archetypes and leveraged action to explore shared problems and propose "levers" to deal with them.

CONCLUSION

Why Use These Strategies?

We have asserted that the learning organization and other management strategies that complement it will promote the goal of effective collaboration between libraries and information technology organizations. This goal is necessary for a variety of reasons: to improve and coordinate customer service, to facilitate change, to improve technology planning and services, and to build organizations that are capable of learning and growing. These approaches are not quick fixes, however, but long-term strategies that require committed leadership. In order to sustain these efforts, managers must commit to ongoing training of the workforce in team concepts, process redesign, systems thinking, advocacy and inquiry skills, and building shared vision. Leaders must develop their personal goals which include commitment to working on the relationships among the collaborating entities. New and expanded roles for staff, openness to change, ability to analyze processes and systems, willingness to expose and discard outmoded assumptions, and the encouragement of dialogue and an open flow of information are all necessary for success.

Beyond providing some mechanisms for more successful working relationships between these two groups, there are broader reasons to build learning organizations, committing ourselves and our institutions to a lifelong attempt to understand and shift the ways we think and behave. Some of these reasons are outlined in *The Fifth Discipline Fieldbook*: because we want superior performance, to improve quality for our customers, for competitive advantage, for an energized, committed workforce, to manage change, for the freedom to speak the truth, because the times demand it, and because we recognize our interdependence (Senge et al., 1994, pp. 9-12). All of these reasons speak to the situation that libraries and information technology organizations face today and in the future.

Where To Begin?

When a university, college or other organization decides to commit to using the disciplines of the learning organization, employing teams, striving for quality services, and improving processes, the next question to answer is where to begin. Central to all the management strategies we have described is the idea of teams as effective vehicles for developing shared vision and promoting synergy. A first step, therefore, is a thorough understanding of what teams are, promoted in a program of training in team structure and techniques (discussion, dialogue, advocacy, and inquiry, for example) as well as management commitment to guiding and supporting these teams with necessary resources and direction. Another early step in the process of building a learning organization is for managers to work from personal visions of the future to shared visions of what the organization can be and can accomplish.

The next steps will depend in part on the type of organization, the organizational culture, and the specific results to be accomplished. For example, highly rational cultures, like those found in computing and in libraries, may want to begin with the structured approach of systems thinking. This graphical method also lends itself to visual display for group discussion. Information technology organizations and library systems staff may find, in addition, that computer models and simulations of situations and dilemmas are helpful.

If there is a need to move especially rapidly because of a crisis or mandate for change, the executive teams of each organization may decide to begin the learning effort and assume most of the burden of change during the early phases as happened with DePaul University and Gettysburg College. If there are chronic problems that need to be addressed immediately, the best approach may be to use systems thinking to uncover fundamental causes, involving staff at every level in each organization which is experiencing the problem. After some understanding of underlying causes is established, work with mental models and team learning can expand more broadly throughout the organization.

Some organizations start with a Total Quality approach as did Oregon State University and the Maricopa Community College District. Then, with a thorough understanding of teams and process improvement, staff are able to move forward more successfully with the disciplines of the learning organization. Another approach is to use mental models to uncover the inhibitors to collaboration and effective team functioning while engaging in training in systems thinking to uncover archetypal problems and to identify possible leveraged actions. With more open dialogue established, the techniques of team learning—which incorporates advocacy, inquiry and dialogue—can help to promote building a shared vision.

This approach of learning a few disciplines simultaneously or in close succession is the one being taken in Seattle University's Information Services. In practice, the disciplines are so entwined, that it is difficult to deal with one and not at least allude to others. Also, by introducing concepts and then exploring each one in more depth, understanding increases and repeated practice accrues cumulative benefits. A commitment to ongoing training of existing staff and orientation of all new staff to the concepts and culture are critical to ensure that improvements are sustained. As one staff member at Seattle University commented, "Let's continue this training regularly or we'll slip back into our old ways."

Senge asserts that changing the way people think and interact is a radical change that can only be accomplished by a true commitment to a shared vision and team learning among all staff. Nonetheless, managers must initiate and sustain the effort through their personal vision, resource commitment and training. Executive mandates will at best produce compliance; commitment must be built, not dictated. Significant change in the way people think and relate requires tools and ongoing practice with those tools. Achieving successful collaboration is not easy, but it is a worthy goal. We believe that there are certain strategies that not only facilitate the collaborative process but also promote organizations that are flexible and responsive to changing times.

The theme of library/information technology collaboration is a popular one. Numerous case studies document schools which have attempted collaborative efforts, benefited from them and described the lessons learned. Chances for successful collaborative projects, however, are increased if certain strategies are employed from the outset. Many of these techniques are already familiar as part of current management trends for using teams, promoting quality, reengineering the organization, and developing a learning organization. These strategies include:

- focusing on client needs first
- providing and sustaining management support
- developing and articulating joint mission statements and service agreements that are more than just paper documents
- planning for change and continuous process improvement
- building flexibility into organizational structures

- considering benchmarking and outsourcing as possible leveraged actions
- negotiating ways to achieve synergistic effects
- starting with small projects before moving to more ambitious collaborative efforts
- uncovering unproductive assumptions, promoting team learning, and developing shared vision.

NOTES

1. Senge (1990, pp. 200-201)—When advocating your view:

- Make your own reasoning explicit (i.e., say how you arrived at your view and the "data" upon which it is based)
- Encourage others to explore your view (e.g., "Do you see gaps in my reasoning?")
- Encourage others to provide different views (i.e., "Do you have either different data or different conclusions, or both?")
- Actively inquire into others' views that differ from your own (i.e., "What are your views?" "How did you arrive at your view?" "Are you taking into account data that are different from what I have considered?")

When inquiring into others' views:

- If you are making assumptions about others' views, state your assumptions clearly and acknowledge that they are assumptions
- State the "data" upon which your assumptions are based
- Don't bother asking questions if you're not genuinely interested in the others' response (i.e., if you're only trying to be polite or to show the others up) When you arrive at an impasse (others no longer appear to be open to inquiring into their own views):
- Ask what data or logic might change their views.
- Ask if there is any way you might together design an experiment (or some other inquiry) that might provide new information.

When you or others are hesitant to express your views or to experiment with alternative ideas:

- Encourage them (or you) to think out load about what might be making it difficult (i.e., "What is it about this situation, and about me or others, that is making open exchange difficult?")
- If there is mutual desire to do so, design with others ways of overcoming these barriers.

2. Butterfield (1991, pp. 50-59)—Deming's 14 points:

1. Create constancy of purpose toward improvement of product and service.
2. Adopt a new philosophy.
3. Cease dependence on mass inspection.
4. End the practice of awarding business on the basis of price tag.
5. Improve constantly and forever the system of production and service.
6. Institute training on the job.
7. Institute leadership.
8. Drive out fear.
9. Break down barriers between departments.
10. Eliminate slogans, exhortation, and targets asking for zero defects and new levels of productivity.
11. Eliminate work standards that prescribe numerical quotas. Substitute leadership.
12. Remove barriers that rob hourly workers of their right to pride of workmanship.
13. Institute a vigorous program of education and self-improvement.
14. Everybody in the company must work to accomplish the transformation.

3. By permission of CAUSE, the association for managing and using information resources in higher education. "Copyright CAUSE 1994. This paper was presented at the 1994 CAUSE Annual Conference held in Orlando, FL, November 29-December 2, and is part of the conference proceedings published by CAUSE. Permission to copy or disseminate all or part of this material is granted provided that the copies are not made or distributed for commercial advantage, that the CAUSE copyright notice and the title and authors of the publication and its date appear, and that notice is given that copying is by permission of CAUSE, the association for managing and using information resources in higher education."

4. Willow and Wilco are trademarks of the University of Washington. They are copyrighted, but are available free of charge.

REFERENCES

Aebersold, D., and G.A. Haaland. 1994. "Strategic information Resources: A New Organization." *Proceedings and Archives of CAUSE '94*. [Online]. Available gopher://cause-gopher.colorado.edu/00/exchange-library/.documents/cnc9418.txt.[3]

Association of Academic Health Centers Study Group on Information Science. 1991. *Integrated Information Management Systems in Health Care*: Washington, DC.

Balzer, J. 1994. *The Learning Action Plan; A New Approach To Information Technology Planning In Community Colleges*. Boulder, CO: League for Innovation in the Community College and Cause.

Benke, Jr., and R.H. Hermanson (ed.). 1992. "Trends in Education, TQM In the Classroom." *Management Accounting* (October): 14-15.

Bleed, R. 1995. "Our New Leadership Responsibility: Building a Learning Organization." Personal correspondence. [E-mail] Abstract of paper to be presented at EDUCOM '95, Portland, OR (January).

Brown, M.G. 1992. *Baldrige Award-Winning Qualifications: How to Interpret the Malcolm Baldrige Award Criteria.* Milwaukee, WI: American Society for Quality Control, Quality Press.

Butcher, K. 1993. "Total Quality Management: OSU's Experience." *Journal of Library Administration* 18(½): 45-56.

Butterfield, R.W. 1991. "Deming's 14 Points Applied to Service." *Training* (March): 50-59.

Chan, S. 1994. "Strategies for Restructuring IT Organizations." *Proceedings and Archives of CAUSE '94.* [Online] Available gopher://cause-gopher.colorado.edu/ORO-21851-/exchange-library/.documents/cnc9456.txt

Crosby, P.B. 1979. *Quality Is Free.* New York: McGraw Hill: 15.

Deming, W. E. 1982. *Quality, Productivity, and Competitive Position.* Cambridge, MA: Massachusetts Institute of Technology, Center for Advanced Engineering Study.

Ewell, P.T. 1993. "TQM and Academic Practice: The Idea We've Been Waiting For?" *Change* (May/June): 49-55.

Fuller, S. 1993. "Creating the Integrated Information Infrastructure for the 21st Century at The University of Washington." Warren G. Magnuson Health Sciences Center, Seattle, WA.

Hammer, M., and J. Champy. 1993. *Reengineering the Corporation: A Manifesto for Business Revolution.* New York: Harper Business: 11.

Hughes, J.R. 1994. "New Age Leadership: How to Make It Work." Paper presented at Library Solutions Conference, Urbana-Champaign, IL.

Kanter, R.M. 1994. "Collaborative Advantage: The Art of Alliances; Successful Partnerships Manage the Relationship, Not Just the Deal." *Harvard Business Review* 72(4): 96-100.

Katzenbach, J.R. 1993. *The Wisdom of Teams: Creating the High-Performance Organization.* Boston: Harvard Business School Press.

Kiesler, S. 1994. "Working Together Apart." *Cause/Effect* 17(3): 8.

Lowry, A.K. 1994. "The Information Arcade at the University of Iowa." *Cause/Effect*: 44.

Osborne, D., and T. Gaebler. 1992. *Reinventing Government: How the Entrepreneurial Spirit is Transforming the Public Sector.* Reading, MA: Addison-Wesley.

Senge, P.M. 1990. *The Fifth Discipline: The Art & Practice of The Learning Organization.* New York: Currency Doubleday.

Senge, P.M., A. Kliner, C. Roberts, R.B. Ross, and B.J. Smith. 1994. *The Fifth Discipline Fieldbook: Strategies and Tools for Building a Learning Organization.* New York: Doubleday.

Seymour, D. 1993. "Quality on Campus: Three Institutions, Three Beginnings." *Change, the Magazine of Higher Learning* (May/June): 14-28.

"Uwired—Electronic Learning Communities at The University of Washington." 1994. [Online World Wide Web document]. Available http://www.cac.washington.edu:1183/uwired

Watts, R.O. 1990. *Report on Library Computing at the University of Washington.* University Advisory Committee on Academic Computing: 1.

"Willow Information Center: Washington Information Looker-Upper Layered Over Windows." 1994. [Online World Wide Web document]. Available http://www.cac.washington.edu/willow/home.html

Woodsworth, A. and T. Maylone. 1993. "Reinvesting in the Information Job Family: Context, Changes, New Jobs and Models for Evaluation and Compensation." *Cause Professional Paper Series, No. 11 PUB3011.* Boulder, CO: Cause.

CAN THE COLLEGE LIBRARY BECOME A LEARNING ORGANIZATION?

James W. Marcum

Amid the vast literature of total quality management and organizational change resides a coherent argument for the value of deliberate organizational learning as an effective path to adaptation for competitiveness and survival. The library profession has paid little attention to this argument, and those assuming that libraries will survive indefinitely in their familiar form have no motivation to pay attention. Librarians less sanguine about the future should consider familiarizing themselves with the idea. To begin with the basics, the best short definition of the learning organization comes from David Garvin: "an organization skilled at creating, acquiring, and transferring knowledge, and at modifying its behavior to reflect new knowledge and insights" (1993, p. 80). The operative words here are "skilled" and "modifying its behavior to reflect new knowledge." All organizations—and certainly all libraries—make, use and communicate knowledge. How well they do so, and the extent to

Advances in Library Administration and Organization,
Volume 14, pages 39-62.

which they utilize the knowledge to adapt and improve their operations, is the issue at hand.

The concept of the learning organization has become popular in the few years since the publication of Peter Senge's *The Fifth Discipline: The Art and Practice of the Learning Organization* in 1990. Indeed, it could be said that an industry has grown up around the concept, judging by the number of new books on the topic. To list a few of the popular titles, there is by Peter Kline and Bernard Saunders (1993), *Strategic Readiness: The Making of the Learning Organization* by John C. Redding and Ralph F. Catalanelo (1994), *Sculpting the Learning Organization: Lessons in the Art and Science of Systemic Change* by Karen E. Watkins and Victoria J. Marsick (1993), *Re-Educating the Corporation: Foundations for the Learning Organization* by Daniel R. Tobin (1993), and *The Learning Edge: How Smart Managers and Smart Companies Stay Ahead* by Calhoun W. Wick and Lu Stanton Leon (1993). Related studies are beginning to appear, such as *Modeling for Learning Organizations* by John D. W. Morecroft and John D. Sherman (1994), reporting how software programs can effectively be used to model organizational learning, to experiment, measure processes, and facilitate conscious development. Peter Senge and his associates have recently reasserted their dominance of the field with the release of an extensive, practical, hands-on field resource for developing learning organizations, *The Fifth Discipline Fieldbook* (1994).

Many of these volumes, including the *Fieldbook*, are designed to guide a manager or a team through the process of transforming their organizations into learning organizations. And many academic libraries doubtless have begun—or will undertake—such a process. But first it is prudent to survey the territory before venturing too far into such a transformation.

REVIEW OF THE LITERATURE

The issue defined as "organizational learning" dominated the field prior to Senge's book. There were limitations and problems with this inquiry, and Senge has essentially ignored much of this research without significant criticism. Nevertheless, the "learning organization" did not spring full-blown from the mind of Zeus-Senge but has developed over many years, and it is accessible through a few serious reviews of the literature. One of these, by Barbara Levitt and James G. March (1988), looks back from the broader, sociological perspective as far as an 1848 Danish study, though most of the literature included dates from the 1960s forward. The thrust of their review is to spell out different approaches to the question of how organizations learn. Essentially, they outline three different approaches, which can be labeled simply as history, diffusion, and ecology.

People in organizations hold "memories" of how the organization came to be the way it is and to do the things it does. These memories can be accurate or wildly misleading. Stories, paradigms, and superstitions characterize members' perception of the organization and its various departments. These memories can be uncovered by probing into the various routines and processes of the organization; some past success or problem solved can often be uncovered to explain why the process exists. This history, or "organizational saga," as it has been described by Clark (1972), can either be durable or fragile. It can be a strength of the organization, but often is a weakness. Routines frequently militate against change and learning. Overcoming them can be daunting, as Levitt and March (1988) point out. Information technology and teams are powerful tools to that end as will be seen.

Two more comments about organizational memory are in order. Levitt and March point out the inherent danger in "competency traps," where a successful solution to a problem in one situation can lead to false confidence in the technique in a different circumstance, particularly where specialization has taken root. Successfully refining an inferior process can negate the implementation of a superior process, delaying a needed change. The second comment is this author's: History properly understood and applied amounts to a dialogue between the present and the past (the organizational memory) which illustrates and improves the understanding of both. Such a dialogue should be useful in most situations where an objective review of events uncovers solutions that were implemented for political reasons or misinterpreted. Organizational history and organizational memory are not the same thing.

Diffusion is learning from others. Organizations and their departments learn from others, including unions, government agencies, customers, and trade associations. The diffusion of technology is a well-studied and documented phenomenon (Rogers,

1983). For this paper it will be assumed that in academic libraries learning is transferred primarily through the associations and work of professional librarianship, through the accreditation process, and through the movement of professional personnel.

Finally, there is the trend of adaptation, or the ecology of the organization's interaction with other organizations within its environment. This concept is more thoroughly discussed in our second review of the literature of organizational learning, this one focused on business management, by Fiol and Lyles (1985). They treat the topic as one of environmental alignment, or adapting and improving to remain competitive; an organization must be able to learn, unlearn, and change.

The literature review by Fiol and Lyles emphasizes contexts and problems. They stress that while there remains no accepted model of organizational learning, there is much agreement on a number of issues. For example, there is agreement that corporate culture creates an environment that can nurture or repress learning. An environment characterized by a healthy tension between change and stability is favorable to learning; too much of either condition can inhibit learning through information overload at one pole or inflexibility at the other. The relationship of individual learning versus organizational learning has been studied. Sometimes individuals can influence the establishment of new routines, for example, thereby shaping organizational memory. The structure of the organization is critical. Hierarchy favors routines and stifles the free flow of information. A more decentralized, organic structure fosters change and learning.

The latter reviewers discuss directly, and the former pair imply, the difference between lower-level, behavioristic learning, and higher learning. Basic learning works as "functional rationality," and is inescapable. But when the learning is reflected upon and is used to adjust overall rules and norms of behavior it becomes higher level, or what Argyris (1993) calls "double loop" learning. At this point what the organization has learned is put to use to adapt how things will be done in the future. It is in this manner that a learning organization gives evidence of its existence.

A third study of the literature of organizational learning was written simultaneously with Senge's *Fifth Discipline*, and has accordingly been overlooked. This study, by Huber (1991), is organized around how an organization acquires knowledge, distributes information, interprets knowledge, and preserves information through organizational memory. Huber is quite critical of the lack of comprehensiveness in the field, of how experiments and studies have often been completed without knowledge of other efforts, a trend illustrated shortly. He believes that our understanding of information distribution, interpretation, and organizational memory are inadequately developed and require further study. Only the concept of organizational acquisition of knowledge is adequately understood by the discipline, according to Huber. (This could also be why Senge's systems approach has met so little resistance; his emphasis on team learning, shared vision, and mental models addresses many of these weaknesses.)

Methods used for knowledge acquisition, to spell out Huber's argument, can be quite varied. Organizations begin with a certain amount of congenital, inherited knowledge. They expand that understanding internationally through experience, experimentation, and self-appraisal, and add to that knowledge gained unintentionally. They learn through searching, scanning, and observation, and even learn vicariously, through second-hand, informal information. Our understanding of this topic is extensive, according to Huber, in contrast with our knowledge of knowledge distribution, utilization, and archiving.

This review of the literature provides a model for the learning organization. The model includes sources of learning (memory, diffusion, and adaptation), and ways of learning (congenitally, experientially, experimentally, vicariously, and through self-appraisal), as well as setting out other essential issues and problems, namely organizational structure, culture, strategy, and flexibility. Troublesome problem areas include the relationship of individual learning to organizational learning and the difficulty of effective higher level, or double-loop, learning.

It is also worth noting that among the approximately 100 citations in the review by Levitt and March and the 50 items cited in the article by Fiol and Lyles, only about fifteen sources were cited in both, if we give partial credit for different articles by the same authors. This can be taken as evidence of the limitations of professional scholarship and research noted by Huber. His review, with its 200 citations, is both broader and more thorough than the first two, yet it encompasses only half of the citations used by Fiol and 40 percent of those used by Levitt. So even Huber, with his claim to greater comprehensiveness, is not free of the limitations of disciplinary bias. Nevertheless, these reviews have great value in surveying the subject and providing a model for further discussion.

PRESCRIPTIONS FOR DEVELOPING LEARNING ORGANIZATIONS

A recent survey of 1,359 managers identified four basic types of learning organizations, those that acquire competence through training and learning, those that utilize experimentation, those using Total Quality Management techniques to achieve continuous improvement, and those using scanning and benchmarking to expand their boundaries (Rheem, 1995). Analysis of the literature suggests a further simplification to a mere two approaches to developing such entities. These can be labeled intervention (in which we arbitrarily lump the systems approach) and innovation. Most of the research, writing, and experience falls into this category of intervention. Another way of expressing the difference is to contrast the metaphors of building (or designing) a learning organization with growing one.

Intervention: Building a Learning Organization

Peter Senge and many of the gurus of organizational learning rely on top management and intervention to make the transformation happen. To be sure, Senge sets forth a new definition of the type of leadership required (1990a, pp. 339-360, 1990b). The proposed model for a leader is one that values the roles of designer, steward, and teacher and that assigns a new responsibility to ensure that learning occurs in the organization. Many will object to classifying Senge's systems approach in this manner since much of it is directed to individual and team development. But the approach is sufficiently complicated to demand professional, or at least highly trained interveners, lending some justification to matching this approach with others involving direction and intervention from the top.

Other books complement this perspective. Argyris entitles his recent book *Knowledge for Action: A Guide to Overcoming Barriers to Organizational Change*, but it is knowledge applied by those in power. The heart of the book is in four chapters on "Diagnosis and Intervention in Organizations" targeted at consultants working in organizational change. He assumes that, if the leader does not lead, he must be managed; and he includes a chapter on "managing the CEO" to offer guidance to that end. Kanter, Stein, and Jick (1992), an influential voice for organization change, offer "10 Commandments" for executing change which emphasize the creation of a shared vision and common direction, creating a sense of urgency, emphasizing a strong leader role, assuring political sponsorship, developing "enabling structures," and communicating, involving people, and being honest. They allow that grass-roots innovation plays an equal role with a crisis event in triggering change, but the burden of the work relies on top-down leadership (pp. 383-383, 498ff).

A closely related trend is the Total Quality Management (TQM) movement with its emphasis on continuous improvement. W. Edwards Deming (1993), the chief guru of this major trend in business management, consistently drove home the point that management was the problem, but implicitly he also assumes that management must provide the solution. He championed a "system of profound knowledge" encompassing an adequate understanding of systems, variation, a theory of knowledge, and psychology. Other overviews of TQM in America stress the link of learning and quality transformations (Greene, 1993, pp. 216-243; Schmidt and Finnegan, 1992, pp. 233-251). This literature normally assumes that corporate leadership will authorize and lead the TQM effort.

A recent collection of studies of organizational change and redesign, involving more than a dozen leading scholars in the field, resulted in a fine book summarizing the state of the art. The dozen chapters of the collection are all predicated on change being a management-driven process. The need for more teamwork and for more processing and analysis of information are acknowledged, but managerial attitudes and leadership remain the focus of the work (Huber and Glick, 1993).

One critique of the rational, intervention model threatens to unhinge its dominance. In his recent *Crisis and Renewal* (1995), David Hurst argues that learning and performance are not compatible, but countervailing trends. Learning occurs early in an organization's saga as egalitarianism and teamwork foster innovation. But, inevitably, if the organization is to flourish, the practices of efficiency, professionalism and hierarchy will be adapted. It will only be when constraints bring about an organizational crisis that the learning mode will again prevail. Hurst's topic is not organizational learning, per se, but he makes a major contribution to the field.

Despite this caveat, the intervention model will likely remain dominant because of the American penchant to leave it to individual leaders and bosses to solve our problems. The consulting industry, which is a potent force in this field, tends to support this trend since the quickest way to gain access to a client firm is to persuade top management that they can solve the firm's problems and make management look good. Some of the best thinking coming from people like Senge, Kanter, and Argyris on learning organizations and organizational change operate within this model. Brian Joiner (1994) operates under this assumption in his new work, *Fourth Generation Management*. An influential new book on competitive strategy, Hamel and Prahalad's *Competing for the Future* (1994), starts by challenging senior management to envision their industry ten years into the future. They point out that "the bottleneck is usually at the top of the bottle "to stress the hazards of inadequate top management, but managerial direction is assumed through most of their book. They argue that intelligent leadership is "the key," and top managers must view the organization in new ways.

The distinctions between the intervention model and the innovation model should not be overdrawn. There is much overlap in practice and strategy between the two models. Senge, Roberts, Ross, Smith, and Kleiner stress team learning, shared vision, mental models (held in common), and self-mastery; their *Fifth Discipline Fieldbook* (1994) is stuffed with ideas, exercises, and practices by which individuals and teams can sharpen their skills and develop learning organizations. The distinctions may almost be unconscious. But some practitioners operate on assumptions of top management (or consultant) direction, while others think in terms of creating collaborative environments and designing information infrastructures to permit organizational learning to happen indigenously, to grow and develop spontaneously. There is a big difference.

Informated Innovation: Growing a Learning Organization

While the dichotomy between intervention and innovation is not absolute and the distinctions between them are sometimes subtle, it is useful to distinguish an emerging, if yet poorly articulated, alternative approach to fostering learning organizations. This approach can be labeled informated innovation, or growing the learning organization. This approach utilizes five complementary ideas—multiple intelligences, the informated organization, information technology, innovation, and knowledge management—to create the conditions required for learning organizations to develop.

Howard Gardner's influential book, *Frames of Mind* (1983) established firmly the concept of multiple intelligences. People learn in many ways. While some flourish in the logical world of data, others work better with spatial (visual) concepts or musical tones and rhythms, through mathematical logic personal interaction, or the kinesthetic world of sports and physical activity. Most people have capabilities in several intelligences, but some have unique powers in one or another mode. Such people may have done poorly in school and are often found laboring in niche jobs rather than in positions of high visibility. The implications are clear in a world of change and uncertainty. There is no one best way of learning, perceiving, or solving problems. Collaborative problem-solving and teamwork are essential for organizations to adapt to their chaotic environments. The quiet nonparticipant in most team discussions may provide the solution to the intractable problem on the crucial occasion with a high level of uncertainty. All of the talents of all members of the group are essential to the learning organization. "Communities of commitment" is the descriptive term offered by Kofman and Senge (1993) as the ideal of the transformed organization. Fragmentation and competition are the enemy. Structures, cultures, and controls that hinder collaborative learning are potentially catastrophic. Accordingly, hierarchies are being flattened and bureaucracies dismantled in favor or networks or similar organic structures in many organizations, as management gurus like Drucker (1985), Pinchot and Pinchot (1993), and Peters (1992) love to point out.

The second formative idea is that of the informated organization. In her seminal work, *In the Age of the Smart Machine* (1988), Zuboff explains how information and "intellective" skills have transformed the workplace. Automation is not the key term here; automation just replaces human routines with computer routines. Informating technology goes further. It generates information about the process, adding a flow of information that allows reflection on how the process is working. It makes the process transparent, which transforms the nature of work. Informating strategies understand the power of intellective skills and seek to create a learning environment where those skills can develop fully. The problem is that an informated organization undermines traditional controls and structures of power because intellective skill development requires that people become their own authority, a condition inimical to managerial authority. The informated organization is a learning community; learning is the new form of labor and is necessary for productivity (Zuboff, 1988, pp. 9-12, 301-310, 390-395).

A brief excursion is needed to link a related issue to this discussion. The issue is the role of professions. Professions are usually knowledge-based, so there is an assumption that they will play a central role in the age of information. Indeed, one prognosticator envisions professions as playing an enlarged role in the future, to the point of serving as social mediators and displacing some traditional government functions (Benveniste, 1994). Others demur. More than a decade ago Schon (1983) spelled out the limitations of and challenges to professional knowledge, a situation calling for professionals—and their clients—to become reflective about their work and decisions. Greene (1993) offers a more serious critique. In *Global Quality* he attributes a large share of the burden for the lack of competitiveness of many American organizations to the limitations of professional training and thinking. He places the blame for this narrow specialization—which he compares unfavorably to Japanese practice—at the doorstep of our academic culture (pp. 639-675). All professionals, including academic librarians, must reflect on our training, traditions, and practices as we contemplate our future. We must not assume that what has been will always be.

The emerging dominant role of information technology is another stream that merges into the flow being developed here. This trend encompasses communication technology—with its new model of interactive communication displacing the linear model that rose to power with television in the 1950s—(Rogers, 1986) and its progeny, the all-embracing new media with its vast potential to enrich the quality of our lives (Brand, 1987; Forester, 1987). On another level, the new technology is globalizing business as well as culture and in many cases has completely transformed entire industries (Bradley, Hausman, and Nolan, 1993). Closer to home, the new technology demands and facilitates collaboration among individuals and groups at unprecedented rates and levels, as Michael Schrage explains in *Shared Minds* (1990).

For the individual organization, information technology raises challenges at two quite separate levels. At the strategic level, top managers must develop a vision linking the new technology with their core competencies to arrive at a strategy that encompasses positioning the firm, redesigning the organization, and utilizing human capital in order to appropriately align the business with technology for competitive advantage. This is a costly but essential task for which few managers are adequately prepared (Keen, 1991). At the micro level, it is incumbent that work processes be reengineered to embrace and accommodate the new technology. More and more business activity and production is fostered by or results in information products. Human skills, knowledge, and expertise are fundamental in this endeavor to develop and improve "total quality" products (Davenport, 1993).

An entirely new world of organizational development awaits the computer literate and technologically venturesome. This world encompasses computer modeling to map what a team or an organization knows, to simulate theories and concepts, to aid and measure learning, to explore future scenarios, and to foster systems thinking. These possibilities, and others, are discussed by Senge and other specialists in the collection of articles edited by Morecroft for the impressive *Modeling for Learning Organizations.*

The fourth element in this argument relates to innovation and its diffusion. A precise definition of innovation is still wanting. For Rogers it is an idea, practice, or object that is perceived as new (1983, p. 11). Drucker offers a definition that is economic or social rather than technological. He contends that anything that changes the wealth-producing potential of already existing resources is an innovation (1983, pp. 31-33). Quinn (1992) equates innovation with the first practical application of an idea in a culture (p. 293). Senge distinguishes between invention (something that works in the lab) with innovation, meaning that it can be replicated extensively at reasonable cost (1990a, pp. 5-6). While these definitions are not the same, ideas, objects, and practical application are elements common to these different definitions.

There is more agreement on how innovation is generated. Multiple, free-flowing, interacting ideas with extensive participation from everyone are basic. Ambiguity is another essential factor because it generates much new information (Wheatley, 1992, pp. 113-115). Multiple small starts and creative borrowing are essential elements for

Tom Peters (1988, pp. 192-283). Organizational factors that hinder innovation include large size, centralized structures, and formality; interconnectedness and organizational "slack" foster innovation (Rogers, 1983, pp. 358-361). Innovation within organizations can occur only by breaking bureaucratic rules, according to Pinchot and Pinchot (1993), and that can only happen when people care about their work and their organization (pp. 31-33).

A new study of the relationship of knowledge to innovation by Leonard-Barton (1995) spells out four key innovation activities for organizations. They are shared problem solving, frequent experimentation, extensive importation and use of technological knowledge from outside, and empathetic learning from the customer (pp. 59-212). Garvin's (1993) prescription is similar: problem-solving, experimentation, learning from history and experience, learning from others, and diffusion. Certain structures (nonbureaucratic) and practices (borrowing, experimentation, teamwork) are evident in all these descriptions, as is the application of the innovation in the real world.

One component of innovation that should not be overlooked in the model described here is envisioning the future. Much of the work done in this regard has been led by futurists or change masters. Fulmer (1994) calls for high-participation envisioning to "invent" the future. Such efforts are outstanding learning exercises and allow the entire organization to "own" the vision that guides the change process.

Another point about innovation comes from a longitudinal study of the characteristics of major innovations. Utterback (1994) concludes that innovations come in two forms: piecemeal, marginal changes resulting from efforts to continuously improve a product, and breakthrough innovations that transform an industry. The latter usually come from outside the industry, often from small companies. To cite one example, the dominant Underwood typewriter design was made obsolete by another model, the IBM Selectric developed by an outsider company, which in turn was pushed aside by word processors from Wang, Apple, and Tandy. Higgins (1995) notes that companies are beginning to emulate this by putting "old hands" on refinement and continuous improvement projects, and newcomers on breakthrough endeavors (pp. 141-166). The lesson should not be lost on organizations like libraries that are currently in a dominant, unchallenged position in their fields.

The final component of informated innovation is the growing focus on the management of technological information. An accomplished management guru like Tom Peters can dash off four chapters on "knowledge management structures" for his new book, skipping glibly from admonitions to abolish central staffs to achieve greater agility, to networking company archives, to facilitating computer-augmented collaboration, to the systematic tapping of expertise (1992, pp. 382-447). For ordinary folks wondering what they are supposed to do on Monday morning, more focused approaches may be more useful. How much does your organization know? Can it use the knowledge effectively? Roger Bohn (1994) suggests starting simply by measuring a process and working through stages of knowledge, from awareness to measurement to management to full understanding. The more advanced the stage of knowledge the greater the "know why" and the better information can be managed.

The conscious process of managing technological information is a recent development. Some preliminary spadework can be attributed to Itami's study, *Mobilizing Invisible Assets* (1987). His purpose was to consciously align "information-based" resources like consumer trust, brand image, corporate culture, and management skills with corporate strategy into something he labels "strategic dynamics." He labeled "technological fit" as one cornerstone of this endeavor. Nonaka (1991) comes at the problem from an entirely different perspective. He is interested in how knowledge can be "spiraled" upward from an individual's tacit knowledge into explicit knowledge that can be articulated and shared. Free access to information and a certain amount of organizational redundancy are important components for the "knowledge-creating" organization.

In occasional articles in *Fortune,* Thomas Stewart (1991, 1994) has popularized the notion of "intellectual capital," which amounts to leveraging invisible assets to achieve greater value or competitive advantage. In a disappointing book on the subject William Hudson (1993) argues for intellectual honesty as necessary for nurturing creativity and out-thinking the competition. Such honesty encompasses humility, acknowledging what is not known, and accepting criticism (pp. 155-162). But more is at stake than management attitudes. Greene (1993) promotes the use of "quality" software, process empowerment rooms for group and concept development, and knowledge management techniques to link the organization's learning to current technology (pp. 461-583). When we include "understanding the organization and how it learns" as a component of knowledge management, there is a seminal model offered by Nevis, DiBella, and Gould (1995). They distinguish the stages of acquiring, sharing, and using knowledge, and spell out the basic orientations of learning organizations (such as organizational culture, experience, and core competencies) as well as listing ten "facilitating factors" ranging from scanning, measuring for performance gaps, experimentation, continuing education, involved leadership, and a systems perspective. This comprehensive model is fresh and will prove useful to many venturing into this field.

Some progress has been made in bringing knowledge management systems into the academic library, but the cutting edge will likely be found in Australia rather than in this country. A special issue of *Library Hi-Tech* recently covered neural networks, expert systems, and artificial intelligence and their probable impact on the library in the future. New media, widespread use of standard markup language, and books that "talk to each other" are rapidly coming online (Weckert and McDonald, 1992). A related, and ongoing problem for academe is the relationship of libraries and computer centers, but that issue is beyond our scope (Branin, D'Elia, and Lund, 1993; Pitkin, 1992).

Much remains to be done before competence in managing technological and intellectual resources becomes anything but rare. Organizations failing to tackle this complex problem will assure that they will eventually be inadequate and lack competitiveness, even though at present the level of understanding of this process in organizations is quite limited. Perhaps librarians can contribute to this endeavor, for their own benefit as well as the benefit of their customers and partners. Such accomplishment would give the profession a new "lease on life," to be sure.

All of these pieces fit together into a colorful, comprehensive mosaic that can be described as informated innovation. Such innovation is not totally spontaneous; certain prerequisites are essential, and these will only be present in the structured organization if there is top management support. These prerequisites include an extensive information infrastructure, the extensive exchange of ideas and information, and a flexible organizational structure. A specific outcome is not guaranteed, which will cause many to resist the approach. But in conditions of uncertainty a preordained outcome is precisely what is not appropriate since few individuals or teams will develop a vision that is appropriate for any extended period of time. The gardener may have a vision of what is desired when the tree is planted, but too much trimming and shaping can be counterproductive. The organism must be allowed to find its own way and take its own shape. The assumption here is heavily influenced by Wheatley: If ideas are encouraged and their exchange promoted and allowed to flow freely, then innovation will happen and the organization will adapt and compete effectively. This "spontaneous generation" is ultimately far healthier than any leader-generated innovation, particularly considering the mobility and dismal track record of organizational leadership today.

PRESCRIPTIONS FOR ACADEMIC LIBRARIES

Academic librarians have seriously engaged in applying Total Quality Management techniques and processes into their operations. The Association of Research Libraries sponsored a First International Conference on TQM and Academic Libraries in Washington, DC in April 1994, attended by more than 100 participants. Numerous programs on benchmarking, quality management, service improvement, and related topics were held. Sessions on quality management appear in many national and state library association meetings. An internet discussion group on TQM in libraries is operating. A few libraries, notably that of Arizona State University, have undertaken major restructurings. A good number of articles applying TQM principles to academic libraries have been authored by Donald Riggs (1993) and others.

Efforts to apply organizational learning techniques to libraries are more limited. One effort to apply the principles to an academic consortium was reported by Hightower and Soete (1995). They proposed a twelve-step procedure by which consortia could learn from successes and failures and adapt accordingly. The steps emphasize planning, adequate communication, flexibility, and system maintenance. Shelley Phipps (1993) discusses the ideas of Senge and how they can be applied in a university library setting. Hert (1994) relates the issue to training and the need to revamp services to encompass the potential of the Internet. The territory is no longer virgin, but is not yet extensively cultivated.

Meeting the Criteria

To begin, the question must be asked: Should academic libraries seek to become learning organizations? Are they not learning organizations already? They obviously access, communicate, and generate information. But to what extent do they learn from their work, and apply that learning to adapt their behavior? Lacking a serious survey or study, those questions can only be answered subjectively. There may well be as many answers to the question "to what extent are academic libraries learning organizations?" as there are academic libraries. This approach apparently leads us toward a dead end.

Another approach serves our purposes better, and that is to draw prescriptions from the review of the literature and the characteristics of learning organizations outlined above. Most of these prescriptions are useful whether the transformation is a leader-directed intervention or a more organic innovation. Each library staff or department can rate itself as to the current state of their organizational learning, and then set tasks for itself where there is need for improvement. Incidentally, there is a conscious effort here to offer an alternative model to the prevailing "five disciplines" systems model of Senge, as is consistent with the informated innovation approach proposed here.

1. *History versus Memory:* Organizational memory can be faulty and misleading. A study of the organization's history, or saga can throw light on those problems. But the history must be studied to that end. Is the library conscious of when it became professionalized? How it became automated? How its collection developed? When and how its organizational structure was established? To what extent is the current structure bureaucratic? A step used in many of the guides to establishing learning organizations discussed elsewhere is a careful analysis of the existing culture, behaviors, and core competencies of the organization. It is important to understand these factors as a precursor to any change strategy.

2. *Diffusion:* How does the organization get its information? How active are the librarians in academic and professional meetings? Do conference attendees report back on what they have learned? Is this information shared widely throughout the organization? What kinds of files are being kept? What journals are read, by whom, and

how is this information shared? Is there any kind of database of "best practices" of comparable libraries, even at the level of shared "pathfinders," bibliographic instruction techniques, collections policies, and solutions to difficult but frequently asked reference questions? Is there any mechanism, such as an annual "benchmarking day" where conference attendees report on best practices and good ideas used elsewhere?

3. *Adaptation:* How much effort goes into improving customer service, particularly by asking for suggestions through a suggestion system or focus groups? How has college instruction changed in the last decade? Is book readership increasing or decreasing, and why? What changes have occurred in patterns of information access and usage? What is the pattern of change in the selection of materials from print to other media? What do the students and faculty "want" or "need?"

4. *Bureaucracy versus Network:* Is information limited to some sort of "need to know" basis or is it "public?" Does a librarian have to "follow policy" in dealing with an unusual situation or are they empowered to "satisfy the customer" and resolve ensuing issues later? How about a staff member in that same situation? Does the organization underrate its people? Is there an underlying effort to "control" people and situations, or is there an assumption that people will "do the right thing" with an accompanying grant of considerable latitude?

5. *Double-Loop (Higher) Learning:* Are problems discussed fully or covered up? Is the messenger "shot" or commended? Is someone blamed when things go wrong, or does the entire organization "own" the problem and set seriously about fixing the system and practices that caused it? Are unexpected failures investigated? Unexpected successes? (Drucker, 1985).

6. *Intervention versus Innovation:* Is the direction for change coming from a top administrator or from a team (or several teams) carving their own way through the jungle? If teams are used, do they have the resources to commit to experiments? Do they have free access to all needed information? Where are the visible "champions" of change, in management or on the "front lines?" Can a team form spontaneously to address a problem, or is "authorization" required?

7. *Participation and Professionalism:* These two items are linked together here because of the high level of sensitivity on the part of librarians to the status of the profession. Are ideas considered

on their merit, regardless of their source, or do the comments and views of professional librarians carry extra weight? Are the full talents of all members of the staff fully utilized?

8. *Technology and Strategy:* Does the library have a vision of what it will be doing in 2005? (Keep in mind that the PC "appeared" a decade ago.) If college "papers" are predominantly multimedia, will the information gathering be done in the library? Will it be gathered through a "gateway" operated by the library? Who will be meeting the information needs of the campus? Since genuine "seers" of the future are rare indeed, the best approach to this effort is a high-participation effort on the part of the entire organization, as suggested by Fulmer (1994) and Higgins (1995).

9. *Technology and Process:* Does every member of the staff have the training and expertise to adapt their routines through computer programs or telecommunications? Are they encouraged to get with other staff members in order to analyze, study, and improve the work that they do on a daily basis? Are they being trained in new software and systems regularly? Do they understand "process reengineering?" Obviously, a requisite for this activity is an extensive, ongoing continuing education commitment by the organization for all of the staff.

10. *Experimentation:* Are individuals (and small groups of two or three) given time and resources to just "play" with an idea or a technique? When was the last time the reference area was reorganized? The tech room? What would happen if students were sent *Choice* cards for suggestions rather than faculty; would circulation of new books rise or fall? How about focus groups to review and recommend journals in a field (without reference to current subscriptions)?

11. *Collaborative Problem Solving:* Do small groups cluster spontaneously to deal with problems or questions from a colleague, on the spot and without notice? Are managerial decisions made with major input from appropriate staff members, or are they "announced?" Is there some creative tension generated by the exchange of viewpoints among people with different skills and professional outlooks? Are student workers given problems to solve, or at least included in task forces and investigations? What would happen if students were put in charge of forming "focus groups" to deal with a problem? Is such a process conceivable in your library?

12. *Knowledge Management:* Peter Drucker and Tom Peters and other pundits argue that knowledge is the most valuable resource of an organization and the most essential for its future competitiveness. If that is so, when will library management catch on and pay as much attention to intellectual resources as they do to the budget and the collections and to the systems and equipment? Knowledge can only be utilized by people. Information must be gathered and made available through some type of knowledge management system. The same is true of expertise. A database of expertise of all kinds should be available to the library, and the larger the organization the more valid and necessary this becomes.

But cataloging the resources is just the beginning; the key is to adapt them into services to meet customer needs.

James Brian Quinn (1992) describes an intelligent enterprise as "a highly disaggregated, knowledge and service based enterprise concentrated around a core of set knowledge or service skills" (p. 373). The college library fits that description nicely. But there is a bit of a static quality about that description since there is no explicit call for utilizing the learning to adapt procedures. And so the question is, how well does the individual college library practice the prescriptions listed above? Can the academic library become a learning organization? It will be necessary to take a little medicine.

Directions

Obviously Senge is required reading in this field, which is not to say that everyone in the organization can benefit from his seminal book, *The Fifth Discipline.* His basic concept, of five disciplines of personal mastery, mental models, shared vision, team learning, and systems analysis is the starting point for most current research and practice. That does not mean the book is an easy read. His recent *Fifth Discipline Fieldbook* is the product of multiple authors and is designed for professionals or highly trained practitioners. Both books should be available as resources on the shelf for team leaders, but both are idiosyncratic and are difficult beginning "texts" for any limited or modestly funded undertaking.

The popular titles listed at the start of this paper have been produced by consultants from the newly-emerged "profession" promoting the learning organization. Many have a useful idea or unique approach to some part of the problem, but generally they are hastily done and uneven in quality. Wick's and Leon's *Learning Edge* (1993) was a very early effort and has been superseded by other works. The Tobin volume is competent and contains useful tools and exercises. The argument by Redding and Catalanello in *Strategic Readiness* (1994) is a powerful one: The best way to be prepared for the uncertainty of the future—reflecting the influence of Margaret Wheatley—is to have a highly educated, committed, and competent work force. The book contains many useful ideas, but its approach is not obviously designed to serve as a text or book of common readings for organizations undertaking the journey. *Sculpting the Learning Organization* by Watkins and Marsick (1993) works both sides of the theory-and-practice street competently and is recommended for consideration. The thrust of the book is linking individual learning with organizational development, and many ideas and exercises are offered to that end. The simple organization and style of *Ten Steps to a Learning Organization* by Kline and Saunders (1993) makes it a useful text for a course in developing the technique for participants of varied backgrounds and levels of education. Higgins' *Innovate or Evaporate* (1995) is a highly useful guidebook, offering numerous illustrations of successful corporate innovations as examples. Larger organizations with computer and systems expertise should consider software programs for learning and knowledge management such as those covered in the book on modeling by Morecroft and Sherman. Interestingly, most of these works tend to rely less heavily—than TQM books, for example— on management direction for their implementation.

One issue remains to be mentioned, namely quality service with its client-centered orientation. The fact that libraries are service-oriented organizations militates for paying some attention to the extensive literature of service quality. Outstanding service requires extensive training or learning in some form. This is an extensive subject, but *The Service Quality Handbook* edited by Scheuing and Christopher (1993) would serve as a valuable resource on this movement. There is a plethora of guidebooks on the market promising to improve an organization's service delivery. One that is unique in its combination of scholarly research and practical application is Collier's *Service/Quality Solution* (1994). He encompasses quality methods, strategy, innovation, and what he calls interlinking (which is virtually identical to systems management).

The journey into the future is fraught with challenges, where the options are, as succinctly put by Hamel and Prahalad, to become drivers, passengers, or road kill. They argue persuasively in *Competing for the Future* (1994) that the successful organization will participate in shaping its future environment by becoming a distinctive deliverer of needed services. But their vision is focused on the leader-led transformation. As we have seen, a style of participatory, informated innovation is the better bet to overcome problems and exploit opportunities. Leadership will remain important, as will organizational culture and technological acumen. But the best guarantee of success is to have a highly skilled and motived "community" of librarians and staff dedicated to a collective vision of what the future will be, and who are increasingly adept at proactively shaping the environment even as they simultaneously adapt their processes and behaviors. Academic libraries that survive the journey will be conscious, and acknowledged, learning organizations. Can we do this? No comprehensive response is possible. What is likely is that academic libraries that are vital ten years from now will be very different, collectively, and varied, individually, from what exists today.

REFERENCES

Argyris, C. 1993. *Knowledge for Action.* San Francisco: Jossey-Bass.

Benveniste, G. 1994. *The Twenty-First Century Organization.* San Francisco: Jossey-Bass.

Bohn, R.E. 1994. "Measuring and Managing Technological Knowledge." *Sloan Management Review* 36(1): 61-73.

Bradley, S.P., J.A. Hausman, and R.L. Nolan. 1993. *Globalization, Technology, and Competition: The Fusion of Computers and Telecommunications in the 1990s.* Boston: Harvard Business School.

Brand, S. 1987. *The Media Lab: Inventing the Future at MIT.* New York: Penguin.

Branin, J.J., G. D'Elia, and D. Lund. 1993. "Integrating Information Services in an Academic Setting: The Organizational and Technical Challenge." *Library Hi-Tech* 11(4) (44): 75-83.

Clark, B.R. 1972. "The Organizational Saga in Higher Education." *Administrative Science Quarterly* 17: 178-184.

Collier, D.A. 1994. *The Service/Quality Solution.* New York: ASQC/ Irwin.

Davenport, T.H. 1993. *Process Innovation: Reengineering Work Through Information Technology.* Boston: Harvard Business School.

Deming, W.E. 1993. *The New Economics.* Cambridge, MA: MIT.

Drucker, P.F. 1985. *Innovation and Entrepreneurship.* New York: Harper and Row.

_____. 1993. *Post-Capitalist Society*. New York: Harper Business.

Fiol, C.M., and M. Lyles. 1985. "Organizational Learning." *Academy of Management Review* 10:4: 803-813.

Forester, T. 1987. *High-Tech Society: The Story of the Information Technology Revolution*. Cambridge, MA: MIT.

Fulmer, R.M. 1994. "A Model for Changing the Way Organizations Learn." *Planning Review* 22(3): 20-24.

Gardner, H. 1983. *Frames of Mind: The Theory of Multiple Intelligences*. New York: Basic Books.

Garvin, D.A. 1993. "Building a Learning Organization." *Harvard Business Review* 71(4): 78-91.

Greene, R.T. 1993. *Global Quality: A Synthesis of the World's Best Management Methods*. Milwaukee, WI: ASQC/Business One Irwin.

Hamel, G., and C. K. Prahalad. 1994. *Competing for the Future*. Boston: Harvard Business School.

Hert, C.A. 1994. "A Learning Organization Perspective on Training: Critical Success Factors for Internet Implementation." *Internet Research*, 4(3): 36-44.

Higgins, J.M. 1995. *Innovate or Evaporate*. Winter Park, FL: New Management.

Hightower, C., and G. Soete. 1995. "The Consortium as Learning Organization: Twelve Steps to Success in Collaborative Collections Projects." *Journal of Academic Librarianship* 21(2): 87-91.

Huber, G.P. 1991. "Organizational Learning: The Contributing Processes and the Literature." *Organization Science* 2(1): 88-115.

Huber, G.P., and W.H. Glick. 1993. *Organizational Change and Redesign: Ideas and Insights for Improving Performance*. New York: Oxford University.

Hudson, W.J. 1993. *Intellectual Capital: How to Build It, Enhance It, Use It*. New York: John Wiley.

Hurst, D.K. 1995. *Crisis and Renewal*. Boston, MA: Harvard Business School.

Itami, H. 1987. *Mobilizing Invisible Assets*. Cambridge, MA: Harvard University.

Joiner, B.L. 1994. *Fourth Generation Management: The New Business Consciousness*. New York: McGraw-Hill.

Kanter, R.M., B.A. Stein, and T.D. Jick. 1992. *The Challenge of Organizational Change: How Companies Experience It and Leaders Guide It*. New York: Free Press.

Keen, P.G.W. 1991. *Shaping the Future: Business Design through Information Technology*. Boston: Harvard Business School.

Kline, P., and B. Saunders 1993. *Ten Steps to a Learning Organization*. Arlington, VA: Great Ocean.

Kofman, F., and P. Senge 1993. "Communities of Commitment: The Heart of the Learning Organization." *Organizational Dynamics* 22(2): 5-23.

Leonard-Barton, D. 1995. *Wellsprings of Knowledge: Building and Sustaining the Sources of Innovation*. Boston: Harvard Business School.

Levitt, B., and J.G. March. 1988. "Organizational Learning." *Annual Review of Sociology* 14: 319-340.

Morecroft, J.D.W., and J.D. Sterman. (eds.) 1994. *Modeling for Learning Organizations*. Portland, OR: Productivity Press.

Nevis, E.C., A.J. DiBella, and J.M. Gould. 1995. "Understanding Organizations as Learning Systems." *Sloan Management Review* 36(2): 73-85.

Nonaka, I. 1991. "The Knowledge-Creating Company." *Harvard Business Review* 69(6): 96-104.

Peters, T. 1992. *Liberation Management: Necessary Disorganization for the Nanosecond Nineties*. New York: Alfred A. Knopf.

_____. 1988. *Thriving on Chaos: Handbook for a Management Revolution*. New York: Alfred A. Knopf.

Phipps, S.E. 1993. "Transforming Libraries into Learning Organizations—The Challenge for Leadership." *Journal of Library Administration* 18 (3/4): 19-37.

Pinchot, G., and E. Pinchot. 1993. *The End of Bureaucracy and the Rise of the Intelligent Organization*. San Francisco: Berrett-Koehler.

Pitkin, G.M., (ed.) 1992. *Information Management and Organizational Change in Higher Education: The Impact on Academic Libraries*. Westport, CT: Meckler.

Quinn, J.B. 1992. *Intelligent Enterprise: A Knowledge and Service Based Paradigm for Industry*. New York: :Free Press.

Redding, J.C., and R.F. Catalanello. 1994. *Strategic Readiness: The Making of the Learning Organization*. San Francisco: Jossey-Bass.

Rheem, H. 1995)."The Learning Organization: Building Learning Capability." *Harvard Business Review* 73(2): 10.

Riggs, D.E. 1993. "Managing Quality: TQM in Libraries." *Library Administration and Management* 7 (Spring): 73-78.

Rogers, E.M. 1986. *Communications Technology: The New Media in Society*. New York: Free Press.

_____. 1983. *Diffusion of Innovations*. 3rd ed. New York: Free Press.

Scheuing, E.E., and W.F. Christopher. (eds.) 1993. *The Service Quality Handbook*. New York: AMACOM.

Schmidt, W.H., and J.P. Finnigan. 1992. *The Race Without a Finish Line: America's Quest for Total Quality*. San Francisco: Jossey-Bass.

Schon, D.A. 1983. *The Reflective Practitioner: How Professionals Think in Action*. New York: Basic Books.

Schrage, M. 1990. *Shared Minds: The New Technologies of Collaboration*. New York: Random House.

Senge, P.M. 1990a. *The Fifth Discipline: The Art and Practice of the Learning Organization*. New York: Doubleday/Currency.

_____. 1990b. "The Leader's New Work: Building Learning Organizations." *Sloan Management Review* 32(1): 7-23.

Senge, P.M., C. Roberts, R.B. Ross, B.J. Smith, and A. Kleiner. 1994. *The Fifth Discipline Fieldbook*. New York: Doubleday/Currency.

Stewart, T.A. 1991. "Brainpower." *Fortune* 123(11): 44-46ff.

_____. 1994. "Intellectual Capital: Your Company's Most Valuable Asset." *Fortune* 130(7) (October 3): 68-74.

Tobin, D.R. 1993. *Re-Educating the Corporation: Foundations for the Learning Organization*. Essex Junction, VT: Oliver Wight/OMNEO.

Utterback, J.M. 1994. *Mastering the Dynamics of Innovation: How Companies Can Seize Opportunities in the Face of Technological Change.* Boston: Harvard Business School.

Watkins, K.E., and V.J. Marsick. 1993. *Sculpting the Learning Organization: Lessons in the Art and Science of Systematic Change.* San Francisco: Jossey-Bass.

Weckert, J. and C. McDonald. (eds.) 1992. "Artificial Intelligence, Knowledge Systems, and the Future Library." *Library Hi-Tech* 10:1-2.

Wheatley, M.J. 1992. *Leadership and the New Science: Learning About Organization from an Orderly Universe.* San Francisco: Berrett-Koehler.

Wick, C.W., and L.S. Leon. 1993. *The Learning Edge: How Smart Managers and Smart Companies Stay Ahead.* New York: McGraw-Hill.

Zuboff, S. 1988. *In the Age of the Smart Machine: The Future of Work and Power.* New York: Basic Books.

INVESTING IN HUMAN RESOURCES:
STAFF TRAINING AND DEVELOPMENT AT THE UNIVERSITY OF BRITISH COLUMBIA LIBRARY

Erik de Bruijn and Margaret Friesen

INTRODUCTION

Nothing will be as important to the quality of library and information services provided to scholars and students within colleges and universities as the quality of people recruited, retrained, retained, and supported to manage and deliver these services (Abell and Coolman, 1982).

In more and more academic libraries today, growing costs and shrinking budgets inevitably lead to fewer staff. Yet the volume of work continues to increase, the pace of technological change is escalating, and the information needs of library users are becoming more sophisticated. Library administrators and supervisors must therefore ensure that their remaining staff have the necessary skills and knowledge to meet these challenges.

Advances in Library Administration and Organization,
Volume 14, pages 63-94.

The costs of not providing staff training and development are high, and represent a potential waste of human resources and talent. Job dissatisfaction, boredom, isolation, inefficiency, low productivity, high turnover, and an inability to attract and retain high caliber staff members are among the consequences of ignoring human resource development. A formal staff training and development (STD) program is increasingly seen as a cost-effective means of ensuring that library staff can work at maximum effectiveness to fulfill the library's mandate and continue to have rewarding and interesting careers.

Staff training and development refer to two interconnected functions which provide both necessary job-related skills to an organization's staff and opportunities for personal and professional growth. Specifically, staff training implies the acquisition of those particular skills or competencies which enable staff members to perform the responsibilities of their positions as effectively as possible. Staff development encompasses those activities which assist staff members to grow as individuals, prepare themselves for increased levels of responsibility, and attain long-range professional and career goals.

Despite a long history of STD programs in industry and government, however, few academic libraries have developed and instituted a comprehensive STD program. The experience of the University of British Columbia Library in planning and implementing such a program may serve as a model for other academic libraries.

REVIEW OF THE LITERATURE

While the general literature on STD is extensive, much less has been published specific to libraries, particularly academic libraries. A review of recent library-related STD literature did not find any single model of a comprehensive plan—a program that addresses training and development needs of both professional and support staff, provides training at various levels for all subjects and skills, and uses a wide range of training methods. Instead it found useful guidelines and benchmarks, recommendations for policies and procedures, and examples of training needs surveys. In addition, the literature provided models of pilot projects and programs for specific groups, on specific topics, and for specific events, many of which involved the participation of staff committees. A number of these are discussed below.

Guidelines and Benchmarks

In 1992 the American Library Association published comprehensive guidelines for staff development programs which still serve as an excellent starting point for STD program planning (Lipow and Carver, 1992). Ken Haycock (1994) also provides guiding principles for staff development, including such key themes as philosophy and goals, focus, context, planning, support, content and processes, rewards and incentives, and evaluation. Another valuable source of information is the study of the practices of twenty-five successful companies by consultants Bennett and O'Brien (1994). They determined that there are twelve fundamental building blocks which lead to successful "perpetual learning." These include the methods of structured training, on-the-job-learning, and nontraditional forms of training, such as peer training, mentoring, and learning-by-doing training (action learning). An important point is raised by Susan Jurow (1992), who advises that in a changing information technology environment, libraries must devote financial resources for STD. She notes that training programs are needed in three particular areas: technology, interpersonal skills, and leadership skills.

Patricia Iannuzzi (1992) emphasizes the need for unleashing staff potential at all levels in the organization and lists a number of mechanisms that can be used in-house to encourage leadership development, such as task forces and coordinator positions. Epple, Gardner, and Warwick (1992) provide twenty tips for success in preparing a staff training program for automated systems. Nofsinger and Lee (1994) describe mentoring roles that senior librarians can employ to train entry-level reference librarians. The eight-step contract learning process described by Ruth Patrick (1990) still provides an effective foundation for reference librarians who wish to develop a self-directed plan for their own continuous long-term learning.

The Carlson Library at the University of Toledo developed a continuing education program, mostly with in-house resources, that was planned and implemented by an elected committee. No special budget was allocated initially for specific activities, although a special fund for faculty development became available later and was used to sponsor lectures and workshops (Phillips, Freimer, and McLean, 1988).

Finally, Smith (1992) paints a rather unflattering picture of the library profession's current continuing education "ecology," describing it as "event-focused" and lacking in continuity. He advocates a "green movement" to change present practices, and emphasizes the need for all levels of library staff to participate in turning librarianship into a "learning profession."

Model Programs for Reference Training

Earlier reviews of reference training models have observed that the literature on continuing education for reference librarians was sparse. For example, Cromer and Testi (1994) were frustrated by the lack of substantive information about programs for acquiring knowledge of specific subject areas. They describe a continuing, integrated program at the University of New Mexico Centennial Science and Engineering Library. The program forms part of existing reference role responsibilities and uses a variety of learning methods, including formal training, partnering at the reference desk, tours, tutorials, subject-specific projects, and subject-related hands-on exercises. This model addresses the diversity of the subject knowledge required as well as the need for flexibility in subjects and timing. The integrated approach results in continuity, builds on previous expertise, and provides opportunities for individual practice and participation in both presentation techniques to the group as well as hands-on learning of the subject matter. This model improves on an earlier one, described by Testi and Bordeianu (1993), which used staff exchanges and peer training methods. Although there were some advantages in this unstructured and voluntary approach, the authors advocated a more formal program.

Model Programs for Training for Automation

Of all the programs described in the literature, model programs for training for automation are the most numerous and diverse in methodology. An online public access catalogue training program at Rutgers University Libraries was developed to facilitate the transition from one automated system to another. The planning committee identified ten critical elements and twenty pointers for success for effective training programs. Key aspects were program content and design, training environment, scheduling, and follow up.

The special problems of training library staff for automation in a decentralized system, where branches are often sparsely staffed, were addressed at the University of Kentucky Libraries (Goode and Vass, 1989). Essential elements for success were the inclusion of librarians from the branches on the original committee, the breakdown of preparation tasks into projects, and the scheduling of workshops consisting of easily digestible units of training on a continuous basis. As in the peer training model for reference librarians at the University of New Mexico, committee members accepted the responsibility for planning workshops for particular topics. These were followed by on-site consulting, where all staff were trained using hands-on techniques. At the same time, the committee developed a guide that reviewed the material covered earlier by the workshops and on-site presentations. Follow-up interactive workshops were presented after one year. The authors concluded that the committee approach was not the ideal model but did have advantages in involving staff from the beginning, helped to create an in-house group of consultants, and resulted in a more integrated library organization through the interaction of the people involved in planning and presenting the training sessions.

At the University of Arizona, the library provided both the resources and the environment for staff to learn computer skills in their own Staff Creativity Lab. Lab learning was only one part of the overall staff training program (not described in this article) and addressed all skill levels on an ongoing basis (Glogoff, 1994). The University Libraries at Virginia Polytechnic Institute and State University embarked on a three year training program to help staff "navigate...through the virtual information space of the electronic environment." To ensure adequate access to equipment, it was accompanied by the installation of two microcomputers for every three employees. All staff members participated in the program, and the library developed a cadre of in-house trainers who followed up the formal sessions with peer training. The program recognized the continuous nature of training in an integrated electronic environment, viewing training as a process, not just an event, and resulted in a network of experienced users and trainers (Kriz and Queijo, 1989).

At the University of Houston, a variety of techniques was used to train staff for online reference searching. Some individuals attended vendor-sponsored regional workshops and then trained others back home, some programs used self-paced instructional materials, one program taught technical skills to staff who helped end-users with their own online searching. A program for the use of CD-ROM based indexes was the most structured of all, consisting of a 10-hour package, primarily demonstration, reinforced with hands-on practice (Wilson, 1989).

Training programs for multicampus and multilibrary networks have been developed for ILLINET member libraries (Hammerstrand, 1989) and for University of California Melvyl libraries using Medline (Renford, 1989). Both programs employ the "train the trainers" or pyramid approach to reach large numbers of staff. Formal programs for automation training were used at the University of Delaware (Glogoff, 1989) and Boston College Libraries (Cronin, 1989). At the latter, training for a new and integrated library system was the full time responsibility of the automation librarian during the migration phase and continued after implementation to provide continued updating to staff.

Model Programs for Specific Target Groups

At the University of Tennessee, a curriculum development project uses a computer-assisted method for training all newly-hired student assistants and support staff (Bayne, 1993). The curriculum covers six topics at the introductory level: orientation, access to periodicals, computers in libraries, acquisition and organization of collection materials, reference services, and resource sharing.

Specially-designed institutes, seminars, or projects are also used to deliver STD to specific target groups. For example, research library administrators attend the UCLA Senior Fellows Program, which lasts for several weeks, to debate leadership issues (Lynch, 1994). A group of junior level librarians, professional staff without library backgrounds, and computer staff focused on technology and the future at the Columbia University Libraries Staff Development Seminar (Harris and Lewis, 1991). Recently graduated librarians from three different Chicago research libraries attended the Professional Development Program, which the Council on Library Resources funded for three successive years (Trevvett, 1991).

At the unit planning level, a specific just-in-time training program was used at the University of California at San Diego to train managers undertaking performance reviews with their staff. George

Soete (1992) describes the specific training tool employed to focus on the "writing skills needed to develop effective performance goals, objectives, and self-reviews." The program provides a practical model of contract learning, self-directed planning, and goal-based self review.

While none of the training and development initiatives reviewed are comprehensive solutions for all the STD needs of academic library staff, their individual components can be combined to create a plan for a continuing program which successfully addresses the needs of all library staff, regardless of level or functional specialization. In developing its STD plan and program model, the University of British Columbia Library has used the experience of other libraries as a foundation, enlarging and expanding upon it, and integrating it with the STD experience of other labor-intensive organizations.

THE UNIVERSITY OF BRITISH COLUMBIA LIBRARY

The UBC Library, located in Vancouver, British Columbia, Canada, is a large, decentralized academic research library organized into functional and subject reference units. The current full-time equivalent (FTE) staff consists of 87 librarians, 8 management and professional (M&P) staff, 247 support staff, and 48 FTE student assistants. While turnover among librarians and M&P staff is low, 27 percent of support staff positions change hands each year, as well as about 30 percent of student assistant positions.

For many years, the UBC Library dealt with both staff training and staff development needs on an ad hoc basis. No formal staff training and development program was in place, and there was no central budget for training or development activities. This does not mean that considerable training and development activities did not take place, but rather that they were handled on an individualized basis when specific needs arose, and were funded from "soft" money. Generally speaking, those individuals who requested training or whose supervisors requested it for them received it, and specific training sessions were provided to staff who were faced with new technology and equipment, but there was no organized library-wide plan to train and develop staff consistently.

DEVELOPMENT OF A PLAN

In response to recommendations made in 1988 by an External Library Review Committee and in agreement with the library's 1991 Strategic Plan, responsibility for staff development and training was centralized and formally assigned to the Assistant University Librarian (AUL) for Administrative Services. In 1991 a Staff Training and Development Committee was formed, chaired by the AUL, which included librarians and support staff from both public and technical service units. This committee had the mandate to develop a plan for a STD program suitable for the library and its staff by April 1992.

During the summer of 1991 a Training Needs Survey (Appendix A) was designed and sent to all staff. The results of that survey were analyzed in the fall, and provided the committee with information about the needs and priorities of staff for training which would help them in the workplace. In October 1991 the committee met with Susan Jurow, Director, Office of Management Services, Association of Research Libraries, who advised the committee that the major emphasis should be on training that meets organizational needs, such as, training which provides the skills which enable staff members to perform their jobs. However, individual needs for development and continuing education should also be addressed to enable staff to fully contribute to the organization's attainment of its goals. She advised the committee that it should use a five-year time frame for the development and implementation of a comprehensive STD program. A long-range goal would be the appointment of a Staff Training and Development Officer who would plan and coordinate training activities and supervise implementation.

The committee recognized that in the interests of effectiveness and economy it had to look beyond library and even university resources in developing an STD program. The program should be pro-active in making use of training and development resources provided in the community, by other organizations and libraries, and by professional associations. At the same time, the development of an in-house cadre of experts with training skills who could pass on their knowledge was also highly desirable. Finally, to assist with individual career management, supervisors and staff members would be encouraged to agree on training and development objectives as part of staff members' annual goal setting and performance reviews.

The committee completed a draft plan by the late spring of 1992. The draft was reviewed by the library administration and was circulated to all staff for comment and suggestions. In August 1992 the final version was approved by the library administration and copies were distributed to all staff members.

THE PLAN

The plan recognizes human resource development as an investment and exhorts the library to make this investment in its human capital resource in reasonable proportion to its investment in collections, information technology, and facilities. The plan outlines goals and objectives, assigns responsibilities, establishes program levels, and describes expected results of STD initiatives.

Goals and Objectives

1. To maintain and develop a staff of the highest quality which can respond to the demands of today's work environment as well as prepare itself for the challenges of the future.
2. To provide high-quality library-oriented training which will give staff members the skills and knowledge they need to perform their responsibilities effectively.
3. To offer fair and equitable training and development opportunities to all library staff members.
4. In cooperation with all levels of staff members, to create a supportive climate which provides training and developmental opportunities to staff members to assist them in fulfilling the information needs of library users and to provide scope for career and personal growth.

Responsibilities

Planning and providing for staff training and development are basic responsibilities of line supervisors and managers. The greater part of training will take place within individual operating units. Division/branch heads and supervising librarians are responsible for ensuring that their staff members receive the training they need to perform their duties. They will be encouraged to discuss training and development needs with their staff at least once a year during goal setting and performance review meetings, and to develop individual and unit training plans. They will be asked to forecast unit requirements for training and to forward these to the AUL for administrative services to assist in developing the library's training plan for the year and to ensure that the best use is made of the staff training and development budget.

Staff members are responsible for informing their supervisor of training and development needs. During goal setting and performance review meetings, they should ensure that their supervisors are aware of any training and development activities they have completed, whether within or outside the university. Staff members should ensure that such information is included on their resumes or in their personnel files.

The office of the AUL Administrative Services will coordinate training and development activities which transcend individual unit requirements and are common to the whole library system. The office will provide information about courses, workshops, and other development opportunities, facilitate in-house workshops, schedule staff orientation sessions, liaise with both on- and off-campus organizations which provide training, obtain training aids, and materials, provide administrative and clerical support for training and development activities, and monitor and control expenditures.

The Staff Training and Development Committee will provide assistance and advice to the AUL Administrative Services, participate in planning and creating programs, and monitor staff training and development activities. It will serve as a forum for the discussion of training and development needs and the library's annual training plan. The committee will be representative of the library's staff, including both support staff members and librarians, and will serve as a channel of communication for training and development concerns.

Program Levels

The training and development program will consist of the following phases: (1) orientation and socialization to the institution; (2) core skills training to perform assigned responsibilities; (3) reinforcement and enhancement of learned skills; (4) training and development to cope with change and/or new roles, and (5) career development and succession planning, including training opportunities for experienced or plateaued staff members.

Orientation and Socialization

The orientation and socialization program for new staff members will consist of three parts, designed to familiarize the staff member with the university, the library, and the individual work unit where the staff member is employed. The first phase, provided by the university's Department of Human Resources, will give new staff members an overview of the university and its mission, and provide necessary employment, staff benefit, and bargaining unit information.

The second part, to be held at regularly-scheduled intervals, will be provided by the library. It will officially welcome the new staff member to the library, give an outline of the library's organization, mission, and responsibilities, demonstrate how the staff member's position relates to these, provide an introduction to and tour of various functional sections of the library, and provide additional information about training and development opportunities. An important part of this phase will be to articulate the library's values and communicate a synopsis of the library's strategic plan to the new staff member.

The third part will be carried out by the individual unit head or supervisor to whom the new staff member reports. This will include physical orientation to the workplace, including the location of lunch and washroom facilities, emergency exits, instruction in fire and other emergency procedures, provision of first aid and safety information, and an introduction to co-workers in the unit, and to staff members in other units with whom the new staff member will be in contact.

Results: Staff members will have an overview of the library's operations, be able to relate their responsibilities to the library's mission, be integrated into the organizational culture of the library, be familiar with their physical work environment, be aware of emergency and safety procedures, and be familiar with applicable conditions of appointment, benefit programs, and bargaining unit membership.

Core Skills Training for Job Performance

Skills training encompasses the skills, knowledge, and techniques a new staff member needs to perform her or his duties successfully. Each individual's needs will be different, resulting from varied educational, training, and experiential backgrounds, and an individualized approach will be most appropriate. Heads and supervisors will need to work with new staff members to determine skills training needs that must be fulfilled for successful job performance, and to schedule the necessary training.

The bulk of this training will occur within the operating unit where the staff member works. This is the most appropriate place for teaching the skills and techniques needed to perform the duties of the staff member's position. Some skills will lend themselves to a more organized and centralized approach. Circulation and serials check-in training for unit staff, for example, will be more effectively handled by skilled cadre staff from the circulation and order divisions. Such divisions will have training included as part of their function. General familiarization with the online catalogue, for example, will be best handled on a library-wide basis as well.

Other skills are most effectively taught by other organizations on or off campus. Word processing, electronic mail, and supervisory and management skills, all of which are not unique to the library's operations are examples of these. For instance, Continuing Studies offers a variety of wordprocessing and microcomputer courses, the Disability Resources Center provides training on working with people with disabilities, the Department of Human Resources provides basic supervisory training, and the Office of Management Services of the Association of Research Libraries provides a comprehensive program of management training for librarians. This does not preclude the development of in-house training programs in these areas if the demand for such training is high, the facilities and physical space are available, qualified library staff members can act as trainers, and such an approach is cost-effective.

Results: Staff members will be fully trained in the skills and techniques they need to know to perform their responsibilities and to operate the equipment they must use. They will have at least a general and basic knowledge of online files and commands, the library's internal electronic message system, and the library's classification system. Supervisors and managers will receive supervisory and management skills training.

Reinforcement and Enhancement of Learned Skills

Without practice and reinforcement, learned skills soon fade away. An important part of the training program will be refresher and advanced training which reinforce and enhance skills previously learned. The need for such training for individual staff members will be established when the individual and head or supervisor discuss the staff member's training needs for the coming period and develop an individualized training plan, usually as part of a performance review discussion. Refresher and enhancement training for online systems, wordprocessing, customer service, and supervisory skills, for example, will be scheduled on a periodic basis.

Results: Periodic refresher training will ensure that staff members review and retain learned skills and competencies. The development of a training plan for each staff member through consensus will ensure that staff members build on the base of what has been previously learned, and have the opportunity to gain wider knowledge and more specialized skills and abilities. Enhancement training will contribute to each staff member's mastery of her or his responsibilities.

Training and Development for Change and New Roles

The library's strategic plan calls for a staff which is sensitive to changes in the information market place and which is aware of new directions in research, teaching, and scholarship. The library's staff will be faced with ambiguity and uncertainty as the library's role changes and develops, and as new services and new technologies are implemented to facilitate user access to information. New skills will be required and new roles will become available for staff members as service priorities shift, and state-of-the-art technology is introduced.

Change can be viewed as positive or negative, and it is important to ensure that staff members are provided with training on coping with change, so that change is not perceived as a threat. Continuing training will be made available to assist staff members in focussing on the opportunities provided by change—opportunities which may make their jobs more interesting, challenging, and rewarding. Not only must staff members receive training on coping with change in relation to job responsibilities, but also in relation to the effects of change on the individual person. Training staff realize that organizational and personal well-being go hand-in-hand, and that personal or life skills training, such as stress management, contributes to the effectiveness of staff members in the workplace.

At the same time, staff will be trained for new roles and responsibilities as these become available. This is in keeping with the library's view of its human resources as an asset to be developed, and its commitment to internal staff development. Preparation for such new roles will take various forms—on the job training, self- or peer-instruction, workshops, short courses, and more formal educational programs. Coupled with this commitment to career development is the recognition that as responsibilities increase, so will compensation and classification. Training and development must occur within the context of applicable collective agreements.

New roles and new services often imply the use of new technology. The adoption of such technology must be preceded or be concurrent with adequate staff training. Not only must staff members be trained in the use of equipment such as microcomputers or workstations: they must also be trained in the use of application systems and software. Such training can occur on-the-job, but a preferable option is through the provision of short courses, so that instruction and learning can take place in a context free from the pressures of the normal workplace. Changes in methods of operation brought about by the use of new technology, and the adoption of the new technology itself, may be subject to the terms of collective agreements. Changes in job responsibilities brought about by the use of new equipment or processes often lead to changes in compensation and classification.

Results: Staff members at all levels will be fully trained in coping with change in the workplace, and will react to change in a creative and flexible manner, viewing change as an opportunity for innovative improvements in library services. They will receive training which will help them cope with the effects of change on themselves. There will be an emphasis on both the personal and organizational well-being of all staff members. Staff members will be trained for new roles and responsibilities which become available. Compensation and classification will adequately reflect individual staff members' responsibilities. New technology will be introduced in accordance with the requirements of collective agreements, and all staff members will be fully trained to use both new hardware and software.

Career Development and Succession Planning

In selecting new staff members, the library carefully assesses each individual applicant's long-term potential for contributing to the library's mission and goals. The library is therefore naturally committed to providing opportunities for career growth to its staff members. For that reason, the library will provide staff training and development opportunities which will yield long-term as well as short-term benefits to both the organization and the individual. The library will support and encourage continuing education, research, and professional development, and make time available to staff members, subject to the constraints of budget and collective bargaining agreements. It will provide training which will assist staff members in qualifying for greater responsibility within the library system. This will provide a pool of qualified internal applicants when higher level positions become available. Such positions will be filled in accordance with the terms of the relevant collective bargaining agreements.

For certain positions, it may be appropriate to solicit, encourage, and identify potential successors and to provide them with the necessary training and education. Not only will this permit a smooth and speedy transition when the position becomes vacant, but the presence of trained understudies will protect the library from the loss of critical knowledge and skills caused by the sudden and unplanned loss of key individuals. Moreover, it will provide a pool of trained individuals who can act as temporary replacements during periods of vacation, leave, or illness. A successor training program must be carefully designed to avoid favoritism and exclusion, and is probably most applicable to significantly specialized professional and management positions.

Changing demographics, poor economic conditions, and a smaller staff have led to reduced turnover and fewer opportunities for career advancement. There are more applicants for fewer senior positions, and many staff members are faced with the fact that they will remain in their current positions or at their current levels of responsibility for a long time. More than ever before, careers are peaking while individuals are at a relatively young age. Boredom, fatigue, career plateauing, and burnout must be addressed for both support staff and librarians if the library is to use its human resources as effectively as possible. Individual needs for development and growth must be meshed with organizational needs, and must be recognized by supervisors and managers. While change and new technologies may provide refreshment and stimulation for some staff members, for others such alternatives as job rotation, job enrichment, or job enlargement may be appropriate. The library's training and development program will support such opportunities by providing staff members with new or enhanced skills to work in new areas or undertake different responsibilities.

Results: The library will demonstrate its commitment to career development and progression for all staff members through an emphasis on long-term as well as short-term training and staff development. Individual staff members will be viewed in terms of the long-term contribution they can make to the library as a whole in a variety of capacities. A pool of trained staff members will be available when more senior or specialized positions become vacant. Understudies will be trained for key managerial and specialist positions. Cross-training and staff development will facilitate job exchange, job rotation, and job enrichment to counteract the effects of career plateauing, burnout, and stagnation. Individual needs for growth, variety, and development will be satisfied, and will be seen to contribute to the effectiveness of the organization.

IMPLEMENTATION AND PROGRAMMING

Participation and Activities

With the plan and the results of the Training Needs Survey in hand, the STD Committee launched its program in the fall of 1992. The committee developed contacts with program suppliers and other campus training groups and took advantage of new or overhauled campus training programs wherever possible.

In keeping with the advice of Susan Jurow, the major emphasis of the first year's program was to address the first three phases of training described above. During the second and third years, while training activities to meet these needs were continued, more attention was paid to meeting the needs for fourth and fifth phase training. For example, during the third year, the STD program placed added emphasis on courses that would help staff to adapt to changing roles and changing career paths, including new skills in management, leadership, and information technology.

During the first year of the program 678 participants attended 171 STD sessions. In the second year 647 participants attended 270 STD sessions. While participation was almost the same as the year before, a greater diversity of courses was offered. In the third year 1,100 participants attended 240 STD sessions.

Orientation and Socialization

As a first step to address orientation and socialization training needs, the library's internal orientation program was revised. It now consists of a printed information kit, a presentation by members of the library administration of one and one half hours, a two-hour tour of the main library and the library processing center, and individually selected "open house" tours of two divisions or branch libraries of 30 minutes each. This program supplements the physical orientation provided by division/branch heads as well as the two orientation sessions for new staff sponsored by the university's human resources.

Core Skills Training for Job Performance

Training activities during the first year included a wide variety of computer skills and supervisory and management skills. The committee approved 132 requests to attend computer skills courses provided by Continuing Studies. Courses were chosen by the individual, with approval for time off from work given by the supervisor. The majority of courses were for introductory microcomputer skills and word processing, but the range of courses was broad, including spreadsheets and database management. Using Continuing Studies resources to meet these training needs was a cost-effective way for the library to meet its core skills training objectives, with the cost averaging $112 per individual course registration. Two new computer skills courses related to the new version of the library's online catalog were launched in-house with library staff as trainers. The first consisted of informal "on the road" shows presented to all staff by library systems staff on new features. The second consisted of peer training for specific online searching skills presented to public service librarians.

Human Resources' Managerial and Other Skills Training Program (MOST) courses were first offered in January 1993 and became the basis for core skills training in supervision and management. Eighty-eight staff members attended thirteen different courses. The two most popular topics were assertiveness training and conflict resolution training, followed by topics on performance reviews, coaching, and quality awareness. These courses cost an average of $31 per individual course registration. Like the computer skills courses, they were self-selected, open to all levels of staff, with approval for time off given by the supervisor.

In addition, library staff attended free on-campus courses such as disability awareness training, offered by the Disability Resource Center, and ergonomics awareness, offered by Occupational Health and Safety. Seven group sessions were attended by 168 staff members. Finally, to fill in training needs that could not be met by on-campus sources, the committee contracted with a local facilitator to present the Myers-Briggs personality assessment methodology to 20 staff members in-house, and paid registration fees for 25 staff members to attend three off-campus seminars on performance management and time management.

During the second year, the Computer Skills and MOST courses offered on campus were supported routinely, the first category at an average cost of $80 per individual course registration and the second at an average cost of $38. Three hundred and fifty participants attended courses in these categories. In addition, introductory Internet courses were offered in-house to approximately 100 staff members in three sessions. During the third year, Computer Skills and MOST courses were attended by 298 participants. In addition, seven in-house programs were offered by library trainers. These included sessions on personal security, the online catalogue, the Internet, FreeNets, copyright and photocopying, and cash handling. Ninety-six staff members attended sessions on interpersonal effectiveness, including valuing diversity, communication skills, conflict resolution, and customer services.

Reinforcement and Enhancement of Learned Skills

During the first year a number of individual requests for courses such as customer service training, intermediate microcomputer skills training, and intermediate Internet training were supported. During the second year, a larger number of requests for off-campus training were supported, including such subjects as advanced cataloguing skills, the OCLC Interlibrary Loan system, interpersonal communications skills, and total quality management. During the third year, 36 staff members attended refresher sessions on human resource management, such as selection interviewing, employee relations, motivating staff, negotiation skills, and quality management.

Training and Development for Change and New Roles

During the first year two in-house training programs were developed and presented by library staff: system wide circulation service enhancements and cross-cultural communication skills for front line staff and monitors. In addition, 80 employees attended two sessions on organizational change facilitated by Shelly Phipps of the University of Arizona Library.

During the second year three external programs addressed training for change and new roles, focusing on the electronic library, the national information policy, and advanced management skills. One of the MOST courses, Employee Relations, was specifically adapted to the library's needs by human resources staff. Three sessions were attended by 60 librarian and support staff supervisors, many of whom had had no previous formal training in this area. During the third year 45 staff members attended sessions on teaching and training roles to prepare themselves for new liaison and facilitation responsibilities.

Career Development and Succession Planning

During the first year several programs addressed this phase of training for individual staff members: 18 librarians attended the ARL Basic Management institute in Washington State, the Preservation Assistant attended several courses on enhanced techniques for preserving materials, several individuals took advanced training on Unix, and several librarians attended the Western Canada Film and Video Showcase in Banff. During the second year, four programs addressed career development, including library instruction techniques, multi-type library networks, records management, and advanced preservation training.

During the third year 45 staff members attended sessions on leadership development, such as problem solving, time management, process improvement, managing stress, strategic planning, leadership styles, decision making, risk taking, delegating, and ethics. Another 45 staff members attended specialized courses to develop technical skills on such topics as media librarianship, preservation, resource sharing, Pacific Rim resources, freedom of information legislation, accounting, copyright, records management, electronic texts, and advanced searching. In addition, support was provided to 96 staff members to attend one or both of the two major conferences which were held in Vancouver that year: those of the Canadian Library Association and the North American Serials Interest Group.

Staff Training and Development Coordinator

The position of a half-time staff training and development coordinator was created (Appendix B), reporting to the AUL for Administrative Services. The coordinator chairs the STD Committee (Appendix C) and coordinates all staff training and development activities within the library, develops in-house courses and training aids where appropriate, and manages the plan. The STD coordinator controls and authorizes expenditures and also tracks other internal training initiatives to form a composite picture of training activities. These include training initiatives of the Librarians' Association, travel grants for training or development approved by the Librarians' Travel Grants Committee or by the library administration.

The coordinator is also a member of the University's Managerial and Other Skills Training Program (MOST) Committee. She negotiates customized courses for in-house delivery with the Human Resources and Continuing Studies Departments. She monitors programs offered by the Faculty Development Committee and the Faculty of Commerce's Executive Programmes Division, and assesses them for applicability to the library. She also maintains liaison with the UBC Librarians' Association professional development subcommittee.

Budget

No STD plan can succeed without the support of senior management and without a commitment of adequate financial resources. The UBC Library Administration recognizes that its human resources are a vital asset and a key contributor to the success of the library's mission. Accordingly, it has established an annual STD budget of $60,000 (or about $170 per FTE library staff member, excluding student assistants). The budget is used to cover the cost of all in-house training activities, external training, staff development activities, workshops, and related travel, subsistence, and accommodation costs. The objective is to increase the budget initially to 1 percent of library human resource expenditures, with a further goal of 2 percent of such expenditures.

The budget is allocated according to the priorities for the year. Usually about half of the $60,000 is allocated for the on-campus MOST and Computer Skills sessions and the remainder is allocated for individual requests. However, allocations can be adjusted to meet the needs of specific groups or to take advantage of resource opportunities. For example, in 1994 a significant portion, about 20 percent, was allocated for attendance at two major conferences described above.

In addition, a separate budget provides opportunities for librarians to travel to conferences and meetings of learned societies and professional associations. Allocations from this budget are made by the Librarians' Travel Grants Committee, which reports on its expenditures to the AUL for administrative services. The annual budget of $11,500 is not adequate to fully meet all the costs of professional travel, and librarians can only be partially reimbursed for their expenses. A future goal is to increase this budget to a minimum of $30,000.

Communications and Approval Procedures

Training needs are identified through periodic surveys (Appendix D), STD Committee initiatives, supervisors' recommendations, administrative recommendations, by staff through formal annual goal setting and performance reviews, and by constant informal communications, often through electronic mail. The objective is to make decisions on approvals as quickly and nonbureaucratically as possible. Most communications, applications and approvals are initiated using internal electronic mail. Individuals and/or supervisors send their requests to the Coordinator as soon as they assess needs or as they come across a training opportunity. The STD Committee develops priorities for some of the major themes of the year as well as approving significant portions of the budget for these priorities and for on-campus courses. Individual approvals are validated by the coordinator in consultation with the manager/ supervisor, the AUL for Administrative Services, and the Financial and Budget Manager. For individual requests requiring unusual expenditures, the coordinator consults with other members of the library administration before authorizing the financial commitment.

For library programs and MOST courses, staff in the librarian's office, including the human resources assistant, provide registration support. The human resources assistant is an ex-officio member of the Staff Training and Development Committee and often coordinates logistical requirements, such as booking meeting facilities, arranging for refreshments, and so forth.

Training Methods and Resources

Training methods and styles vary, depending on the purpose of the training or learning, the timing, and the level of skills to be acquired. Principles of programming for adult education are followed, such as competency-based education, self-directed planning, focus on learning, life-long learning, and new (and traditional) delivery systems (Knowles, 1980). Examples of new STD delivery systems include video conferences, videotapes, self-directed learning through online electronic workshops, model simulations in group settings, one-on-one tutoring, and computer labs.

The training resources of other on-campus organizations are employed wherever suitable. These include the Computer Skills training programs organized by the university's Continuing Studies, and three programs offered by the university's Human Resources Department: the Managerial and Other Skills Training (MOST) program; the Better English Skills Training (BEST) program; and Occupational Health and Safety courses. In addition, individuals may select courses offered by the Disability Resource Center and the Faculty of Commerce's Executive Programs.

Where appropriate, on-campus courses may be customized for in-house delivery. In addition, new in-house programs have been designed and delivered, and unique needs have been satisfied by sending individuals for specialized training at both on-campus and off-campus venues.

SUMMARY

The UBC Library, like other academic libraries, is and will continue to be a labor-intensive service organization with the major part of its budget used for human resources. Rather than an expense to be minimized, however, such an expenditure should be viewed no differently than expenditures on collections or facilities, namely as an investment which provides long-term benefits to the library's clientele—faculty, researchers, students, and the community. The library's staff should be recognized as significant partners in the academic enterprise of the university, and, as any other asset, should be used as effectively as possible. An investment in staff training and development, even in times of financial constraint, makes it possible for individual staff members to contribute at their full potential. In so doing, they can best provide the information services which advance the quality of research and teaching at the university.

To attain its goal of excellence in supporting teaching and research and in keeping with the university's pledge to be a model employer, the UBC Library is committed to encouraging and supporting the training and development of its staff. The library recognizes that these activities promote both personal and organizational well-being, and has allocated the necessary resources to provide training and development opportunities for all staff members.

The UBC Library's STD plan defines training and development in its broadest sense, aims to cover all training needs from recruitment to the exit interview, and is designed to address all levels of learning, from introductory to expert, for all library staff. It builds on the benchmark practices advocated by a number of staff training and development practitioners and draws on, combines, and expands on the planning and programming models found in the library literature.

As a university library model, it is probably unique in several respects, specifically by formalizing programming, budgeting, and assigning responsibility for planning and coordination in a long-term and continuing context. After three years of implementation, it still adheres to the principles outlined in its plan, but remains flexible and evolutionary in its response to changing individual needs and organizational dynamics.

APPENDIX A

UBC Library Training Needs Survey

The UBC Library Training and Development Committee is surveying all Library staff to determine what training programs the Library should offer. Please fill in this form and return it to **Peggy Ng, Librarian's Office, Main library** by August 15.

TOPICS:

	Useful in current job	Useful for career development	Not relevant

1. LDMS Training

introduction to LDMS	____	____	____
tips and tricks for searching	____	____	____
advanced searching	____	____	____
specific files (i.e. Microlog, Headings, Bibliography)	____	____	____

Please list the file(s) you would like to learn more about. _____

other _____

2. Human Resources Department Workshops
    (programs available through UBC Human
    Resources)

management skills	____	____	____
personnel appraisal	____	____	____
time management	____	____	____
"Training the trainer" skills	____	____	____

3. Personal Skills

supervisory skills	____	____	____
stress management	____	____	____
written communication	____	____	____
public speaking	____	____	____
conducting meetings	____	____	____
creative thinking	____	____	____
interviewer/interviewee skills	____	____	____
counseling skills	____	____	____
budgeting skills	____	____	____
grant proposals writing	____	____	____
assertiveness	____	____	____
coping with change in the workplace	____	____	____
other!	____	____	____

4. Technological Skills

introduction to microcomputers	____	____	____
hard disk management	____	____	____
word processing	____	____	____
personal file management (like EndNote & ProCite)	____	____	____
spreadsheet	____	____	____

	Useful in current job	Useful for career development	Not relevant
statistical software	_____	_____	_____
online searching of remote databases	_____	_____	_____
desktop publishing	_____	_____	_____
communications software	_____	_____	_____
electronic messaging systems and networks (Internet etc.)	_____	_____	_____
database management programs	_____	_____	_____
keyboarding skills	_____	_____	_____
office equipment operation (fax, photocopiers etc.)	_____	_____	_____
a-v equipment operation (VCRs, remote computer setup)	_____	_____	_____
preservation of materials	_____	_____	_____
other	_____	_____	_____

5. People Skills

communicating with people from different cultures	_____	_____	_____
serving and working with people with disabilities	_____	_____	_____
working with problem patrons	_____	_____	_____
teaching skills	_____	_____	_____
telephone skills	_____	_____	_____
conflict resolutions in the workplace	_____	_____	_____

6. General Interest

first aid	_____	_____	_____
CPR	_____	_____	_____
rescue skills	_____	_____	_____
copyright	_____	_____	_____
information malpractice	_____	_____	_____
disaster procedures	_____	_____	_____
library ethics	_____	_____	_____
research methods	_____	_____	_____
preservation of materials	_____	_____	_____
evaluating library services	_____	_____	_____

Please tell us **which** position you currently hold:

LA I____ LA3____ Clerical____ How long have you worked at the UBC Library? ____

LA2____ LA4____ Secretarial____ In which service group do you work? _____

Librarian____ Other (please specify) _____ Public Services____ Tech Services____

APPENDIX B

University of British Columbia Library

Position Description

Librarian

Revised: January 1995

Administration

Position Number: 287

Divisional Title: Staff Training & Development Coordinator (50%)

SUMMARY OF RESPONSIBILITY

To plan and implement the library's staff training and development program for professional and support staff.

Qualifications

A graduate degree in library science from an accredited institution in addition to an undergraduate degree in an appropriate discipline. Formal training and experience in teaching and curriculum development. Proven management skills and relevant library experience. Ability to demonstrate leadership and innovation. Familiarity with staff training and development needs and opportunities.

Relationships

Works under the general direction of the Assistant University Librarian for Administrative Services and in cooperation with other assistant university librarians, heads, managers, coordinators and colleagues. Consults with and chairs the Staff Training and Development Committee. Participates as a member of the Library Planning and Management Council.

Duties

1. In consultation with the Assistant University Librarian for Administrative Services and the Staff Training and Development Committee, plans and implements a comprehensive program for staff training and development.
2. Plans, develops, and implements in-house programs where appropriate.
3. Supports training and development programs offered by other on-campus resources, for example, Human Resources MOST (managerial and other skills) Program, Computer Skills, and so forth.
4. Supports individual training and development needs from off-campus resources where appropriate.
5. Prepares and manages the budget for the library's staff training and development programs.

Standards of Performance

A cost-effective staff training and development program which meets the needs of both the library and its staff, and which assists in providing excellent services to the library's clients.

APPENDIX C

Staff Training and Development Committee
Terms of Reference

Purpose

To review and monitor the library's staff training and development plans and programs, and to recommend changes to the library administration. To provide advice, guidance, and feedback to the Staff Training and Development Coordinator on staff training and development plans and programs. To assist with the implementation of the staff training and development program.

Membership

Members will include librarians, management and professional staff, and support staff from both public and technical services units, as well as individuals with expertise in information technology, frontline services, management, and UBCLIB training. The AUL Admin. Services, the Human Resources Assistant, a representative from UBCLA, and a representative from CUPE 2950 will be ex-officio members. The committee will be chaired by the Staff Training and Development Coordinator.

Selection and Term of Office

Members, excluding ex-officio members, will be appointed by the library administration from among those volunteering to serve. The selection will ensure adequate representation from all staff groups and areas of expertise. The term of office will be two years, but can be extended.

Reporting Relationship

The committee will report on its activities to the library administration through the AUL Administrative Services.

Terms of Reference

1. To review and monitor the library's staff training and development plan, and to recommend changes to the library administration.
2. To prepare an annual program and budget for staff training and development activities for approval by the library administration.
3. To provide advice, guidance, and feedback to the STD Coordinator on staff training and development plans and programs.
4. To assist the STD Coordinator with the implementation of the staff training and development program.
5. To evaluate the effectiveness of programs offered.
6. To maintain an awareness of staff training and development activities in general, and to provide information to and feedback from colleagues.

APPENDIX D

Staff Training and Development Survey

To: All Library Staff
From: Staff Training and Development Committee

We need your help in planning training programs for 1993/4. **Please assist** the Committee by answering the following questions and returning the questionnaire to Margaret Friesen, Chair, STDC, c/o Interlibrary Loan *by* June 15, 1993. **Thank you very much.**

I.   Which courses did you take since Sept. 1992 which were reimbursed by the Library and/ or taken during working hours. Place a tick next to all courses you took. (Do NOT include courses taken with tuition waivers).

    a.   Microcomputer/computer courses:

        _____   1.   MSWord Introductory
        _____   2.   MSWord Intermediate or advanced
        _____   3.   Other word processing
        _____   4.   Level I: Introduction to microcomputers, e.g., DOS 1 , courses on setting up your hard disk, etc.
        _____   5.   DOS 2 or 3, or advanced courses on operating systems
        _____   6.   Spreadsheets
        _____   7.   dBASE or other database
        _____   8.   Internet
        _____   9.   Unix
        _____   10. Desk top publishing
        _____   11. Other: specify

    b.   Interpersonal/management skills (MOST):

        _____   12. Assertiveness
        _____   13. Conflict resolution
        _____   14. Career Planning
        _____   15. Disability Awareness
        _____   16. Quality Awareness
        _____   17. Selection Interviewing
        _____   18. Manager as Coach
        _____   19. Performance Review
        _____   20. Records Management
        _____   21. Introduction to Central Agencies
        _____   22. Negotiating Across Cultures
        _____   23. Racism
        _____   24. Curriculum Design: Teaching in a Diverse Society
        _____   25. Cultural Diversity Training
        _____   26. UBC SuperHost Training
        _____   27. Telephone Courtesy

   c. Other Library-funded programs:

	28.	Focus on Service
_____	28.	Focus on Service
_____	29.	Ergonomics (S. Dodson, convener)
_____	30.	How to Satisfy Every Customer
_____	31.	Performance Management (BCLA)
_____	32.	B. C. Information Policy Conference
_____	33.	Myers Briggs
_____	34.	Priority Management
_____	35.	UBCLIB
_____	36.	Safety/Security (2-day for Safety committee members)
_____	37.	Safety/Security (other shorter sessions, e.g., RCMP)
_____	38.	Safety: fire extinguisher
_____	39.	Organizational issues (Shelley Phipps)
_____	40.	ARL Basic Management
_____	41.	Other: (what did we forget?)

II. Have you used these skills or this knowledge at work? How?

_____

_____

III. If you have *not* used these skills, why not?

_____

_____

IV. What topics do you *need* further training in for your current job or for career progress on campus? Specify:

_____

_____

V. What topics do you *want* training in for personal interest or other career options ? Specify:

_____

_____

VI. Do you supervise, train or coach others?
       _____Yes   _____No

_____

_____

If yes, what skills or knowledge are needed:
a. By you?

_____

_____

b. By the staff you supervise?
Comments: (add a page)

_____

Name (optional) _____

Division/Branch (optional) _____

REFERENCES

Abell, M.D., and J.M. Coolman. 1982. "Professionalism and Productivity: Keys to the Future of Academic Library and Information Services." in *Priorities for Academic Libraries*. San Francisco: Jossey-Bass: 71.

Bennett, J.K., and M.J. O'Brien. 1994. "The 12 Building Blocks of the Learning Organization." *Training* 31(16):41-48.

Cromer, D.E., and A.R. Testi. 1994. "Integrated Continuing Education for Reference Librarians." *RSR: Reference Services Review* 22 (4): 51-80.

Cronin, M.J. 1989. "The Second Time Around: Transition to a New Integrated Library System." *Library Hi Tech* 7(28): 76-77.

Epple, M., J. Gardner, and R.T. Warwick. 1992. "Staff Training and Automated Systems: 20 Tips for Success." *Journal of Academic Librarianship* 18 (2): 87-89.

Glogoff, S. 1994. "The Staff Creativity Lab: Promoting Creativity in the Automated Library." *Journal of Academic Librarianship* 20 (2): 19-21.

_____. 1989. "Staff Training in the Automated Library Environment: A Symposium." *Library Hi Tech* 7 (28): 61-62.

Goode, J.M., and M.M. Vass. 1989. "Training Library Staff for Automation in a Decentralized Library System: The University of Kentucky Experience." *Southeastern Librarian* 39 (Fall):97-101.

Hammerstrand, K. 1989. "Library Staff Training for ILLINET Online." *Library Hi Tech* 7(28): 70-73.

Harris, C.L., and D.W. Lewis. 1991. "The Columbia University Libraries Staff Development Seminar." *Journal of Academic Librarianship* 17 (3): 71-73.

Haycock, K. 1994. "Staff Development in Library and Information Services: Reconfiguring Effective Practice." *Education for Library and Information Services: Australia* 11 (2): 3-16.

Iannuzzi, P. 1992. "Leadership Development and Organizational Maturity." *Journal of Library Administration* 17 (1): 19-36.

Jurow, S. 1992. "Preparing Academic and Research Library Staff for the 1990s and Beyond." *Journal of Library Administration* 17 (1): 5-17.

Knowles, M.S. 1980. *The Modern Practice of Adult Education: From Pedagogy to Andragogy*. Englewood Cliffs, NJ: Cambridge Adult Education.

Kriz, H.M., and Z.K. Queijo. 1989. "An Environmental Approach to Library Staff Training." Library Hi Tech 7(28): 62-66.

Lipow, A.G. 1989. "Training for Change: Staff Development in a New Age." *Journal of Library Administration* 10 (4): 87-97.

Lipow, A.G., and D.A. Carver. (ed.) 1992. *Staff Development: A Practical Guide.* 2nd ed. Chicago: American Library Association.

Lynch, B.P. 1994. "Taking on the Issues in a Changing Environment: The Senior Fellows Program." *Journal of Library Administration* 20 (2): 5-15.

Nofsinger, M.M., and A.S.W. Lee. 1994. "Beyond Orientation: The Roles of Senior Librarians in Training Entry-Level Reference Colleagues." *College & Research Libraries* 55 (2): 161-170.

Patrick, R.J. 1990. "Self-Directed, Contract Learning for the Reference Librarian."
    Reference Librarian (30): 207-224.
Phillips, J.C., G. Freimer, and D.D. McLean. 1988. "A New Direction for
    Continuing Education at Carlson Library." *Journal of Academic
    Librarianship* 13 (6): 340-344.
Renford, B.L. 1989. "Staff Training Systemwide on MELVYL MEDLINE." *Library
    Hi Tech* 7 (28): 73-76.
Smith, D. 1992. "The Greening of Librarianship: Toward a Human Resource
    Development Ecology." *Journal of Library Administration* 17 (1): 37-53.
Soete, G. 1992. "The Rhetoric of Performance Management: A Training Problem
    and Two Solutions." *Journal of Library Administration* 17 (1): 107-118.
Testi, A.R., and S. Bordeianu. 1993. "Staff Exchange in Reference Services." *RSR:
    Reference Services Review* 21 (4): 7-12.
Trevvett, M. 1991. "The Professional Development Program." *Journal of Academic
    Librarianship* 17 (3): 73-75.
Wilson, T.C. 1989. "Training Reference Staff for Automation in a Transitional
    Environment." *Library Hi Tech* 7 (28): 67-70.

EFFECTIVE MENTORING PROGRAMS FOR PROFESSIONAL LIBRARY DEVELOPMENT

Linda Marie Golian and Michael W. Galbraith

INTRODUCTION

Mentoring is an old idea with relevance and meaning in today's world of education, work, and personal development. The term "mentor" has a long and distinguished history. It is synonymous with a wise teacher, guide, and friend. It is the mentor who often makes the difference between success and failure throughout a lifetime of careers.

In Homer's book the *Odyssey*, Odysseus is preparing to begin an epic voyage. He entrusts his son Telemachus to his friend Mentor, who guides Telemachus in the passage from boyhood to manhood. Mentor, an Ithacan elder, often has his body taken over by Athena, the Greek goddess of war, wisdom, and craft. Therefore, when Mentor's body was taken over by Athena, he was given the goddess's

Advances in Library Administration and Organization,
Volume 14, pages 95-124.
Copyright © 1996 by JAI Press Inc.
All rights of reproduction in any form reserved.
ISBN: 0-7623-0098-1

most glorious qualities as he guides Odysseus' son. It was wisdom personified. Mentor's role in this story is instructive, "for he is a classic transitional figure, helping the youth achieve his manhood and confirm his identity in an adult world..." (Daloz, 1986, p. 19).

The purpose of this paper is to examine and describe the mentoring process and highlight how it may be utilized as a means of professional library development. This developmental tool can enhance the professional status of librarians in various career paths and organizational responsibilities. Mentoring is also an effective equalizer in overcoming professional advancement barriers for under-utilized groups such as women and minorities in library leadership roles.

The paper begins by providing various definitions of mentoring and discusses common themes pertaining to all professions. It continues with a brief review of mentoring literature, including contributions made within library science. Types of mentoring, informal and sponsored, are examined next with emphasis placed on characteristics that make mentoring programs effective and the benefits of mentorship. Mentoring roles, phases, and functions are explored, followed by a presentation of critical issues and special concerns in mentoring. Finally, specific library applications of effective mentoring programs are highlighted.

DEFINITIONS AND THEMES OF MENTORING

The literature offers numerous definitions of mentoring, although a single, widely accepted operational definition of mentoring is absent. Jacobi (1991, p. 505) suggests that this "definitional vagueness is a continued lack of clarity about the antecedents, outcomes, characteristics, and mediators of mentoring relationships despite a growing body of empirical research."

In this section a sampling of definitions from education, management, psychology, and library literature is provided as a means of illustrating this definitional dilemma. An operational definition of mentoring drawn from the work of Galbraith and Zelenak (1991) is provided, along with some themes derived from these diverse explanations of mentoring. The following selection of definitions for mentor or mentoring are not exhaustive. It is an attempt to provide a picture of the definitional diversity surrounding these terms as gleaned from the literature of a variety of disciplines including library science.

Higher Education Definitions

The following definitions are provided from selected studies concerned with mentoring in the field of higher education.

- "Mentoring... is a process by which persons of superior rank, special achievements, and prestige instruct, counsel, guide, and facilitate the intellectual and/or career development of persons identified as protégés" (Blackwell, 1989, p. 9).
- "Mentoring as a function of educational institutions can be defined as a one-to-one learning relationship between an older and a younger person that is based on modeling behavior and extended dialogue between them" (Lester and Johnson, 1981, p. 119).
- "Mentoring is a form of professional socialization whereby a more experienced (usually older) individual acts as a guide, role model, teacher and patron of a less experienced (often younger) protégé. The aim of the relationship is the further development and refinement of the protégé's skills, abilities, and understanding" (Moore and Amey, 1988, p. 45).
- "Mentors are colleagues and supervisors who actively provide guidance, support, and opportunities for the protégé. The functions of a mentor consist of acting as a role model, a consultant/advisor, and sponsor" (Schmidt and Wolfe, 1980, p. 45).
- "Mentors have something to do with growing up, with the development of identity" (Daloz, 1986, p. 19).
- "Mentoring is simply the advice from a respected, experienced person provided to someone who needs help" (Heller and Sindelar, 1991, p. 7).

Management/Organizational Behavior Definitions

Research on mentoring in the field of management and organizational behavior provides the following definitions.

- Mentoring is "the process of an older, more experienced member of the organization assuming a paternal, guiding role with a less experienced protégé" (Kogler-Hill, Bahniuk, Dobos, and Rounder, 1989, p. 356).

• A mentor is "a senior member of the profession or organization who shares values, provides emotional support, career counseling, information and advice, professional and organizational sponsorship, and facilitates access to key organizational and professional networks" (Olian, Carroll, Giannantonia, and Feren, 1988, p. 16).

• Mentoring is "a dynamic, reciprocal relationship in a work environment between an advanced career incumbent (mentor) and a beginner (protégé) aimed at promoting the career development of both" (Healy and Welchert, 1990, p. 17).

• "Mentors are influential people who significantly help you reach your major life goals" (Phillips-Jones, 1982, p. 21).

• "Mentoring occurs when a senior person (the mentor) in terms of age and experience undertakes to provide information, advice and emotional support for a junior person (the protégé) in a relationship lasting over an extended period of time and marked by substantial emotional commitment by both parties" (Bowen, 1985, p. 31).

• "A mentor is a person who oversees the career and development of another person, usually a junior, through teaching, counseling, providing psychological support, protecting, and at times promoting or sponsoring" (Zey, 1984, p. 7).

Psychology Definitions

Several definitions of mentoring and mentors are provided from the field of psychology.

• "Mentoring is defined not in terms of formal roles, but in terms of the character of the relationship and the functions it serves" (Levinson, Darrow, Klein, Levinson, and McKee, 1978, p. 98).

• "The terms mentor and sponsor are often used interchangeably to indicate older people in an organization or profession who take younger colleagues under their wings and encourage and support their career progress" (Speizer, 1981, p. 708).

• "A mentor provides encouragement and helps adult learners increase their psychological options through perceiving and using various alternatives" (Schlossberg, Lynch, and Chickering, 1989, p. 121).

Library Definitions

From library literature, several definitions of a mentor emerged. Surprisingly, although a number of articles focusing on mentoring within librarianship exist, rarely do the authors define the term mentoring.

- "Mentor: Someone senior to you in the field who actively works for your advancement. A mentor can also be a role model" (Maack and Passet, 1994, p. 16).
- "A mentor is anyone who enhances, enriches, and encourages the professional development of another member of the profession" (Kaplowitz, 1992, p. 219).
- "Mentoring is...a special relationship within an organization. It extends only to a handpicked few the counseling, role modeling, and interest that might benefit every motivated young employee" (Harris, 1993, p. 37).

As evidenced by these comments, many different definitions of the terms mentoring and mentor exist. Jacobi (1991, p. 506) suggests that "although many researchers have attempted to provide concise definitions of mentoring or mentors, definitional diversity continues to characterize the literature." Merriam (1983) contends that "mentoring appears to mean one thing to developmental psychologists, another thing to business people, and a third thing to those in academic settings" (p. 169). It may be said that it means yet another thing to library science professionals, although it could also successfully be argued that no operational definition for mentoring currently exists within library science.

This paper supports the mentoring definition developed by Galbraith and Zelenak (1991). The authors agree with their suggestion that mentoring is defined "as a powerful emotional and passionate interaction whereby the mentor and protégé experience personal, professional, and intellectual growth and development" (p. 126). They contend that mentoring is a unique one-to-one teaching and learning method that incorporates the basic elements of collaboration, challenge, critical reflection, and praxis.

Definitional Themes

A cursory review of the above definitions would suggest that many of them have some very similar "themes" running through them. The literature suggests that mentoring:

- is a process within a contextual setting
- involves a relationship between a more knowledgeable and experienced individual (perhaps older) and a less experienced individual
- provides professional networking, counseling, guiding, instructing, modeling, and sponsoring
- is a developmental mechanism (personal, professional, and psychological)
- is a social and reciprocal relationship
- provides an identity transformation for both mentor and protégé.

Not all of the definitions have the same focus and meaning. Some of the definitions are rather narrow in perspective. Many do not recognize the essence of a good mentoring relationship, such as the necessity of a reciprocal and developmental process for both the mentor and mentee. Mentoring is not just about giving advice on professional and career advancement and opportunities. It is about dialogue, caring, authenticity, emotion, passion, and identity.

REVIEW OF THE LITERATURE

Mentoring as a tool for enhancing personal and professional growth and development is found in a plethora of settings and disciplines. To understand the process, one must review a selected body of literature from various disciplines.

Teacher and student role development in public education is one area of mentoring that has been investigated (Evans, 1992; Heller and Sindelar, 1991; Neubert and Stover, 1994; Reilly, 1991; Weinberger, 1992; Wilkin, 1992). Mentoring has also been a topic of discussion relating to enrichment possibilities in the student personnel and developmental functions in higher education (Brown and DeCoster, 1982; Jacobi, 1991; Lester and Johnson, 1981; Shandley, 1989).

Mentoring has found its place in higher education settings as well as through improving the instructional process, student and faculty relations, professional enhancement, and faculty development (Berger, 1990; Cohen, 1995; Daloz, 1986, 1990; Evanoski-Orsatti, 1988; Galbraith and Zelenak, 1991; Harnish and Wild, 1993; Schlossberg, Lynch, and Chickering, 1989; Wunsch, 1994).

Mentoring is cited as an important element in understanding the development and growth of men and women (Daloz, 1986; Levinson et al., 1978; Sheehy, 1976). Career development of women in organizations through the ability of mentoring to enhance advancement and increase a person's power, and influence has been the focus of numerous publications (Bolton, 1980; Fisher, 1988; Haring-Hidore, 1987; Kram and Isabella, 1985; Speizer, 1981; Wolfe, 1993). In addition, Bova, (1987), Cohen (1995), Fagenson (1989), Hall and Associates, (1986), Kogler-Hill et al. (1989), Kram (1985), Murray (1991), Phillips-Jones (1982) and Zey (1984), as well as many others, have investigated mentorship in relationship to organizational and career development, leadership potential, and learning within business and industry settings.

Not all researchers view mentoring in a positive light. For example, Darling (1985a) warns the nursing profession of "toxic" mentors and the negative consequences of having a relationship with a mentor with negative attributes. Elsewhere Darling (1985b) provides a discussion on how one becomes a mentoring manager for those who are not a nurse administrator. Prestholdt (1990) provides strategies for developing leadership skills through the mentoring process, and Yoder (1990) attempts to clarify and enhance the understanding of mentoring through a conceptual, analytic approach.

Professional library literature has only recently begun to discuss and report research on mentorship as seriously as with other disciplines. The majority of the literature is directed toward professional and leadership development. Special emphasis on mentoring women for leadership roles within the academic setting has been a primary concern. Mentoring for leadership is now being incorporated into library science graduate school curriculums as a tool for enhancing professionalism and continuous learning. Mentoring is also used as a method for reducing faculty and student turnover in library science programs (Burruss, 1988; Kaplowitz, 1992). Burruss (1988) and Kaplowitz (1992) suggest that strategies aimed at developing such mentoring programs assist young librarians in moving into and through librarianship.

Specific career development and training for women is a major focus of the literature on mentoring (Hunt and Michael, 1984; Logsdon, 1992; Maack and Passet, 1994; McNeer, 1988; Person and Ficke, 1986). In general, mentoring is viewed as a means to an end in the development of the professional talent of women. It is seen as one way of reversing the inverse management situation of women library leaders. Essential in these writings is the notion that women's voices should be heard in relation to concepts such as power, influence, leadership, academic criteria for promotion and tenure, visibility, research, and management. Harris (1993), however, in a thoughtful essay, points out that mentorship programs have failed to catapult enough women and minorities into library leadership roles. Overall, the literature suggests that the development of mentorship programs that address the uniqueness of female library professionals is needed.

The literature provides a wealth of information about mentorship. But, as noted earlier, it provides no comprehensive, yet functional definition of the process (Bogat and Rednar, 1985; Healy and Welchert, 1990; Jacobi, 1991; Merriam, 1983). A clear understanding of what should be the most rational purpose of mentorship and the meaning of the results of these programs is lacking. As a result, mentoring continues to mean different things to different disciplines, and various groups may not concur on how the process should be conceptualized and utilized in promoting the growth and development of mentors and mentees.

TYPES OF MENTORING

There are basically two types of mentoring that take place—informal and formal (or sponsored mentoring). Informal mentoring is a relationship that occurs that is unplanned, and, in most cases, not expected. A certain "chemistry" emerges drawing two individuals together for the purpose of professional, personal, and psychological growth and development. Informal mentoring seems to be a qualitative experience that has great meaning for the parties involved. However, it is very difficult to explain how the mentoring relationship began, developed, and sustained itself and how the process can be replicated. The phenomenology of informal mentoring is a rich area for further inquiry.

The second type of mentoring, sponsored or formal mentoring, is an intentional process that is the result of a planned and operating mentoring program. It is a method designed to reach a variety of specific goals and purposes, defined within the setting in which it operates. The majority of the literature describing sponsored mentoring suggests similar processes or steps in the development and operation of a program (Cohen, 1995; Murray, 1991; Wunsch, 1994; Weinberger, 1992; Zey, 1984):

- Step 1: Recruitment and Screening of Mentors and Mentees
- Step 2: Orientation and Training of Mentors and Mentees
- Step 3: Length and Frequency of Mentoring Relationship
- Step 4: Matching Mentors and Mentees
- Step 5: Continuous Evaluation of Mentoring Relationship

Both informal and sponsored mentoring occurs in nearly every profession. While sponsored mentoring is grounded in a structured and planned program, informal mentoring can provide the same benefits and positive results as those experienced through formal programs. However, informal mentoring can be rather inexplicable and an elusive phenomena. It has great meaning and value for those who have had the pleasure of experiencing and engaging in it, but may never be repeated. It is important to realize that the characteristics, roles, phases, functions, and benefits of mentoring are consistent for both informal and sponsored mentorship.

EFFECTIVE MENTORING CHARACTERISTICS

Although all organizations benefit from the kind of supportive, open climate which encourages mentoring relationships, it is equally unrealistic to believe that all seasoned professionals are capable of being either effective mentors or mentees. Appropriate mentorship pairing, whether informal or sponsored, is perhaps the most crucial element in effective mentoring affiliation. Besides seeking a union of mutual respect, mentors and mentees pursue a professional union based upon personalized preferences of human attributes and characteristics.

Desired Mentor Attributes

It is not uncommon for mentees to initiate a mentoring relationship with someone they admire and aspire to emulate. Mentees selecting a possible mentor should consider someone with several of the following attributes:

- good communication skills
- sound and seasoned knowledge of the organization, including its political structure
- a wide range of professional skills and resources and the willingness to share these skills with others
- time and effort to invest in developing an effective professional relationship
- organizational support, grounded in knowledge that normal work responsibilities will not suffer
- history of encouraging and motivating others
- mutual respect
- reputation for respecting differences in opinions and challenging ideas not people
- previous experience in developing other professionals
- genuine interest in helping others advance (Caldwell and Carter, 1993; Cagrill, 1989; Clutterbuck, 1985; Daresh and Playko, 1992; Kram 1985; Shea, 1994).

Desired Mentee Attributes

Some mentors also actively seek out individuals for professional development relationships. Many mentors desire mentees who are similar to themselves, while others seek individuals with unique strengths and talents that may complement the mentor's abilities (Burruss, 1988).

It is important to realize that even in informal mentoring, most connections occur because of a specific sharing of a common interest, a meeting of the minds, or a spark between two people. Mentors do not view potential mentees as globs of clay awaiting the great master sculptor. In reality, successful mentees are committed professionals who are willing to take responsibility for their career and diligently work towards developing their success. Effective characteristics and attributes that attract the attention of potential mentors include:

- desire to work towards a professional goal
- ability to accept help from others
- good listening skills
- willingness to carry out obligations, activities, and commitments
- desire to learn new things
- desire to see different points of view
- discretion
- ability to object diplomatically
- ability to show appreciation for help received
- eagerness to cooperate
- ability to handle setbacks
- positive attitude
- ability to ask for advice, and actually use it
- not desperate or clingy
- willing to work hard and juggle several tasks at once (Caldwell and Carter, 1993; Cagrill, 1989; Clutterbuck, 1985; Daresh and Playko, 1992; Kram, 1985; Shea, 1994).

ROLES, PHASES, AND FUNCTIONS

The literature describes the role of the mentor in various ways (Bova, 1987; Cohen, 1995; Daloz, 1986, 1990; Galbraith and Zelenak, 1991; Kram, 1985; Murray, 1991; Zey, 1984). It suggests that the mentorship experience goes through various phases and, within these phases or stages, certain functions are performed.

Roles

Within the mentorship process, a mentor may be viewed as playing many different roles that combine and enhance professional, personal, and psychological development. For some the mentor is a role model, advocate, sponsor, counselor, guide, developer of skills and intellect, listener, host, coach, challenger, visionary, balancer, friend, sharer, facilitator, resource provider, confirmor, and/or protector. The label or title that is given to the mentor may be decided, quite frankly, as a result of how well he or she understands the total mentorship process, its phases, and required functions.

Phases and Functions

The phases and functions of mentorship are best understood if discussed together and not as two distinct and separate dimensions of the process. It is within the various identified phases of mentorship that specific functions are performed. Getting "out of tune" with the development aspects of the process can result in a less than positive experience for both the mentor and the mentee.

There has been little investigation of the phases of mentoring from a conceptual and theoretical perspective except for the work of Kram (1985) and Cohen (1995). Kram (1985) examined phases of a mentoring relationship using psychological and organizational factors that influenced career and psychological functions performed at any give time. She suggested that developmental relationships vary in length but generally proceed through four predictable, though not entirely distinct, phases.

The initiation phase is the period in which the relationship is conceived and becomes important to both mentor and mentee. This phase may last for six months to one year.

The second phase is called the cultivation phase and lasts from two to five years. During this phase the positive expectations developed during the initiation phase are continuously tested against reality. The mentor and mentee during the cultivation phase discover the real value of relating to each other and clarify the boundaries of their relationship.

Phase three is called separation. This phase is marked by significant changes in the type of functions provided by the relationship and in the effective experiences of both the mentor and mentee. In addition, it is a time in which the mentee experiences new independence and autonomy, as well as turmoil, anxiety, and feelings of loss. The separation phase lasts from six months to two years.

Kram's final phase is redefinition. It is during this phase that the relationship becomes: a more peer like friendship or one that is characterized by hostility and resentment. In general, the redefinition phase is a recognition by both the mentor and mentee that a shift in developmental tasks has occurred and that the previous mentorship process is no longer needed or desired. It is the moment in which the mentor achieves peer status.

Within these four phases, two types of mentoring functions are rendered. There are career functions, "those aspects of the relationship that enhance career advancement" and psychological functions, "those aspects of the relationship that enhance a sense of competence, identity, and effectiveness in a professional role" (p. 23). Career functions include sponsorship, exposure and visibility, coaching, protection, the assumption of challenging assignments. The psychological functions include role modeling, acceptance and confirmation, counseling, and friendship. In the redefinition phase, little if any career and psychological functions are provided, although, at times, sponsorship from a distance occurs as well as occasional counseling and coaching.

Cohen (1995) also suggests that mentoring should be understood as a dynamic and interactive process that occurs within phases of an evolving experience for the mentor and mentee and offers a somewhat different view of the process. His four developmental phases—early, middle, later, and last—were established to identify the basic issues and objectives of each phase and to suggest the type of mentor behaviors most appropriate for each stage of the relationship. He also developed the "Principles of Adult Mentoring Scale," a 55-item instrument designed to measure the effectiveness level of the mentor. Using this tool, Cohen has identified six essential behavioral functions that fall within these four phases.

Cohen's early phase is a period that focuses on interpersonal development during which the mentor emphasizes "relationship" behaviors with the mentee in order to establish the foundation of trust, non-judgmental acceptance, meaningful dialogue and relevant self-disclosure required to support mentoring. Specific mentor behaviors in this phase are responsive listening, open-ended questions, descriptive feedback, perception checks of feelings, and nonjudgmental sensitive responses to clarify emotional states and reactions. In the middle phase, the mentor emphasizes the accumulation and exchange of information for the purpose of making suggestions about the mentee's current plans and progress in achieving personal, educational, and career goals. Mentor behaviors in this middle phase include questions aimed at assuring a factual understanding of the mentees' present educational and career situation, a review of relevant background to develop personal profile, the asking of probing questions which require concrete answers, the offering of directive comments about present problems or solutions, a restating dialogue to ensure factual accuracy, and fact finding to assist in decision making.

The later phase contains facilitative and confrontive dimensions. The purpose of the facilitative dimension is to assist mentees in considering alternative views and options as they reach their own decisions about attainable personal, academic, and career objectives. The facilitative dimension allows the mentor to pose hypothetical questions to expand individual views, uncover the mentee's underlying assumptions, present multiple viewpoints to generate more in-depth analysis of decisions and options, examine the level of commitment to goals, analyze reasons for current pursuits, and review recreational and vocational preferences.

The second dimension of the later phase includes a confrontive aspect, designed to help mentees obtain insight into unproductive strategies and behaviors and evaluate their need and capacity to change. Mentor behaviors in the confrontive dimension include carefully probing activities aimed at assessing the psychological readiness of the mentee to benefit from different points of view. To do this effectively, the mentor openly acknowledges any concerns about possible negative consequences of critical feedback on the relationship, selects behaviors for meaningful change, uses feedback for impact, and provides reinforcing comments for fostering growth.

Finally, in the later phase the mentor acts more explicitly as a role model to motivate mentees to pursue challenges. Mentors directly encourage mentees to critically reflect on and be faithful to, their personally selected vision and their chosen educational and career paths. This phase also includes various contributions by the mentor, such as:

- sharing self-disclosing life experiences
- offering personal thoughts and feelings, emphasizing the value of learning from unsuccessful and difficult experiences
- sharing selected examples from one's own life,
- furnishing positive support in the mentee's ability to pursue goals
- providing realistic assessment and direction of mentee's progression in achieving goals
- portraying a confident view of appropriate risk-taking for further development
- reinforcing and encouraging the mentee, through statements and personal actions to attain stated objectives.

The final behavioral function of the mentor, is stimulating the mentees' critical thinking process. The mentor assists the mentee in envisioning personal and professional potential for future growth. To do this, mentors encourage mentees as they manage personal and career changes. Effective mentors advocate the necessity of taking the initiative in their transitions through life events. Other essential mentor behaviors include:

- making statements which require reflection on present and future educational, training, and career attainments
- asking questions aimed at clarifying perceptions about personal ability to manage change
- reviewing mentee choices based on reasonable assessment of options and resources
- offering comments directed at analysis of problem-solving strategies
- providing expressions of confidence and remarks that show respect for capacity to determine own future
- rendering encouragement to develop talents and pursue "dreams."

Cohen suggests that the framework of mentor functions viewed within distinct phases that the proposes is designed to explain the general developmental process of mentor and mentee interaction rather than being a rigid sequence or step-by-step progression. The six behavioral functions of the mentoring role should be interpreted as a general blueprint of an evolving interpersonal relationship which include mentor and mentee adaptation and modification.

In general, the mentoring functions, as detailed by Cohen (1995), Daloz (1986), Kram (1985), and many others, is summarized as:

- building and establishing relationships
- providing information and support
- facilitating change
- challenging and confrontive exchanges
- modeling
- visioning

These essential functions of the mentor seem to be relevant whether one is engaged in an informal mentoring relationship or a sponsored (formal) one. The value of this relationship is to be determined by the mentor's art and ability to nurture such a partnership.

MENTORING BENEFITS TO THE LIBRARY PROFESSION

Effective mentoring is a four way exchange, which provides many benefits to the mentor, mentee, library organization, and the library profession as a whole. Similar to other service occupations, librarianship relies upon the ability of its professionals to assist patrons by supporting a wide variety of informational and other service needs effectively, skillfully, and competently. Mentoring programs are just one of many professional development tools which allow the library organization to foster effective skills for providing these services.

However, convincing library administrators about the overall benefits of supporting mentoring programs, and addressing the general misconceptions of these programs, can be difficult. Although in the last ten to fifteen years mentoring programs in education and business have abounded (Bey and Holmes, 1992), it is not uncommon to experience negative reactions and a general lack of support when trying to initiate a program within a library. A clear understanding of the benefits of a mentoring program, including its capacity to help library administrators empower others (Field and Field, 1994), to encourage networking (Swoboda and Miller, 1986), to support an open system of management (Caruso, 1992) and to assist interested librarians in soliciting support from reluctant library administrators is necessary for success.

Mentee Benefits

The professional goal of many individuals is to be successful and satisfied in their career of choice. According to Fagenson (1989), securing an effective mentor helps many individuals achieve this goal. Mentees benefit from a variety of long-lasting and short-term mentoring relationships, as well as informal or sponsored mentoring programs. Often mentees indirectly benefit from the reflective power and respect associated with their mentor. Traditional mentee benefits include:

- a sense of vision about career direction
- personalized recognition and encouragement
- honest criticism and informal feedback
- first hand advice concerning the professional obligations of balancing research, teaching, job assignments, and personal life
- insight into the informal rules of career advancement
- wisdom concerning the informal politics, and pitfalls, of a library organization
- leads for professional committee assignments
- a resource for showcasing one's accomplishments
- insight into how to develop a network of professional colleagues
- introduction to influential people in the field
- nomination and general information concerning awards, scholarships, and grants
- support during promotion and tenure processes
- an experienced ear to listen to and react to professional dilemmas (Hall and Sandler, 1989; Kram, 1985; Shandley, 1989).

Mentor Benefits

One myth associated with mentoring programs is that mentors reap few benefits from the relationship. This myth explains why some qualified library leaders decide not to get involved in mentoring relationships and why some library administrators are reluctant to support mentoring programs. In reality, mentors receive a wide array of professional and personal benefits from mentoring programs.

One specific benefit shared by many mentors is a deep personal satisfaction for repaying what is perceived as a past debt. According to Weber (1980) most mentors had mentors themselves earlier in their careers. They acknowledge that they were successfully mentored during crucial career periods. These relationships have resulted in many professional successes, and these mentors now wish to continue the cycle of support by helping other professionals in similar ways. Moore (1982) summarized this sentiment in his Two Golden Rules of Mentoring:

- Golden Rule #1: "Do unto others what they have done to you!"
- Golden Rule #2: "Do unto others what was not done for you!"

Another crucial benefit for mentors is the ability to build new professional relationships with colleagues. It is not uncommon for a library leader advancing through the ranks of administration to relocate. These moves to various locations, while exciting, often result in a lack of collegial contact and professional isolation. To counter this situation, many library leaders actively seek cybernetic professional relationships, such as mentoring, to build their new local support network, and expand their community of professional associations.

Additional benefits include:

- personal satisfaction from assisting other professionals in their career growth
- fresh ideas and feedback concerning projects in process
- a network of former mentees at other institutions available for quick consultations and support
- increased power and visibility in professional associations through mentee networking
- assistance in effectively managing new projects and those already in process
- cutting edge information concerning the profession the mentor normally would not have time to explore
- personal satisfaction from spotting and developing new talent
- expansion of professional colleague foundation (Burruss, 1988; Clutterbuck, 1985; Hall and Sandler, 1989; Phillips-Jones, 1982; Shandley, 1989).

Library Organization Benefits

It is critical that library administrators realize that institutions, as well as individuals, benefit from mentoring programs. A principle responsibility of any library leader includes the quest of ensuring continuity of leadership for both the organization in which he or she works and the profession (Moore, 1982). By fostering a climate conducive for informal and sponsored mentoring relationships, the library organization benefits from:

- competent and dependable people who continue to grow and meet new challenges and obligations
- increased productivity

- increased commitment, especially from beginning professionals
- lower rates of staff turn over
- team based/facilitative management
- establishment of an organizational esprit-de-corps
- increased effective communication and cooperation among staff and administrative units
- lower incidence of burn out for senior level professionals
- improved community relations, awareness and support (Hall and Associates, 1986; Hall and Sandler, 1989; Shandley, 1989)

Benefits to Librarianship

A desirable component of many professional programs is the availability of internships for students and new professionals as a means of defining, refining, and testing their newly acquired knowledge (Sheldon, 1991). Both informal and sponsored mentoring programs provide opportunities for library students and beginning professionals to meet and interact with others in the field. When supported by a specific library administration or library association, these programs promote professional development and enhance the overall professionalism of librarianship.

Additional benefits for the profession of librarianship supported through mentoring programs include:

- developing a unified professional reputation
- supporting a professional code of ethics
- sharing a vision of professional services
- fostering an understanding of changing trends and technologies within the profession
- building necessary communication and negotiation skills
- supporting social responsibility and the need to incorporate global views
- developing professionals for their next career move (Sheldon, 1991)
- cultivating a sense of inquiry necessary for the growing knowledge base of the profession
- cultivating work place diversity by empowering minorities and women (Garten, 1994).

LIBRARY APPLICATIONS

The various definitions of mentoring, a review of literature, explanations of mentoring types, and the discussions of the roles and phases of mentoring all support a discussion of the effective application of mentoring and critical concerns relating to mentoring programs within library science. This discussion can best be divided among the three areas of library career development that are enhanced by mentoring programs—namely recruitment, burnout prevention, and career advancement.

Recruitment

Traditionally, mentoring is associated with assisting neophyte librarians through the pitfalls and advancements of their first professional assignment. However, before mentoring someone through his or her first library professional position, recruitment into the field must occur (Pollack, 1992).

Mentoring supports two special functions in recruiting new library science professionals. First, it is useful in helping encourage professionals from other fields to consider switching to library science. One of the profession's greatest strengths lies in the diversified backgrounds of its members. For many library professionals, librarianship was not their first career choice. The expertise and first hand experience that these professionals bring into librarianship provide the field with special talents, such as subject specialization, fiscal management, and liaison skills, that are necessary to keep library organizations functioning.

Secondly, mentoring is an essential and integral phase in encouraging talented library paraprofessionals to make the commitment to the profession through the acquisition of a library science degree. Many creative individuals with the potential to be leaders in library science, currently work in libraries as paraprofessionals. It is every librarian's responsibility to encourage these capable people to join the profession.

Currently, many of these individuals are encouraged to join the field through programs sponsored by various American Library Association groups. The Social Responsibilities Round Table Feminist Task Force Mentorship Program for Women of Color and the New Members Round Table Minorities Recruitment Program are two programs deserving special recognition in this regard. Both of these outreach programs seek out talented individuals and encourage them to apply for admission to an ALA accredited MLS program. They provide individuals with information concerning the profession and show them what kinds of financial assistance is available to them in the form of scholarships and grants.

Burnout Prevention

Like other service professions, librarians are prone to suffer from career burnout. Leading causes of career burnout for veteran librarians are techno stress, everyday public service obligations to library patrons, and the various administrative and job responsibilities.

Librarianship faces a challenging future filled with technological advancements which create stressful, frustrating, and sometimes frightening responses from librarians (Massey, 1995; Sullivan, 1992). Besides the traditional pressures of inadequate funding, under staffing, and repetitive job requirements, today's librarians must also confront swift changes associated with new electronic systems and informational products.

The presence of these pressures and their effects are supported by numerous studies concerning burnout and librarians working in public service positions (Blazek and Parrish, 1992). Burnout is a major obstacle to the retention of valued professionals in librarianship, and burnout prevention is a critical issue that every library leader must confront aggressively.

According to Massey (1995), mentoring is a simple and immediate process that can alleviate many of the negative conditions associated with burnout. Mentoring is a tool that encourages the sharing of knowledge, skills, and responsibilities among professionals. It provides a positive forum that helps librarians realize that they are not alone in their feelings and problems, and supports cross-training and team building for continual professional understanding and growth (Keele and DeLaMare-Schaefer, 1984; Massey, 1995).

Career Development/Advancement

In theory, every library administrator's job includes the responsibility for the professional development of subordinates

(Bennett and Shayner, 1988). Library administrators are realizing the satisfactory results that ensue from supporting career development for beginning and middle management librarians through mentoring programs. Although these library leaders understand that career advancement is just as vital for professionals in senior level positions, they commonly overlook mentoring as an effective tool for aiding the development of their senior staff members (Sheldon, 1991).

Realizing this void in career support for senior level professionals, the American Council on Education, and the Council on Library Resources have each developed unique professional development programs. Although quite different, both programs primarily use mentoring for overall program effectiveness.

The American Council on Education created the Fellows Program as a means of acknowledging how higher education, including library management, has become increasingly complex. This program is designed to assist all higher education leaders in acquiring a more sophisticated knowledge of funding, planning, budgeting, personnel management, and legal strategies. Upon the completion of the intensive one year training program, graduates can rely upon the benefit of a national network of Fellows and Mentors to assist them in their continued professional development and daily administrative problems.

Perhaps the best example of mentoring support for senior librarians is a program developed by the Council on Library Resources (CLR). Beginning in 1992 the CLR, in conjunction with the Association of College and Research Libraries Division of the American Library Association, created the New College Library Director Mentor Program. Like other CLR programs, the New College Library Director Mentor Program supports the overall goal of developing library leaders and effective library directors (Roberts, 1986).

First time library directors are paired with experienced directors who serve as coaches, guides, and peers for a designated one year period. New directors begin the program with an intense three day seminar, which is then followed-up with campus visits, telephone support, and electronic mail communications. This successful project has generated interest in, and acts as a model for, other groups who are considering incorporating mentoring into their programs.

CRITICAL ISSUES AND SPECIAL CONCERNS

Responsible utilization of mentoring for career development requires attention to the concerns and critical issues of the specific profession. Several critical issues and concerns of mentoring in the field of library science include women's issues, cross gender mentoring, and organizational climate.

Women and Library Advancement

The issue of equity for women in librarianship is a fundamental mission of the American Library Association's Committee on the Status of Women in Librarianship (COSWL). Although the gender imbalance is slowly equalizing, a few facts supported by COSWL and the Association of Library and Information Science Educators (ALISE) quickly highlight the importance of concern for the status of women in the library science profession. According to a 1992 ALISE Report:

- only 41 percent of all ALA accredited library education programs are headed by a woman dean/director
- 80 percent of library science students were female, but only 48% of the teaching faculty were female
- women hold only 29 percent of the full library science professorships in these programs
- while the majority of all professional librarians are female, the majority (65 out of 104 libraries) of Association of Research Library Directorships are held by males.

Mentoring and modeling are significant processes in the socialization of new professionals to any field. Many beginning female library professionals find few high ranking women who can help them acquire a leadership identity and position in librarianship. It is not unusual for an organization to exist with virtually no women at the highest levels of library administration who are available, capable, or willing, to serve as mentors and role models (Douvan, 1976). When senior level female administrators are available, chances are they have had little experience developing mentoring skills.

The shortage of female role models in advanced positions compounds the problem of limited feedback that newer female librarians receive during their professional climb (Collins, 1983). The number of women seeking upper level library management positions is increasing as they participate more widely in the overall labor force. However, the number of mentoring relationships available to women does not appear to be keeping pace with the increasing number of women wanting or needing mentors. This failure to identify and develop talented women reduces the overall effectiveness of the profession (Noe, 1988).

Mentoring is also an effective tool for achieving equity and creating a critical mass of tenured female library science educators to support the academic culture of the profession. Increasing evidence indicates that the faculty experience of a woman professor is strikingly different from that of her male compatriots, with national data demonstrating that women tend to be promoted and tenured more slowly than their male peers. It is suggested that mentoring programs be designed to couple female faculty who have been successful in achieving tenure and promotion with those new female professionals aspiring to reach these milestones of academic achievement (Johnrud, 1994). In addition, mentoring can be made more successful when it is part of a well conceived set of faculty development activities. Intensive orientation sessions for new faculty, along with frequent teaching in-service courses and colloquia for all faculty help create an environment for effective mentoring (Swenson, 1994).

Cross Gender Mentoring

In an attempt to create equal professional development and career opportunities for women librarians, cross gender mentoring holds great promise (Clutterbuck, 1985). However, this type of mentoring can pose some special personnel problems (e.g., such as unfounded office gossip) if not handled properly by the mentor, mentee, and library organization. The solution is relatively easy, requiring an extremely high level of openness and communication that leaves no room for rumor. An effective formula for cross gender mentoring is:

1. effective organization communication, plus
2. ample publicity, plus
3. organizational support, plus
4. clarity of the relationship's goals and objectives, equals

5. a mentoring relationship that is effective, mutually beneficial and relatively safe from petty office gossip (Clutterbuck, 1985).

This formula provides women mentees equal opportunity to all available mentors without regard to sex. It furnishes female mentees legitimate access to mentors in upper management and helps break down barriers so that cross gender mentoring is not viewed as an improper sexual act. The climate of open communications allows a mentor of the opposite sex to bestow legitimate compliments and praise upon mentees without people wondering about the relationship (Henderson, 1985).

Library Climate

The last special concern regarding the promotion of mentoring programs for library professional development includes fostering true career growth throughout all administrative levels of the organization. Effective library administrators support an open climate of mutual trust and respect within their organizations (Birnbaum, 1988). These administrators create cybernetic environments in which each person helps the organization grow and meet its overall mission, while simultaneously supporting individual growth.

In the real world, this ideal may be a lot harder to accomplish. For example, the library director may support on paper the concept of mentoring programs for professional development, while in actuality supporting only programs that do nothing more than provide beginning librarians with information about membership in professional organizations. Another common scenario occurs when upper management promotes mentoring programs for professional development but is unaware of (or unwilling to confront) the barriers presented by middle managers or others within the organization's bureaucracy. These library environments are not conducive to the development of effective mentoring programs for professional development and career advancement (Burruss, 1988; Kaplowitz, 1992). Effective library leaders realize the enormous benefits of mentoring programs for the mentors, mentees, organization, and library science profession. Along with the new emphasis on total quality management, shared decision making, and increased organizational communications, mentoring programs are finding a prominent position in the everyday management of today's library.

CONCLUSIONS

Society is noticing a growing demand for career development and enhancement in all professions, and mentoring is becoming popular as a tool which can be used in meeting these demands. Informal and structured mentoring programs are currently becoming more common in library schools and organizations. As mentoring has been used more often in other professions, library administrators have come to view this professional development method with new interest. However, like other professions, the field of library science needs to formulate some sort of consensus on the definition of this potentially powerful career development and advancement tool.

As mentoring is further utilized throughout the library science profession fewer negative stereotypes will exist. Wise library science faculty members and administrators will realize the potential of this method, not only for the library science student and beginning professional, but for the career development and enhancement of middle and upper level library professionals. As the field of librarianship prepares for a new generation of leaders and a new century of innovations, the benefits derived from mentoring will expand, and the new technologies of distance learning and services can be used to enhance its effectiveness so that this vital tool can reach an ever greater potential in professional development.

REFERENCES

Association for Library and Information Science Education. 1992. *Library and Information Science Education Statistical Report 1992*. Raleigh, NC: ALISE.

Bennett, S. M., and J. A. Shayner. 1988. "The Role of Senior Administrators in Women's Leadership Development." Pp. 27-38 in *Empowering Women: Leadership Development Strategies on Campus*, edited by M. A. D. Sagaria. New Directions for Student Services, no. 44. San Francisco: Jossey-Bass.

Berger, R. M. 1990. "Getting Published: A Mentoring Program for Social Work Faculty." *Social Work* 35: 69-71.

Bey, T. M., and C. T. Holmes. 1992. *Mentoring: Contemporary Principles and Issues*. Reston, VA: Association of Teacher Educators.

Birnbaum, R. 1988. *How Colleges Work: The Cybernetics of Academic Organization and Leadership*. San Francisco: Jossey-Bass.

Blackwell, J. E. 1989. "Mentoring: An Action Strategy for Increasing Minority Faculty." *Academe* 75: 8-14.

Blazek, R. D., and D. A. Parrish. 1992. "Burnout and Public Services: The Periodical Literature of Librarianship in the Eighties." *RQ* 32: 48-59.

Bogat, C. A., and R. L. Rednar. 1985. "How Mentoring Affects the Professional Development of Women in Psychology." *Professional Psychology, Research and Practice* 16: 851-859.

Bolton, E. B. 1980. "A Conceptual Analysis of the Mentor Relationship in the Career Development of Women." *Adult Education* 30(4): 195-207.

Bova, B. 1987. "Mentoring as a Learning Experience." Pp. 119-133 in *Learning in the Workplace*, edited by V. J. Marsick. New York: Croom Helm.

Bowen, D. 1985. "Were Men Meant to Mentor Women?" *Training and Development Journal* 39(1): 30-34.

Brown, R. D., and D. A. DeCoster. (eds.) 1982. *Mentoring-Transcript Systems for Promoting Student Growth*. New Directions for Student Services, no. 19. San Francisco: Jossey-Bass.

Burruss, M. A. 1988. *Mentoring for Leadership*. Paper presented at the Library Administration and Management Associations President's Program at the Annual Convention of the American Library Association, New Orleans, LA. (ERIC Reproduction Number 304 148).

Cagrill, J. 1989. "Developing Library Leaders: The Role of Mentorship." *Library Administration and Management* 3(1): 12-15.

Caldwell, B. J., and E. M. Carter. 1993. *The Return of the Mentor: Strategies for Workplace Learning*. Washington, DC: Falmer Press.

Caruso, R. E. 1992. *Mentoring and the Business Environment: Asset or Liability?* Brookfield, VT: Dartmouth Publishing Company.

Clutterbuck, D. 1985. *Everyone Needs a Mentor: How to Foster Talent Within the Organization*. London: Institute of Personnel Management.

Cohen, N. H. 1995. *Mentoring Adult Learners: A Guide for Educators and Trainers*. Malabar, FL: Krieger.

Collins, N. W. 1983. *Professional Women and Their Mentors: A Practical Guide to Mentoring for the Woman Who Wants to Get Ahead*. Englewood Cliffs, NJ: Prentice Hall.

Daloz, L. A. 1986. *Effective Teaching and Mentoring*. San Francisco: Jossey-Bass.

_____. 1990. "Mentorship." Pp. 205-224 in *Adult Learning Methods*, edited by M. W. Galbraith. Malabar, FL: Krieger.

Daresh, J. C., and M. A. Playko. 1992. *A Method for Matching Leadership Mentors and Protegees*. Paper presented at the Annual Meeting of the Association for Supervision and Curriculum Development, New Orleans, LA. (ERIC Reproduction Number 344 315)

Darling, L. W. 1985a. "What To Do About Toxic Mentors." *Journal of Nursing Administration* 15(5): 43-44.

_____. 1985b. "Becoming a Mentoring Manager." *Journal of Nursing Administration* 15(6): 43-44.

Douvan, E. 1976. "The Role of Models in Women's Professional Development." *Psychology of Women Quarterly* 1(1): 5-20.

Evanoski-Orsatti, P. 1988. "The Role of Mentoring in Higher Education." *Community College Review* 8(2): 22-27.

Evans, T. W. 1992. *Mentors: Making a Difference in Our Public Schools*. Princeton, NJ: Peterson's Guides.

Fagenson, E. A. 1989. "The Mentor Advantage: Perceived Career/Job Experiences of Proteges Versus Non-proteges." *Journal of Organizational Behavior* 10: 309-320.

Field, B., and T. Field. 1994. *Teachers and Mentors: A Practical Guide*. Washington, DC: Falmer Press.

Fisher, B. 1988. "Wandering in the Wilderness: The Search for Women Role Models." *Signs: Journal of Women in Culture and Society* 13(2): 211-233.

Galbraith, M. W., and B. S. Zelenak. 1991. "Adult Learning Methods and Techniques." Pp. 103-133 in *Facilitating Adult Learning*, edited by M. W. Galbraith. Malabar, FL: Krieger.

Garten, E. D. 1994. "Cultivating Workplace Diversity and Empowering Minorities by Fostering Mentor-Protege Relationships." Pp. 43-62 in *Diversity and Multiculturalism in Libraries*, edited by K. H. Hill, *Foundations in Library and Information Science*, vol. 32. Greenwich, CT: JAI Press.

Hall, D. T. and Associates. 1986. *Career Development in Organizations*. San Francisco: Jossey-Bass.

Hall, R. M., and B. R. Sandler. 1989. *Academic Mentoring for Women Students and Faculty: A New Look at an Old Way to Get Ahead*. Washington, DC: Association of American Colleges.

Haring-Hidore, M. 1987. "Mentoring as a Career Enhancement Strategy for Women." *Journal of Counseling and Development* 66: 147-148.

Harnish, D., and L. A. Wild. 1993. "Peer Mentoring in Higher Education: A Professional Development Strategy for Faculty. *Community College Journal of Research and Practice* 17: 271-282.

Harris, R. 1993. "The Mentoring Trap." *Library Journal* 118(17): 37-39.

Healy, C., and A. Welchert. 1990. "Mentoring Relations: A Definition to Advance Research and Practice." *Educational Researcher* 19(9): 17-21.

Heller, M., and N. W. Sindelar. 1991. *Developing an Effective Teacher Mentor Program*. Fastback no. 319. Bloomington, IN: Phi Delta Kappa Educational Foundation.

Henderson, D. W. 1985. "Enlightened Mentoring: A Characteristic of Public Management Professionalism." *Public Administration Review* 39: 857-863.

Hunt, D. M., and C. Michael. 1984. "Mentorship: A Career Training and Development Tool." *Journal of Library Administration* 5(2): 77-95.

Jacobi, M. 1991. "Mentoring and Undergraduate Academic Success: A Literature Review." *Review of Educational Research* 61(4): 505-532.

Johnsrud, L. K. 1994. "Enabling the Success of Junior Faculty Women Through Mentoring." Pp. 53-64 in *Mentoring Revisited: Making an Impact on Individuals and Institutions*, edited by M. A. Wunsch. New Directions for Teaching and Learning, no. 57. San Francisco: Jossey-Bass.

Kaplowitz, J. 1992. "Mentoring Library School Students: A Survey of Participants in the UCLA/GSLIS Mentor Program." *Special Libraries* 83(4): 219-233.

Keele, R. L., and M. DeLaMare-Schaefer. 1984. "So What do You Do Now That You Didn't Have a Mentor?" *Journal of the National Association of Women Deans, Administrators & Counselors* 47(3): 36-40.

Kogler-Hill, S. E., and M. H., Bahniuk, J. Dobos, and D. Rounder. 1989. "Mentoring and Other Communication Support in the Academic Setting." *Group and Organization Studies*14: 355-368.

Kram, K. E. 1985. *Mentoring at Work: Developmental Relationships in Organizational Life.* Glenview, IL: Scott, Foresman and Company.

Kram, K. E., and & L. A. Isabella. 1985. "Mentoring Alternatives: The Role of Peer Relationships in Career Development." *Academy of Management Journal* 28(1): 110-132.

Lester, V., and C. Johnson. 1981. "The Learning Dialogue: Mentoring." Pp. 49-56 in *Education for Student Development*, edited by J. Fried. New Directions for Student Services, no. 15. San Francisco: Jossey-Bass.

Levinson, D., C. Darrow, E. Klein, M. Levinson, and B. McKee. 1978. *The Seasons of a Man's Life.* New York: Ballantine.

Logsdon, J. 1992. "Need help?...Ask Your Mentor." *Journal of Library Administration* 17(3): 87-101.

Maack, M., and J. Passet. 1994. *Aspirations and Mentoring in an Academic Environment.* Westport, CT: Greenwood Press.

Massey, T. 1995. "Mentoring: A Means to Learning." *Journal of Education for Library and Information Science* 36(1): 52-54.

McNeer, E. J. 1988. "The Mentoring Influence in the Careers of Women ARL Directors." *Journal of Library Administration* 9(2): 23-33.

Merriam, S. B. 1983. "Mentors and Proteges: A Critical Review of the Literature." *Adult Education Quarterly* 33(3): 161-173.

Moore, K. M. 1982. *What to Do Until the Mentor Arrives.* Washington, DC: National Association for Women Deans, Administrators, and Counselors.

Moore, K. M., and M. J. Amey. 1988. "Some Faculty Leaders are Born Women." Pp. 39-50 in *Empowering Women: Leadership Development Strategies on Campus*, edited by M. A. D. Sagaria. New Directions for Student Services, no. 44. San Francisco: Jossey-Bass.

Murray, M. 1991. *Beyond the Myths and Magic of Mentoring.* San Francisco: Jossey-Bass.

Neubert, G. A., and L. T. Stover. 1994. *Peer Coaching in Teacher Education.* Fastback no. 371. Bloomington, IN: Phi Delta Kappa Educational Foundation.

Noe, R. A. 1988. "Women and Mentoring: A Review and Research Agenda." *Academy of Management Review* 13(1): 65-78.

Olian, J. D., S. J. Carroll, C. M. Giannantonia, and D. B. Feren. 1988. "What do Proteges Look for in a Mentor? Results of Three Experimental Studies." *Journal of Vocational Behavior* 33: 15-37.

Person, R. J., and E. R. Ficke. 1986. "A Longitudinal Study of the Outcomes of a Management Development Program for Women in Librarianship." *Advances in Library Administration and Organization* 5: 1-13.

Phillips-Jones, L. 1982. *Mentors and Proteges.* New York: Arbor House.

Pollack, M. 1992. *Recruiting for the Library Profession: A Mentoring/Intern Process.* Chicago: American Library Association.

Prestholdt, C. O. 1990. "Modern Mentoring: Strategies for Developing Nursing Leadership." *Nursing Administration Quarterly* 15(1): 20-27.

Reilly, J. M. 1991. *Mentorship: The Essential Guide for Schools and Business.* Dayton, OH: Psychology Press.

Roberts, D. L. 1986. "Mentoring in the Academic Library." *College and Research Libraries News* 47: 117-119.

Schlossberg, N., A. Lynch, and A. Chickering. 1989. *Improving Higher Education Environments for Adults.* San Francisco: Jossey-Bass.

Schmidt, J. A., and J. S. Wolfe. 1980. "The Mentor Partnership: Discovery of Professionalism." *NASPA Journal* 17: 45-51.

Shandley, T. C. 1989. "The Use of Mentors for Leadership Development." *NASPA Journal* 27: 59-66.

Shea, G. F. 1994. *Mentoring: Helping Employees Reach Their Full Potential.* New York: American Management Association.

Sheehy, G. 1976. *Passages: Predictable Crises of Adult Life.* New York: E.P. Dutton & Company.

Sheldon, B. E. 1991. *Leaders in Libraries: Styles and Strategies for Success.* Chicago: American Library Association.

Speizer, J. J. 1981. "Role Models, Mentors, and Sponsors: The Elusive Concepts." *Signs: Journal of Women in Culture and Society* 6(4): 692-712.

Sullivan, C. G. 1992. *How to Mentor in the Midst of Change.* Alexandria, VA: Association for Supervision and Curriculum Development.

Swenson, C. D. 1994. "Tips on Mentoring in Adult Education." *Professional Tips for Adult and Continuing Education* 3(1): 1-2.

Swoboda, M. J., and S. B. Miller. 1986. "Networking-mentoring: Career Strategy of Women in Academic Administration." *Journal of the National Association for Women Deans Administrators and Counselors* 50(1): 8-13.

Weber, C. E. 1980. "Mentoring." *Directors & Boards* 5(3): 17-24.

Weinberger, S. G. 1992. *How to Start a Student Mentor Program.* Fastback 333. Bloomington, IN: Phi Delta Kappa Educational Foundation.

Wilkin, M. 1992. *Mentoring in Schools.* London: Kogan Page.

Wolfe, M. A. 1993. "Mentoring Middle-aged Women in the Classroom." *Adult Learning* 4(5): 8-9, 22.

Wunsch, M. A. (ed.) 1994. *Mentoring Revisited: Making an Impact on Individuals and Institutions.* New Directions for Teaching and Learning, no. 57. San Francisco: Jossey-Bass.

Yoder, L. 1990. "Mentoring: A Concept Analysis." *Nursing Administration Quarterly* 15(1): 9-19.

Zey, M. 1984. *The Mentor Connection.* Homewood, IL: Dow Jones-Irwin.

A ROLE TRANSFORMED?:
TECHNOLOGY'S CHALLENGE FOR
JOB RESPONSIBILITIES OF
THE REFERENCE LIBRARIAN

Robert R. Burkhardt

The permeation of technology into the reference environment and its possible consequences represent familiar themes in the recent literature of librarianship. Pei-Yu Lin (1992), in an analysis of journal articles pertaining to automation in academic libraries, noted a recent swell in articles related to public services. One commonly held assumption is that information technology has sparked change in the activities of many who perform reference service in college and university libraries, increasing managerial responsibilities and transforming the instructional role.

Among the numerous discussions of this subject are those written by librarians who championed the shift to more extensive computerization in reference. Typically, these writings hailed

Advances in Library Administration and Organization,
Volume 14, pages 125-190.
Copyright © 1996 by JAI Press Inc.
All rights of reproduction in any form reserved.
ISBN: 0-7623-0098-1

technology for offering a broader range of service options and for liberating the reference librarian from the clerical drudgery that seemed an inescapable part of the work.

Recent literature, however, has adopted a more cautious tone. Technology has been charged with compounding the work of reference librarians by expanding the dimensions of certain responsibilities—in the areas of planning, budgeting, training, and communicating—and by altering modes of user instruction. Barbara Farah (1989) illustrated this opinion and concluded, "The developments associated with information technology that reference librarians use demand an interaction and assessment beyond the scope of most professionals' time, and in some cases, beyond their expertise."

As mounting literature continues to portray the struggle of reference librarians to cope with newfound multiple responsibilities, a large part of the issue concerns time management. The relation between the provision of time and perceived effectiveness in reference has been demonstrated. Among the findings of Jo Bell Whitlatch (1990) in her analysis of the reference process was that a significant relationship existed between librarians' impressions of service value and their perception that they had sufficient time to respond to the question. Various authors (Bunge, 1984; Miller, 1984; Goodyear, 1985) depicted the harried reference librarian as one prone to "burnout," "overload," and feeling "out of control."

Many reference librarians (Loomis, Jaros, Jackson, and Gilreath, 1989; Cornick, 1989; Stewart, Chiang, and Coons, 1990) have observed that more time is required for user instruction when online, CD-ROM, and other electronic options are available, even though some (Mood, 1994; Ewing and Hauptman, 1995) argue that continued improvements in technology should result in a diminished teaching responsibility for the library. Judging from accounts in the literature, electronic options are almost always more popular with users than their print counterparts, and librarians typically underestimate their appeal. Beyond the issue of heavy patron demand, users possess widely varying levels of library and computer proficiencies, and rates of learning differ as well. In-house surveys (Goettler, Hawthorn, and McCaskill, 1990) have indicated that CD-ROM users are novices in most cases. Even if they are not, one librarian (Reese, 1990) reported that, in comparison to print services, patrons tend to forget information learned about CD-ROM databases. Regardless of prior experience with a technology, users and librarians are confronted with a daunting diversity of electronic database alternatives, as well as a myriad of access strategies, search commands, and protocols. As William Miller (1984) observed:

> Each new machine also seems to generate additional questions and demand its own quotient of additional time for user instruction. Those of us who work extensively with a variety of machines and a multiplicity of online systems are discovering that although they expand, improve, and redirect many of our efforts, they do not really save us any time.

Based upon the inability to identify the average database and the typical user, Tom Eadie (1992) reported the ineffectiveness of classroom presentations about reference technologies, and suggested that primary attention in the electronic environment be devoted to one-on-one instruction. This instruction could consume as much as one hour per user (Stewart, Chiang, and Coons, 1990). Since a characteristic of using computerized tools can be the generation of an overwhelming quantity of citations, this individualized instruction tends to focus on critical evaluation of sources for relevance and selectivity. Critical thinking is viewed as an essential skill in the electronic library (Kissane and Mollner, 1993).

With online databases, CD-ROM sources, the Internet, and other options accompanying the more familiar reference capabilities of books and microform, selecting the appropriate medium for research can prove a sizable challenge in itself. A review of the literature suggests that a positive association may exist between the degree of variety in reference capabilities and the extent of one-on-one instruction offered, and between variety in capabilities and the extent of instruction devoted to critical evaluation of source material. A search on the Internet reveals a seemingly unlimited mass of databases with a welter of user interfaces, passwords, and access methods, and where database content and means of access can change suddenly and without notice. Multimedia products have been notorious for their lack of standardization and uniformity. When locally loaded databases are added to online catalogs, it is easy for patrons to confuse periodical article citations with books (Carande, 1992). And since new technologies in the reference environment tend not to displace previous forms, the duties of the reference librarian can involve both instruction in the most traditional and the most innovative of formats.

The instructional effectiveness of electronic reference assistance options has proven of limited usefulness to the reference librarian. Help screens are of marginal aid in facilitating search strategy and in the assessment of search results, and most cannot pinpoint a patron's specific need (Carande, 1992). Expert systems require a heavy initial investment of time in the design phase, as well as constant vigilance for modifications. Moreover, it has been observed that they are most effective when applied to unsophisticated, well-trodden problems (Vedder, 1990). In sum, help screens and expert systems may not be the time-savers many anticipated.

In addition to its contribution in changing the direction of and approach to user instruction, technology typically is credited with a major role in dissolving organizational bureaucracy and fostering an atmosphere conducive to collaboration and participation in decision making. A review of the literature suggests that for reference librarians, this participation translates to greater involvement in management functions such as planning, budgeting, and training. Increased communication activity, both inside and outside traditional hierarchical lines, is the vehicle for achieving this involvement. Communication is often regarded as a primary responsibility of the modern librarian (Lancaster, 1983). In 1982, Shoshana Zuboff maintained that computers in the workplace inhibited opportunities for personal encounter and created an isolated work force. In recent years, it is more common to read that increased use of computer technology stimulates collaboration and multiple communication channels in the work environment (Neal, 1987; Drucker, 1988; Lowry, 1992).

Library managers might be expected to resist involving reference librarians in organization-wide decision making, especially since staff participation could contribute to the business of reference work— already difficult to define—becoming even less certain in its responsibilities and thus more difficult to evaluate and measure. Issues of faculty status aside, many managers adopt a participative strategy for a number of reasons: to build acceptance of change and a commitment to the direction of the organization, to improve employee morale, to expand employee perspective, to share the credit or blame for decisions, and in an effort to produce better decisions. In a continually shifting environment, it is increasingly difficult for managers to have the requisite expertise or the time and ability to access information needed. Joanne Euster (1990) remarked that due to explosions in information and knowledge, the leader no longer "knows enough to be truly in charge" unless there is "either superhuman intelligence at the top of the organization, or an incredible amount of coordination and information sharing" (p. 42). Collaboration and participation in decision making from throughout the organization may pose a threat to the traditional academic library structure, a hierarchical organization with specified departments and rife with middle management. The interdepartmental sharing of information and expertise can dissolve organizational boundaries and promote the integration of duties. The online catalog is a technology acknowledged to foster interactions between reference and technical services, two departments that traditionally "speak different languages" (McCombs, 1988, p. 141). Strategies to accomplish a more collaborative atmosphere include use of teams and cross-training, as well as experimenting with alternative organizational structures. These strategies can provide the mechanisms to further broaden responsibilities of the reference librarian and add complexity to job role. Studies in librarianship (Cline and Sinnott, 1983; Henshaw, 1986; Lowry, 1992) suggest a close association between a technological environment and the degree of collaboration in the organization.

The planning process is central to decision making and determining the direction of the organization. Planning entails the development of activities and the coordination of courses of action toward specified and established goals. Activities traditionally associated with planning include formulating goals, designing policies and procedures, and evaluating programs. Budgeting, a closely aligned process, assists in making decisions about resource allocation toward those goals by formally quantifying the resources needed.

Planning and budgeting, once the exclusive province of top administrators, are now widely regarded as highly participative activities. Both management theorists (Peters, 1987) and librarians (Veaner, 1985a; Sullivan, 1991) concur that involving people from throughout the organization in planning is necessary when conditions are highly fluid. In 1985 Veaner predicted that "all academic librarians will be held accountable for the effective, economical use of their assigned resources" (1985a, p. 224). Barbara Schloman (1993) noted the complexity of selection and funding decisions in the "increasingly electronic environment" (p. 100).

As information technology adds variety to the reference environment, the planning and budgeting processes can become quite multifaceted. Librarians must weigh one format versus another in terms of cost, use, ease of access, preservation, storage capability, maintenance, security, and equipment compatibility. Costs associated with the new technology are often difficult to establish. Librarians are confronted with many new questions: Does the price include equipment or only software? Will the library lease or purchase? Are there telecommunication charges or other per use costs? Are there direct charges for upgrading and replacement? If the library subscribes to the print counterpart of the service, should it be retained? Since technologies are expected to coexist with paper in the future and costs for print continue to rise rapidly, can the library budget for and acquire an electronic item without reducing the need for print capabilities? What type of training will be required and how will costs be satisfied? Each technology seems to offer its own set of factors which direct the budget and planning. Given the complexities involved and given that reference librarians are at central service points where they should be aware of patron needs, they may be able to supply expertise as well as a user-oriented perspective. Additionally, managers may believe that participants will more likely accept budgets that they have assisted in formulating.

Information technology also introduces new training challenges. It is widely reported that college and university libraries are utilizing nonprofessionals at the reference desk to handle many questions, particularly those of a ready reference or directional nature. Some libraries have used student assistants for lower level reference queries (Heinlen, 1976). This strategy can provide cost-effective service and allow reference librarians to become more involved in other work, such as the managerial responsibilities described above.

A potential problem with this strategy is the failure to recognize that the training of staff is a significant management responsibility itself, and a considerable amount of time should be devoted to the process if it is to be effective (Veaner, 1984; Anderson and Huang, 1993). Sheila Creth (1986) delineated the numerous responsibilities in planning for training: analysis of the job, establishment of performance standards, identification of training content and training objectives, determination of training sequence, identification of trainers, choice of training methods, and writing the training plan.

In the electronic reference environment, continual training and retraining are vital to remaining abreast of rapid advances. Whether trainees are student workers, nonprofessionals, or professionals, training can present a demanding responsibility for trainer and trainee alike. A support staff member in a Wisconsin academic library who responded to a survey reported, "There is greater pressure to use all the latest technological advances and there does not seem to be adequate time to familiarize oneself with all the programs one needs to know" (Palmini, 1994, p. 126). Creth (1989) concluded that adequate training "will have to accommodate both the traditional and automated environments for the foreseeable future, so librarians will be doubling training requirements rather than replacing current ones" (p. 10).

To summarize, a common assumption in library literature is that the extent of information technology in the reference area has enlarged the job role of the academic reference librarian, so as to encompass a greater emphasis on certain managerial responsibilities and a renewed emphasis on user instruction. It is often posited that these individuals are more frequently engaged in planning, budgeting, training, instruction, and communication activities. However, much of the literature is anecdotal and does not attempt to test the hypothesis. A few case studies exist, but sampling has not been broad enough to demonstrate reliability. Thus far, the association has not been developed fully.

PURPOSE OF THE STUDY

The primary purpose of this study was to survey academic reference librarians and investigate whether differences in reported frequencies of performing certain responsibilities—planning and budgeting, training, instruction, and communication—exist relative to the variation in technological capabilities in the reference environment. A questionnaire that compared respondents' perceptions of frequency in performing responsibilities with their identification of capabilities in the reference department was administered. Statistical tests that estimated the significance of mean differences in those responsibilities among traditional, transitional, and electronic reference departments were conducted.

The secondary purpose of this study was to determine whether there is a difference in the perceived importance of the same responsibilities based on differences in the technological capabilities of various reference departments. This was accomplished by examining perceptions of importance with regard to the relative presence of technology in the work environment, and by testing the significance of difference among group means.

A third purpose of the study was to ascertain the relationship between frequency of personal performance of each responsibility and the importance of that responsibility. This was accomplished by means of correlation analyses comparing responses for each item on indexes corresponding to measures of frequency and ratings of importance.

Null Hypotheses

1. There is no significant difference in perceived frequency of personal performance of planning and budgeting responsibilities by reference librarians in traditional, transitional, and electronic reference departments.
2. There is no significant difference in perceived frequency of personal performance of training responsibilities by reference librarians in traditional, transitional, and electronic reference departments.
3. There is no significant difference in perceived frequency of personal performance of communication activity by reference librarians in traditional, transitional, and electronic reference departments.
4. There is no significant difference in perceived frequency of personal performance of instructional responsibilities by reference librarians in traditional, transitional, and electronic reference departments.
5. There is no significant difference in perceived importance of planning and budgeting responsibilities by reference librarians in traditional, transitional, and electronic reference departments.
6. There is no significant difference in perceived importance of training responsibilities by reference librarians in traditional, transitional, and electronic reference departments.

7. There is no significant difference in perceived importance of communication activity by reference librarians in traditional, transitional, and electronic reference departments.
8. There is no significant difference in perceived importance of instructional responsibilities by reference librarians in traditional, transitional, and electronic reference departments.
9. There is no significant relationship as perceived by reference librarians between frequency of personal performance of each responsibility and the importance of the same responsibility.

It was necessary to make the following assumptions: (a) the responses of librarians represented a true reflection of their perception of the variables under consideration, (b) librarians selected for the study were representative of the population of reference librarians employed in U.S. and Canadian universities holding membership in the Association of Research Libraries, (c) respondents possessed a common understanding of the descriptions of the independent and dependent variables in the study, and (d) administration of the questionnaire developed for this study provided valid information by which stated purposes of the study can be examined. The following were the delimitations: (a) The study was limited to persons performing the duties of reference librarian in the main libraries, or in humanities libraries in the absence of a main library, of ARL university members in the United States and Canada; (b) job responsibilities were limited to those of a planning, budgeting, training, communicating, and instructional nature; (c) since all scales were developed especially for this study, further testing and improvement are needed to insure validity and reliability; (d) valid responses depended upon respondent understanding of questionnaire items; (e) all variables, subjects, and conditions not so specified were considered beyond the scope of this study; (f) significance was defined at the .05 level in all cases.

For this study, a "traditional reference department" is defined as a reference department consisting entirely of paper and microform based resources. Personal assistance and paper and microform based resources limited to a fixed location predominate. A "transitional reference department" is one beginning the migration to electronic capabilities. Print-on-paper represents the primary medium for information, and personal assistance offered by the reference librarian is the primary means of helping the user. Computers are present but have restricted capabilities. The "electronic reference department" is dominated, in terms of identification and use, by electronic sources of information. It is characterized by a wide variety of capabilities in information technology, and by networked access to contents and services both on and off-site. The collection in an electronic department is defined as much or more by quick access to information held remotely as by local ownership of physical holdings.

Although the topic of technology's possible effect upon job responsibilities in reference has received much discussion in the literature, this study represents a formative endeavor to investigate the variation in performance and importance of the responsibilities under study, according to the extent of information technology in the work environment. This study may yield results which will assist in creating evidence associating information technology with certain responsibilities that may be assumed by reference librarians. Results suggest the degree of variation and complexity in reference work, and may assist reference librarians in preparing for the job roles they are likely to fill in the future. Regardless of the presence or absence of such an association, the study generates valuable information regarding the range of job responsibilities and reference capabilities which are perceived to exist in the reference environment. As a result of this work, library managers will have a clearer indication of some of the less traditional responsibilities that reference librarians are performing, and the degree to which they are being performed. This information may be valuable to managers in the job definition and evaluation process. Since there has been avid interest in this subject in recent years, the study should also spawn further research and may have implications in related areas, such as job satisfaction and occupational stress research.

LITERATURE REVIEW

This review is divided into five areas and will focus chiefly on the postulated effects of technology in the library workplace. Sections are presented as follows: (a) the development of reference work, (b) technology and occupational skill levels, (c) technology and burnout in reference work, (d) technology and responsibilities of reference work, and (e) methodological considerations.

Development of Reference Work

According to Richard Miller (1986), reference work in early academia referred, not to work done by the librarian, but to the process of students reading assigned material in the library. The term "reference work" was preferred to the term "research" when applied to undergraduate study.

Samuel Rothstein (1955), a valuable author in tracing the history of reference services, demonstrated that, from the late nineteenth century, the concept of personal assistance was regarded as the core of librarianship. Samuel Green (1876), James Wyer (1930), and Margaret Hutchins (1944) all included "personal assistance" as a key element in their definitions of the nature of the work. That emphasis has continued in the literature to date, despite the significant changes experienced in libraries and in the reference environment through the years. Guidelines set forth in 1979 by the Reference and Adult Services Division of the American Library Association defined reference or information services in terms of "personal assistance provided to users in pursuit of information." In a 1992 work, G. Edward Evans, Anthony Amodeo, and Thomas Carter considered the delivery of "personal service" a reference librarian's chief role (p. 70).

The scope of that personal service has never been especially well defined. In his survey of reference history, Miller (1986) discussed a turn-of-the-century college librarian who was apparently charged with all the duties no one else on campus wanted to undertake. Guy Lyle (1974) strove to codify an array of amorphous and somewhat disparate elements:

> (1) to provide answers to inquiries regarding specific information, (2) to teach students how to use the library in connection with their studies, (3) to provide bibliographical and other reference assistance, (4) to locate material for users whenever these materials may be in the library system, (5) to make available material not in the library through interlibrary loan, and (6) to organize uncataloged material for effective use (p. 91).

Margaret Hutchins (1944) noted the inadequacy of all previous definitions of reference service because they tended to focus on the central objective rather than endeavoring to define the "content or scope" of activity (p. 10). She contended that personal aid did not suffice in characterizing this broad range.

In an effort to organize reference activity, the reference department was created as a separate unit of the library. For Rothstein (1955), these departments did not help develop a focused definition of reference services:

> Reference service cannot be limited to the study of the activities of reference departments. Reference departments may engage in a number of activities, such as maintaining records of government publications, which cannot be construed as "personal assistance." On the other hand, some forms of personal assistance, such as the provision of inter-library loans, may not be a reference department responsibility (p. 4).

Even in the formative years of reference departments, librarians (McCombs, 1929; Wyer, 1930) recognized that reference work carried a number of managerial responsibilities. Included were decisions on who could utilize reference services, collecting policy, the compilation of statistics, publicity, and the procedure for reserve materials.

Another matter which contributed to the difficulty in defining reference service was the debate over the level of instruction to be offered. Given the perceived significance of personal assistance in reference work, user instruction became a primary responsibility. Authors (Wyer, 1930; Rothstein, 1955) identified three distinct philosophies of assistance that they dubbed conservative, moderate, and liberal.

According to the conservative theory, reference librarians could direct patrons to source material, but should avoid furnishing the information directly. Information should be supplied only for those who seemed unable to locate it for themselves.

The moderate approach was exemplified by Charles McCombs (1929), who believed that the role of the reference librarian was to teach patrons which books to use. For this purpose, the compilation of bibliographies and conducting some group lectures were especially useful. Librarians should "refer readers to the proper or probable sources of information" (p. 18). The reader could be "supplied with information" (p. 2), but the librarian should refrain from any interpretation of material for the patron. McCombs acknowledged that some classes of users—such as members of the state legislature—might be deserving of extra attention.

James Wyer (1930) adopted the liberal philosophy, which offered the "fullest possible attention" to user needs (p. 9). He believed that "the conception of reference work which is limited to the resources of one city or even to books and print alone is out of date" (p. 12). Although his words remained an ideal for many of his contemporaries, they presaged the modern stirrings away from the print medium and toward access of information irrespective of format or location.

A clear understanding of the nature of reference work is difficult given the variety of duties and philosophies that have marked its development. An often-read observation is the lack of a consensus as to the components of reference services (Rothstein, 1989; Klassen, 1983). Nonetheless, an analysis of the literature can yield a number of recurring elements.

Wyer's sentiments aside, the traditional reference setting chiefly remained dependent upon a well-stocked local collection. Careful selection of materials was central in providing effective service. Hutchins (1944) maintained that materials selection was as important to reference work as the interpretation of those materials. The collection was print-based: books, periodicals, vertical file materials, microforms. Reference librarians extensively relied upon a set of "reference books" and personal knowledge of their contents (Rothstein, 1955). Access to the collection was primarily through a card catalog with author, title, and subject entries. Interlibrary loan service was a regular function in many libraries, with reliance on a series of union lists. Graduate work in library science represented a primary qualification for reference service (Lyle, 1974; Wyer, 1930).

A variety of methods were utilized to offer instruction in the use of the library and its resources. According to Rutherford Rogers and David Weber (1971), "traditional means" of instruction included "personal reference assistance from a desk, lectures or group tours, handbooks or guidebooks, and selectively prepared bibliographies" (p. 202). The manual preparation of bibliographies and reading lists could constitute a significant part of the work of the reference librarian. These in-house publications were considered particularly important when published bibliographies were scarce and when specific needs for information were expected to recur (Rothstein, 1955).

Limitations of the traditional paper library were reviewed by Michael Buckland in 1992. He concluded that paper is "strictly localized" (p. 10) since it and the user must be in the same place simultaneously, that it can only be used by one person at a time, that it is costly to store, and that it does not facilitate the merging, dividing, or reformatting of information. To Buckland, microforms presented as inflexible a medium as print.

Buckland contrasted the problems inherent in the paper library with two other library scenarios: the "automated library" and the "electronic library" (p. 19). The automated library signified a sort of way station on the road to the electronic library. In the automated library, computers are present but have restricted capabilities. His example is a user only being able to search one online catalog or one online bibliography at a time and separately.

Buckland's electronic library presented extensions of capabilities in the automated library. Electronic full-text predominates, and the catalog is no longer physically separated from the text. In this scenario, materials "can be used from a distance, can be used by more than one person at a time, and can be used in more different ways" (p. 6).

Buckland was not the first to contend that library scenarios were driven by technology. In 1984 Patricia Battin surveyed "three generations of library computing" (pp. 13-15). The application of computers to processing functions represented the first generation. The second generation, highlighted by the online catalog, introduced keyword and Boolean searching capabilities. Among the capability enhancements in the third generation (yet to come when the article first appeared) were local networks linked by a gateway and full-text electronic journals.

The three stages of library development identified by Monica Landoni, Nadia Catenazzi, and Forbes Gibb in 1993 were similar to those of Battin, although the authors considered a broader range of reference applications. The first period, dubbed the "traditional library" (p. 175), represented the preautomation world. The second stage, "library automation" (p. 176), began in the mid-1960s with the introduction of computers for card production and continued with the online public access catalog through online and CD-ROM bibliographic search systems. The "electronic library" (p. 176) signified the next stage where full-text is accessible online, the library can be reached remotely from any site, gateways to other library systems can be accessed, and the library contains electronic books and journals. In this environment, public services become a greater focus of the library.

Four levels of library technology were described in a 1993 report issued jointly by the National Center for Education Statistics and the U.S. National Commission on Libraries and Information Science (Dillon, 1993). The first stage, "automation of library processes" (p. 14), discussed the application of computers to various library functions: acquisition, circulation, cataloging, interlibrary loan. "Access to electronic document surrogates" (p. 18) represented the second stage and included access to the online public access catalog and access to periodical references by online or CD-ROM means. Stage number three, "digitized documents" (p. 19), included the publication of material using desktop publishing and the creation of page images resulting from a digitized document scanner. The final stage signified the completion of the revolution, when electronic became "the dominant form of knowledge representation" (p. 20). According to the author of the report, CD-ROM and telefacsimile machines are transitional technologies.

A number of recent authors have employed the term "electronic library" to describe a scenario in which the capabilities of the library stand in dramatic contrast to those in the traditional paper-based library. The dominant motif is remote access to information. Kenneth Dowlin (1984), an early writer on the subject, defined the electronic library in terms of two cardinal attributes: "the widest possible access to information and the use of electronic technology to increase and manage information resources" (p. 27). Capabilities included an online catalog with all nonelectronic informational forms, online reference assistance, and an assortment of commercial electronic encyclopedias.

Charlene Hurt (1991) regarded the electronic library less as a site than as a "concept of service" (p. 7). According to Hurt, an increasing amount of information will be available electronically due to publication costs and the value of access over ownership. Books will remain viable in the new environment, however.

Mel Collier, Anne Ramsden, and Zimin Wu (1993) contrasted the electronic library with a term often used as a synonym: the virtual library. For these authors, the difference between the two was that the electronic library remained a physical entity (albeit a highly technological one), while the virtual library conveyed an illusion to users that information was local whereas, in reality, it could have been transmitted from any point on the globe. Capabilities of the virtual library included electronic documents and remote access to online public access catalogs from throughout the world.

Barbara von Wahlde and Nancy Schiller (1993) surveyed ARL library directors to identify participation in activities which were reputed to constitute an electronic library environment. Over 80 percent indicated involvement in access to Internet, end-user access to files on or off campus, electronic document delivery, a campus-wide information system, a multicampus OPAC, and the formulation of policies that stress access over ownership. Between fifty and eighty percent were involved in end-user training, a gateway from OPAC to other databases, access to electronic full-text, cooperative development or purchase of electronic files, Internet training, and modified staffing. Less than half reported that they subscribed to electronic journals, provided an electronic mail front-end for patrons to initiate interlibrary loan or pose reference queries, or had a written plan to access resources from a single workstation.

A 1993 survey of ARL libraries (Association of Research Libraries, 1993) indicated ninety-nine percent supplied remote access to the online public access catalog. Over two-thirds included locally mounted databases as a service for remote users, but only twenty-eight percent provided remote access to CD-ROM products at that time. Sixty-four percent reported offering reference service to remote users, usually in the form of electronic mail.

Other capabilities that have been suggested as typifying the electronic or virtual library include expert search systems, hypertext linking of texts and ideas, and searching by natural language. Robert Carande (1992) provides an overview of these and other technologies that are transforming the electronic reference environment.

Technology and Occupational Skill Levels

As indicated in the model of Battin and others, the impact of computerization in libraries first occurred in technical services, the production operations of the library. By the 1980s much writing had surfaced regarding its impact, especially on skill levels, alienation from work, and job role.

The discussion over the effect of automation on level of skill in technical services reflected the "upgrading"/"deskilling" debate in the literature of business and sociology. The "deskilling" position can be traced to Karl Marx. Its most influential advocate in modern times was Harry Braverman (1974), who argued that technology, along with the tenets of scientific management and the division of labor, had routinized work and essentially removed judgment and interpretation from many jobs, alienating the worker from his work in the process. The "upgrading" side found persuasive adherents in Robert Blauner (1964) and in Jon Shepard (1971). Blauner studied four industrial environments and concluded that while assembly-line work can cause skills to erode, automation can produce workers with a more integrated, company-wide perspective and greater involvement in the job. Shepard examined employees in factories and office clerical work, and found that workers in an automated environment experienced less alienation.

The debate was extended to librarianship in the early 1980s. Robert Holley (1981) noted that nonprofessionals performed a greater extent of cataloging in an automated environment, relieving catalogers to perform more supervision, problem-solving, interpretation, and reference work. Influenced by Shoshana Zuboff (1982), Michael Malinconico (1983) maintained that automation diminished personal contact with colleagues, resulting in a sense of isolation at work. A case study of six academic libraries (Hafter, 1986) concluded that catalogers felt isolated from users, even in an online environment.

However, most research in the area of technical services tended to indicate that jobs were enriched throughout the department as a result of automation. According to Michael Gorman (1983), the introduction of the online catalog facilitated a "decentralizing" process and enabled subject catalogers to become more involved with all phases of professional work in their subject specialization: reference, original cataloging, selection, and bibliographic instruction. In a separate study, Karen Horny (1987) reported that after the introduction of the NOTIS system at Northwestern, some work handled by professionals was transferred to support staff, and some support staff work began to be performed by students. Another study (Andrews and Kelley, 1988) reported that paraprofessional positions were upgraded and assigned increased responsibility following the introduction of online cataloging. Marie Bednar (1988) found that with paraprofessionals performing more detailed work, professional catalogers could spend time working in other departments. A survey of public and academic librarians (Intner and Fong, 1991) discovered that many professional catalogers were performing outside traditional departmental confines, but many were also performing administrative duties within the department: recruiting, training, and supervising copy catalogers; and planning departmental policies and budgets.

Regardless of whether jobs in technical services were perceived as enriched or deskilled, surveys indicated that they were changing, both in terms of their numbers and the organizational structure of these areas. One study (Hudson, 1986) reported that half the libraries surveyed had experienced organizational change, whether through staff reallocation, or the addition or subtraction of positions. A much earlier survey (Spyers-Duran, 1979) reported the frequent merging of cataloging and acquisitions functions following automation. Additionally, it found that professional catalogers perceived that staff members embraced the changes. This attitude among support staff was again discovered in a subsequent study (Jones, 1989).

The debate over whether technology affected skill level was not confined to the area of technical services. In 1980 Brian Nielsen reported preliminary indications which suggested that online searching had contributed to an upgrading or "professionalization" of reference work. More time was spent interviewing users, in continuing education, and delegating work, with less time being consumed performing routine duties. Margaret Stieg (1990), on the other hand, maintained that computers threatened to make reference service "more uniform, more rapid, and less individualized" (p. 46) and to reduce reference librarians to the status of technical assistants. The literature of reference librarianship would adopt another perceived effect of technology as a more prevalent theme: stress and burnout.

Technology and Burnout in Reference Work

Typically, the area of reference services was one of the last in the college or university library to experience the inroads of automation. Whereas the literature of technical services suggested that computerization had improved the task environment and occupational roles and relationships, the literature of reference services tended to view technology as a disrupting force and a significant stressor in the workplace. "Burnout" became a term frequently applied to reference librarians.

Herbert Freudenberger (1974) is often credited with applying the term "burnout" to mental health and stress research. He defined it as "to fail, wear out, or become exhausted by making excessive demands on energy, strength, or resources" (p. 159). In the first thorough treatment of the subject, Christina Maslach (1982) associated burnout with the helping professions. According to Martha Rader (1981), burnout also characterized organizations with "periodic information overload" (p. 373). Mary Ann Westerhouse (1979) found that the frequency of role conflict was an important predictor of burnout. Librarians, more specifically reference librarians, seemed to be ideal candidates for the syndrome.

Christina Maslach and S.E. Jackson (1981) conducted a factor analysis as part of their research relating to burnout. It revealed three factors significantly associated with burnout: emotional exhaustion, depersonalization, and personal accomplishment. The Maslach Burnout Inventory was constructed and found to be a reliable and valid measure of burnout.

"Technostress," a related term coined by Craig Brod (1982), is a "condition resulting from the inability of an individual or organization to adapt to the introduction and operation of new technology" (p. 754). Technostress was believed to result from a number of factors: insecurity over continued employment, a change in work responsibilities, unrealistic expectations about the benefits of technology, poor planning or implementation, a lack of adequate training, and demands on time (Bichteler, 1987; Kupersmith, 1992). Performance anxiety, information overload, role conflicts, and organizational factors (the lack of adequate resources, for example) were identified by John Kupersmith as the components of technostress in the reference environment.

One of the earliest writings (Watstein, 1979) concerning burnout among librarians summarized a workshop on the subject. The author listed suspected causes of librarian burnout, and among them was the new responsibility of database searching.

Charles Bunge (1984) perceived low morale and burnout among working reference librarians. He concluded that the multiplicity of difficult-to-use database options, as well as an increasing variety of patrons and user insistence upon quick and concise delivery, contributed to reference librarians feeling frustrated, inadequate, and insufficiently stimulated.

The research on burnout in library literature depicts conflicting findings. In part, this is due to some of the studies employing flawed methodology. One study (Haack, Jones, and Roose, 1984), surveyed reference librarians attending a conference in order to discover the prevalence of burnout. The results indicated a high incidence of burnout among those surveyed, but this could have been anticipated given that a presentation on the subject preceded the administration of the questionnaire.

On the other hand, a survey of university reference librarians by Nathan Smith and Veneese Nelson (1983) found little correlation between responses measuring challenge of the job and those producing a burnout quotient. A study of corporate librarians published the following year (Smith and Nielsen, 1984) found a low level of burnout, especially when the sample was compared to other professional groups who had utilized the same instrument, the Maslach Burnout Inventory.

The Maslach Burnout Inventory was employed again to ascertain burnout among reference librarians in large public libraries, to correlate burnout with measures of role conflict and role ambiguity, and to compare results with a similar survey of teachers (Birch, Marchant, and Smith, 1986). The study found a substantial incidence of burnout among the group of librarians, an essentially similar level to that of the teacher-group. However, the librarians demonstrated a higher correlation between role ambiguity and role conflict than did the teachers. Following regression analysis, both predictor variables contributed significantly to burnout among the librarians.

In a series of interviews with special librarians responsible for online activity, Julie Bichteler (1986) found a low incidence of technostress. Instead, respondents reported pleasure and satisfaction with their work. While the author commented that this represented a lower level of burnout than had been reported for other groups of workers, such a conclusion would be difficult to support since the methodology of Bichtele's study was substantially different from the others cited.

A survey of librarians representing all functions of the academic library employed a reliable, valid instrument to measure stress levels (Wood, 1989). Librarians scored in the normal range on four of six criteria tested, and in the lower than normal range on the other two. One of the low scores represented a measure of stress due to change, suggesting to the authors that librarians embraced change due to technology.

Given the lack of a consistent and sound methodological approach in many of these studies and the conflicting findings which resulted, it is difficult to reach any conclusions based upon available literature. Nonetheless, the issue is discussed often in the literature of librarianship, as is evident by the recent publication of a monograph on the subject (Caputo, 1991).

Technology and Reference Responsibilities

In the literature of reference services, a prominent hypothesis suggests that technological change is a primary contributor not only to stress levels directly, but also indirectly through changes in responsibilities of reference work. As noted in the Introduction, much of this literature is theoretical.

Samuel Huang (1993) presented an effective distillation of the problem. He noted that as changes in technology operated to transform reference services, reference librarians became involved in more administrative work, especially pertaining to budgeting, staffing, and training. The nature of user instruction was changing too, with reference librarians operating like "personal advisors" (p. 2). In addition, they continued to perform all the duties encompassed in traditional reference work (Huang, 1990). According to Jennifer Cargill and Gisela Webb (1988), changes in communication patterns are also important to note, with technology shaping organizational relationships. The section that follows will focus on a set of responsibilities prominently identified in the literature as significant in the new reference environment: planning, budgeting, staff training, user instruction, and communication.

Communication

Reference librarians cannot effectively assume managerial responsibilities until access to information for decision-making is decentralized. Traditionally, however, academic libraries have been structured in a bureaucratic, hierarchical fashion, facilitating a clear chain of command, accountability, and the performance of repetitive, routine tasks. Top administrators assumed responsibility for planning and for most of the decision making. Beverly Lynch (1979) championed the bureaucratic model for libraries, preferring it for reasons of efficiency. The departmental and divisional forms of bureaucratic structure continue to be widely accepted methods for organizing libraries.

The research of Tom Burns and G.M. Stalker (1961), however, has indicated that mechanistic structures, such as bureaucracies, are ill-suited to rapidly changing environments. Under these conditions, organic systems were recommended, where more work was performed in groups and communication permeated all levels and departments of the organization. Jay Galbraith (1974) maintained that in conditions of task uncertainty, more information must be processed. He also supported the creation of lateral relationships, including the use of liaisons, teams, and task forces. For Peter Drucker (1988), the basis of the "new organization" was information. Communication extended in all directions, and teams were frequently employed to solve problems. F.W. Lancaster's description of the future library (1983) gave prominence to the librarian as communicator, especially outside conventional library walls.

A number of authors credited technology with creating new organizational relationships in libraries. Sharon Walbridge (1991) discussed the online public access catalog as a tool that facilitated dialogue between those who create the catalog and those who interpret it. Rod Henshaw (1986) presented a case study of how introducing computerization into a university library opened new channels of communication and decentralized management responsibilities. A survey of staff at one university library found that a majority believed information technology had fostered working relationships among departments and provided a "more interdependent, cohesive, and communicative" environment (Lowry, 1992, p. 121). In another survey, respondents from four university libraries reported that automation had improved interdepartmental communication (Cline and Sinnott, 1983).

However, some believed that computerization created an adverse effect on communication patterns. Based on a number of interviews representing many different organizations, Shoshana Zuboff (1982) concluded that information technology reduced personal interaction and promoted feelings of isolation.

Changes in communication patterns did not ordinarily produce new organizational structures, at least in the short term. The results of a recent questionnaire sent to college and university library directors revealed that almost two-thirds continued to be structured along traditional lines with separate public service and technical service departments (Buttlar and Garcha, 1992). This represented little change from an ARL survey conducted almost a decade earlier (Association of Research Libraries, 1985). A survey of information processing in academic libraries concluded that librarians (McClure and Samuels, 1985) tend to adhere to traditional sources and hierarchical roles, preferring to rely upon other professionals rather than nonprofessionals for information.

According to Charles Lowry (1992), one significant consequence of the computerized environment is "common access by all members within an organization to the information produced by the organization," or the "electronic text" (p. 103). The most frequent example of the "electronic text" in library scholarship is the online catalog, and it is often used to illustrate how it has promoted the integration of public and technical services. Gillian McCombs (1986) supplied a number of ways in which catalogers and reference librarians could develop a keener awareness of each others' work. Catalogers could work at the reference desk, provide bibliographic instruction, and "brainstorm" with reference staff. Reference librarians could become more involved in catalog creation and design. James Neal (1987) reported that at Penn State, catalogers worked in public service departments where they functioned as subject specialists who provided reference assistance, bibliographic instruction, online search help, and collection development, as well as cataloging.

But, mechanisms for achieving an integration of responsibilities have been reported in library literature infrequently, and the results of the studies have been tentative and often speculative. At Brown University, a number of committees and task forces composed of individuals from various departments engaged in problem solving with each group being assigned a distinct charge (Taylor, 1984). Committee appointment was based upon expertise, interest in the committee charge, or an individual's role in the organization. According to the library director, the process was beneficial in that it brought a variety of viewpoints to an issue, and staff members gained an organization-wide perspective. Another article described the creation of a quality circle organized to improve cataloging processes and work flow in a public library (DeSirey, Dodge, Hargrave, Larson, and Nesbitt, 1988). The authors reported that the quality circle approach encouraged conceptual thought about work and involvement in the planning process. However, a second quality circle at the library failed due to personality problems among the participants. A case study of cross-training in an ARL library concerned the participation of two bibliographers and a pair of catalogers in a discussion of procedures and issues germane to each area (Gossen, Reynolds, Ricker, and Smirensky, 1990). Since the project was intended as a temporary experiment, a total of only eighteen to twenty hours was expected of each participant. The authors concluded that the experiment improved interdepartmental understanding and promoted new lateral lines of communication, although they refrained from speculating how long such benefits might last.

Planning and Budgeting

The responsibility to communicate across the organization in an effort to gather information can prepare workers for involvement in other responsibilities such as planning. In discussing the possibilities of the electronic library, Kenneth Dowlin (1984) wrote, "At no time in history has there been a greater need for planning for library and information services" (p. 108). Barbara von Wahlde (1993) believed that "effective, pro-active planning will be an essential part of developing the virtual library" (p. 33), since planners would have to decide which traditional services would be retained and which would be discontinued so as to afford newer technological capabilities. However, Brice Hobrock (1991) noted that libraries have traditionally not been characterized by effective planning and that planning skills have not generally been considered an important attribute for library managers. One problem has been that most libraries have been quite myopic, viewing "services, collections, policies, and procedures from the internal perspective of the library" (Gater, 1991, p. 89).

A work which enjoyed great popularity in academic circles during the 1980s was George Keller's *Academic Strategy* (1983). The book helped to popularize the term and concept of "strategic planning" in higher education. Keller believed that strategic planning should constitute a calculated means to anticipate and react to the multiple environments shaping American colleges and universities through carefully planned resource allocation and utilization. One major force he identified was the gain in new technologies, and the impact they were having on the college library.

Michael Malinconico (1984) remarked that the rise in technology introduced several new considerations for library planners. For instance, the limited life of a system should be recognized, and plans should be made for how the transition to its successor would be accomplished. In his view, new systems should "be depreciated and resulting expenses should be included as part of the cost of operation" (p. 335). In addition, changes in technology and in other external or internal factors made it difficult to anticipate the future with any confidence. According to Betty Taylor, Elizabeth Mann, and Robert Munro (1988), other difficulties included projecting the types of personnel needed as well as future user patterns. Von Wahlde (1993) suggested that if, as projected, library effectiveness will be measured by access rather than ownership, measuring that access will be a challenge indeed. David Lewis (1995) remarked that libraries may need to recognize that it may not be economically feasible to provide the same high quality service to all types of users, further complicating the situation.

As a consequence, Maureen Sullivan (1991) believed that planning would entail much more conceptualization than ever, and that library managers lacked sufficient knowledge and time to solve problems and make correct decisions. In her view, the manager should become more of a facilitator, with the staff becoming a "partner or participant" in the process (p. 75). A 1989 ARL review of the strategic planning process in libraries (Gardner, 1989) commented that while planning had traditionally been viewed as a duty for top management alone, libraries now were involving staff from throughout the organization. In the opinion of Donald Riggs (1984), staff involvement in planning could stimulate acceptance of change. Jack King (1987) contended that the participation of reference librarians in the process was critical since they "represent the library user" (p. 195) whom the technology was designed to serve.

A potential problem with involving staff is that it could be very time-consuming. A case study of the planning process at the Wayne State University Library (Mulhare, 1991) mentioned a planning team of twenty-three individuals from throughout the organization, who attended a series of planning retreats. A number of work groups were created to perform research and writing. Later, these groups were reconfigured to address key areas such as staffing and collections. The complete process took sixteen months. Additionally, a review of the process at Pennsylvania State University (Cline and Meringolo, 1991) indicated that the ongoing nature of the process cost an extensive investment of time.

As with planning, a guiding premise in writings about budgeting for libraries is that the budgeting process benefits from the involvement of staff. For example, Barbara Schloman (1993) stated that in order to enable reference departments to be equipped for the future, "the work of managing reference belongs to the entire professional staff of the department." In an article published in 1985, a trend perceived by Allen Veaner (1985b) was that more librarians would assume management responsibilities, and a central part of these responsibilities was "managing institutional time and money" (p. 300). David Lewis (1994) urged that reference librarians be extended "clear budgetary and programmatic authority" in order to "maximize" their effectiveness (p. 451). Unfortunately though, the literature contains a dearth of surveys, case studies, or other research to support this observation. Most of the writing about planning and budgeting either delineates the process or forecasts changes that may occur.

Many management texts link budgets with planning. In an article which summarized the budgeting process, Dale Montanelli (1987) explained that budgets essentially state goals and objectives, along with a method for attaining the objectives if financial resources are furnished. According to James Benson (1987), the process includes "identifying programs of service, establishing objectives for each program, setting priorities, and measuring performance toward the achievement of the objective" (p. 7).

As the number and variety of electronic reference services increase and as they become more prevalent in libraries, budgeting becomes exceedingly complex. Edwin Clay (1987) maintained that for each different informational format, reference librarians should consider in the budget database selection, staffing, training, comparison with print, and whether fees would be charged. Each of these criteria involved a set of additional factors. For example, when selecting a database, Schloman (1993) emphasized the following considerations: whether to lease or purchase, requirements of hardware and software, copyright, and licensing of the site. Marcia Pankake (1986) reviewed the requirements of an adequate online budget, which included not only the costs of searching but also "reference tools like database directories, search manuals, publicity, demonstration searches, absorbing mistakes, training sessions and other costs" (p. 236). Richard Meyer (1993) offered guidelines in choosing between formats (such as CD-ROM and online): data purchase and storage, hardware and software utilization, maintenance, and the time of staff. Potential nondollar costs that he identified but could not calculate included "user effort in the form of multiplicity of interfaces and learning requirements, friendliness of the interface, power of the retrieval software, response time, availability of campus-wide access, and linkage to library holdings" (p. 175). Nancy Eaton and Nancy Crane

(1987) discussed how to compute the per search costs for end-user CD-ROM databases, end-user online services, and mediated searches. Following approval of the budget, expenditures must be monitored. It is no wonder that Michael Buckland (1988) associated the difficulty of the budgeting process with changes in technology. One reason authors called for broader participation in budgeting was that managers lacked the "full information and data" needed to make informal decisions about technology (Cline, 1987, p. 55).

Training

Staff training is another administrative responsibility that is postulated to increase in importance as technological capabilities change. Shoshana Zuboff (1991) defined training in the "posthierarchical period" as "empowering the front lines with information, intellective skills, and the opportunity to act on what they can learn" (p. 6). From the 1970s until very recent years, the emphasis on training in reference has been directed toward nonprofessionals. Numerous studies examined the use of nonprofessionals in reference as a potentially cost-effective approach to answering lower level queries and as a means of enabling professionals to perform an expanded managerial role.

In a 1975 article, Laura Boyer and William Theimer surveyed reference librarians representing academic libraries in the United States to ascertain the use of nonprofessionals at the reference desk. Over two-thirds of the libraries reported such a practice. Eighty percent did not provide formal in-service training, although most had some informal training program: either a tour, general orientation, or other method.

A 1984 survey of academic reference librarians in Illinois (Courtois and Goetsch) and a 1990 survey of public library directors (Jahoda and Bonney) produced results similar to those of Boyer and Theimer, although in the latter survey three-fourths reported using nonprofessionals. In neither study did many respondents report the existence of a formal training program.

Recently, librarians representing ARL and Carnegie Classification libraries were surveyed on scheduling paraprofessionals in reference (Oberg, Mentges, McDermott, and Harusadangkul, 1992). With eighty-eight percent responding affirmatively, the authors considered the issue "resolved" (p. 232).

Jeffrey St. Clair and Rao Aluri (1977) analyzed reference questions in a university library to ascertain professional abilities necessary for a successful response. The questions were classed into four categories: directional, instructional, reference, and extended reference. Results showed that over forty-four percent were directional, and another eighteen percent were of the simple instructional type. The authors concluded that trained nonprofessionals could successfully answer at least sixty-two percent of questions asked.

However, a survey of library patrons (Murfin and Bunge, 1988) generally found low satisfaction with the performance of paraprofessionals in answering reference questions, both with respect to the desired information provided and the quality of service extended. Among other results, the authors discovered that paraprofessionals were more likely to give brief attention to users, and they were less likely to determine whether patrons felt they had succeeded or to identify problems in communication.

As the literature indicates, one reason that nonprofessionals may not be more successful is that they are not likely to receive any systematic or extensive training. Some writers suggest that reference librarians simply cannot find the time to conduct satisfactory training. In a case study describing the use of paraprofessionals in reference work, the author reported that one of the problems with the experience was the time that had to be invested in "mentoring at the desk and on-the-job teaching" (Hammond, 1992, p. 101). Thomas Wilson (1989), after reviewing a training program at the University of Houston, observed that "many valid projects compete for time and priority within a reference department." He continued, "Training left to whim usually will not happen, and training without preparation is a waste of time" (p. 69).

The recent view is that all librarians and staff should be involved in training and that it should be continual (Stafford and Servan, 1990). Hugh Cline and Loraine Sinnott (1983) advocated that training be reviewed whenever a new technology is introduced. A case study of British public libraries (Craghill, Neale, and Wilson, 1989) found that information technology promoted a more serious and more professional view toward training. In a discussion of training in the electronic library, Sheila Corrall (1993) maintained that all staff—professionals and nonprofessionals alike—should participate in staff development, and training should concern "both technical expertise and people oriented skills" such as communication and teamwork competencies (p. 74).

Instruction

Unlike the activities of planning, budgeting, and the training of staff, the instruction of library users has long been considered a primary responsibility of the reference librarian. In the early 1980s, the advent of end-user searching along with the development of more user-friendly systems, caused some in the profession to fear the loss of status as an intermediary between information and the patron (Nielsen, 1982). Elizabeth Frick (1984) rejected this argument because she believed that the librarian's interpretation was needed to add value to the information. According to Carol Tobin (1984), librarians would not become obsolete because they would be needed to assist in selecting databases and formulating search strategy, especially in an electronic environment.

Supporting this view was the research of Sara Penhale and Nancy Taylor (1986), who compared undergraduate end-user searches with those of reference librarians. The librarians performed more sophisticated searches, produced more citations, and generated more relevant citations.

In 1985 the Reference and Adult Services Division of the American Library Association developed a set of goals for instruction in an online setting (Johnston and Clarke, 1992). The four principal goals were: "to know which on-line systems are available and what each system represents; to analyze each information need and to develop a search strategy appropriate to the need and the system; to operate the system in an efficient manner; and to understand how to interpret the search results and how to obtain the needed information" (p. 229). As electronic reference capabilities advanced, users would experience increasing difficulty meeting these objectives.

The literature strongly suggests that one consequence of end-user searching is a need for one-on-one instruction. Alice Littlejohn (1987) conducted a survey of end-users, and they indicated that individualized instruction made the greatest contribution to their searching knowledge. The 1990 book *Public Access CD-ROMs in Libraries: Case Studies* contained a number of accounts acknowledging the importance of one-on-one instruction in an optical disc environment. At Vanderbilt, the time needed for instruction was perceived to increase substantially, perhaps because patrons must be adept at so many facets of electronic research, "not only the individual commands and content of a system, but the concepts of online searching as well" (Resse, 1990, p. 47). Most libraries that aspired to continue the classroom instruction approach expressed disappointment in the lack of interest by the users. Tom Eadie (1992) contended that, as the "Virtual Library" draws nearer, the effectiveness of group instruction will diminish since patrons will require "highly specific instructions" (p. 110).

As technology became a presence on the reference scene, accounts of searching problems began to surface. It seemed almost as though each new capability offered brought with it at least one new difficulty that some users had trouble surmounting. A survey of online catalog users (Lawrence, 1986) noted the following problems: finding the correct subject, conducting a search by subject, using truncation, determining strategies for reducing a quantity of citations, interpreting displays, remembering items on and absent from the catalog, scanning a lengthy display, and stopping the display. Research indicated that subject searches were performed more often using an online catalog than with the traditional card catalog (Markey, 1986), and searching by subject proved especially troublesome. In a study of online catalog searching in a large academic library (Lancaster, 1993), the searcher with the most experience could identify only about half of the needed items.

As capabilities were added to a technology, users became perplexed. For example, when journal contents databases appeared on the catalog, users had difficulty distinguishing the database they were using (Wallace, 1993).

With the move to CD-ROM products in reference service, librarians detected sizable increases in use, as patrons were no longer constrained by telecommunications costs. A need for much more instruction ensued, and librarians began noting the length of time attending to this type of patron (Bonta and Kallin, 1989). At Brock University, it was discovered that CD-ROM assistance took more time than instructing a patron as to the use of a print index (Macdonald, Marshall, and Auer, 1990). At the University of Utah, librarians reported users needed up to twenty-five minutes of individualized instruction (Youngkin, McCloskey, Daugherty, and Peay, 1990). Librarians at Auburn University commented that staff must teach CD-ROM users "everything from the layout of the keyboard and operation of the printer to Boolean logic and the concept of controlled vocabulary" (Childress and Boosinger, 1990, p. 83). In addition, a "minimum level of service skills"—printing citations, changing ribbons and paper, and so forth—was required of those who were responsible for CD-ROM or any computerized technology (Cornick, 1989, p. 147). Many librarians were confronted with an unexpected time management problem.

As information formats multiplied and diversified and as they offered a much broader range of choices for accessing resources, many perceived the instructional role of the librarian to be even more critical. Kelly Collins and Sharon Takacs (1993) dubbed this new role "teacher of information structure" (p. 49).

A part of this instruction continued to focus on concepts such as Boolean logic that had been capabilities of previous technologies, but a special emphasis on critical evaluation of sources began to develop. With a broad range of choices in the market, the effective library user had to be expert in judging the relevance, quality, and availability of information. For instance, Walt Crawford and Michael Gorman (1995) suggested that establishing the authenticity of text in an electronic environment posed a significant challenge. Many authors believed that assisting the patron in evaluation of source material represented an important new responsibility for the reference librarian (Evans, 1992; Oberman, 1991; Kissane and Mollner, 1993). For Evan Farber (1995), complicating matters was that many computer users may be susceptible to the "'gee-whiz' factor, the mystique of the computer, its apparent infallibility, which will cause users to be even more unquestioning than they are now about the information they get" (p. 31).

A big question became "How do we teach standards of judgment and evaluation when students have access to so much information?" (Turner, 1990, p. A15). Problems in the electronic library included assisting remote patrons, the varying access strategies and protocols represented in the Internet and other networks, and the sheer proliferation of databases. Ilene Rockman (1993) debated how to teach users about Internet since it encompassed gateway systems, electronic discussion groups, online library catalogs, campus information systems, bulletin board services, and FTP archives. In addition, the Internet has proven highly unstable, as databases appear, disappear, and change locations daily.

Methodological Considerations

Early investigations of work performed by reference librarians focused on analysis of reference queries. The research of Dorothy Cole (1946) is one example of this approach. Cole studied reference questions posed during one month in thirteen libraries, based upon recorded data. Then, she classified the questions by subject, historical period, and type (book reviews, directory-type information, etc.). The author remarked, "No precise and exact formula for evaluating reference work has yet been devised; furthermore, the nature of the reference process seems to preclude the possibility of such an accomplishment" (p. 45).

Abram Lawson (1969) undertook a broader approach. He used recorded data and work diaries to ascertain the range and frequency of activities performed by reference departments in two university libraries, and then associated these activities with the objectives of both the reference departments and libraries through questionnaires and interviews. Although a variety of activities was revealed, Lawson concluded that less than half of work time of professionals was devoted to professional-type duty.

Cynthia Duncan (1973) surveyed reference librarians in Indiana colleges and universities to determine differences in opinions between colleges and university librarians regarding the following: the category of personnel (professional or nonprofessional) who is performing reference tasks, the category of personnel who should be performing reference tasks, the frequency with which reference-related tasks are performed by each personnel category, and the perceived degree of importance of various tasks. Data were collected through a questionnaire measuring respondents' impressions. Duncan found that college and university librarians devote approximately one-fourth of their time to nonprofessional tasks, and activities pertaining to planning and budgeting ranked particularly high in terms of perceived importance.

In the mid-1970s Danuta Nitecki (1976) directed a questionnaire to reference librarians in order to ascertain attitudes toward the computerized retrieval of information. In one of the questions on her instrument, a range of reference activities was presented, and participants were asked to describe how often they should perform each one. Categories of frequency included a great deal, a moderate amount, a little, and once. According to responses, instructional activities took up the bulk of reference librarians' time.

The following year, a study by Edward Reeves, Benita Howell, and John Van Willigen (1977) sought a self-assessment from reference librarians of their own duties. Staff representing a single university library reference department were interviewed to discover the range of activities they performed, to what extent their activities involved specialization and social interaction, and the estimated frequency with which each activity occurred. From this data, another series of interviews was developed, and staff were asked to rate each activity on the bases of importance, interest, complexity, and the degree to which the respondent was self-confident concerning performance capabilities. According to perceived importance, training student assistants as well as various instructional responsibilities scored especially highly.

Nancy Emmick and Luella Davis (1984) developed a questionnaire that was mailed to reference librarians throughout the United States and Canada. The intent was to "define the characteristics of the occupation of reference librarian, including elements of duties, responsibilities, work loads, status, measures of performance, and the like" (p. 68). In addition to staffing the reference desk, other primary duties were identified as the preparation of bibliographies, coordinating library instruction, serving as faculty liaison, interlibrary loan, and maintaining vertical files.

In her survey conducted from 1982 to 1983, Paula Watson (1986) aimed to collect data on reference staffing and organization, and to identify reference department functions in academic research libraries. The questionnaire was administered to members of the Large Research Libraries and Medium-Sized Libraries discussion groups from the American Library Association's Reference and Adult Services Division. Information sought pertained to staff size, hours of operation, number of questions answered, amount of online searching activity, budget and collection size, and principal functions performed. The following functions were cited as most often performed (in terms of respondent percentage): online services, orientation activities, preparation of bibliographies, "selection for the general collections and liaison work with teaching departments," preparation of exhibits, and vertical file maintenance (p. 49). Respondents were also asked to estimate FTE staff allocated to principal functions in the reference department; results indicated that instructional services and collection development required the most professional staff. Instructional methods most often employed were the preparation of guides, point-of-use assistance, the "general tour," and short lectures and courses (p. 67).

Charles Bunge's survey (1986) investigated the duration of shifts at the reference desk and the extent of the work week spent at the desk by reference librarians. Regarding the latter, each participant was asked to report the number of hours per week in "public contact" (including on-desk, bibliographic instruction, and online searching). Respondents were given a range of choices from which to select: 13-15 hours, 16-18 hours, and so forth.

A questionnaire developed by Jeanie Welch (1988) endeavored to identify a variety of characteristics of reference librarians, including length of time at the reference desk, as well as staff numbers, salaries, qualifications, and skills and responsibilities. The population was limited to reference librarians representing public and academic libraries in the state of Texas. Among academic librarians, the responsibilities of user education, preparation of library guides, collection development, and online searching were most frequently mentioned. The results were similar to those of the national survey of Emmick and Davis (1984).

In the study of Terrence Mech (1988), reference librarians from four similar-sized college libraries maintained a record of duties performed and the amount of time devoted to them for five typical work days. Not surprisingly, the answering of reference questions was the most time-consuming activity. Depending upon the library, however, a number of other duties were assigned as well: interlibrary loan, government documents, archives, cataloging, and so forth. The author explained that because of the wide variation in situations, it was "difficult to establish reasonable expectations or norms" (p. 286) for reference librarians. He also noted that respondents cited meetings as the third most time-consuming activity. Nonetheless, he feared that insufficient time was being devoted to planning, especially given the dramatic change in the library environment.

Rebecca Schriener-Robles and Malcolm Germann (1989) employed a mail questionnaire to investigate the responsibilities of reference-bibliographers in academic libraries of medium college size. Respondents were asked to specify the number of hours per week devoted to selected activities. While reference, research, and collection development were again most frequently mentioned, a mean of almost two hours per week was spent on serving as a faculty liaison. Participating on library, university, state/regional, and national committees consumed a weekly average of 3.0, 1.7, 1.5, and 1.3 hours, respectively.

In her investigation of the role of the reference librarian, Jo Bell Whitlatch (1990) focused on the evaluation of user assistance. To determine value of service, over 200 reference transactions were assessed both from the perspective of the user and the reference librarian. For the most part, users associated a different set of predictor variables with service value than did librarians. Information technology in reference was not a part of the study.

In a series of "yes/no," "more/less," and other questions producing dichotomous responses, Peggy Johnson (1991) asked the heads of technical services in ARL libraries a broad range of general questions dealing with technology in the library workplace. For example, respondents were surveyed as to problems resulting from automation, and whether coordination and communication had increased throughout the organization. Results indicated increased lateral communication among various levels and areas, and particularly between technical and public services.

Carol Tenopir and Ralf Neufang (1992) interviewed reference librarians from "several" ARL reference libraries (methodology not stipulated) to gather their impressions regarding the effect of electronic options on the "(1) work environment, (2) formal instruction of users, (3) the fundamental nature of reference work" (p. 54). Although results are not reported in terms of data, the authors extract comments from the interviews to support their conclusions that technology has in general promoted a reference environment that is busier, one that requires more individualized instruction and teaching of concepts and search structure, and a more satisfied workforce and user group.

Elizabeth Winstead (1994) surveyed all employees of three libraries at a single university about their reaction to some of the perceived consequences of automation in the library. Most respondents believed that automation increased communication activity outside the library but did not result in a "diffusion in decision-making." A majority favored participative management and perceived the importance of communication skills. Ninety-six percent responded that a need for additional training accompanied automation. Reference service was not specifically addressed in the study, nor were responses compared to opinions about the extent of technology in the workplace.

Summary

It has been widely theorized, in the literature of librarianship as well as in that of other disciplines, that technology—especially computer technology—contributes to significant change in the work environment. Many previous library studies regarding this issue have focused on changes in skills and stress levels.

Another substantial body of writing discusses technology and its possible impact on the performance of certain job responsibilities of reference librarians. The literature on this subject is characterized by much speculation, and hypotheses linking reference responsibilities to technology have not been tested directly. Previous surveys appear purely descriptive or methodologically flawed, and case studies provide insufficient breadth of response. The topic continues to spark much interest.

METHODOLOGY

The population selected for this study was limited to the 108 academic libraries in the United States and Canada holding membership in the Association of Research Libraries (ARL). Subjects included the head of reference services from each library in the sample. Names of these subjects were obtained from the current *American Library Directory* (1994). The main library building on each campus was the focus of the study. When no main library could be identified, the facility housing central humanities collections and services was substituted. An additional appropriate sample of professional reference librarians representing each library was also included. The number of these subjects was based upon the total number of professional staff per library as noted in data available in *ARL Statistics* (1994).

One hundred four of 108 reference heads were reached by telephone, and all expressed an interest in participating in the study. After gathering names and addresses of additional subjects, surveys were mailed to 262 potential respondents. A mail questionnaire was employed in an effort to gather data to test the hypotheses. The design of an original instrument was required for this research, since another study of this specific nature could not be located in the literature.

The questionnaire developed uses a Likert-type scale to measure the dependent variables of the study: the perceived importance and frequency of performing communication, instruction, training, and planning and budgeting. A review of the literature suggested these activities and responsibilities were associated with the independent variable: the perception of the capabilities of information technology in the respondents' working reference environment. The dependent variables were measured by participants responding to a series of statements reflecting dimensions of the responsibilities and activities under study. Respondents were asked to assess the frequency with which they performed each statement, as well as the relative importance to the role of reference work each statement was perceived to have. Responses were coded and converted to interval level data for scoring.

To measure the independent variable, the instrument contained descriptions of three scenarios reflecting varying levels of technological capability in reference services. Multiple sources in the literature presented the evolution of libraries in terms of three phases: the traditional paper-based library, a transitional phase, and the electronic library. The descriptions of the scenarios provided on the instrument approximate the three phases found in the literature. An investigation of the literature also suggested to the researcher that capabilities of reference service can be reduced to three primary dimensions—information content, access method, and assistance—and that by assessing the nature of these dimensions in each scenario, one can account for much of the change in reference work. In order for respondents to fully assess capabilities in their working reference environment, the instrument provided a continuum ranging from the traditional library (beginning at level zero) to the electronic setting (ending at level 10). For each dimension, respondents were asked to rate the reference capabilities in their workplace from zero to ten, using the scenario descriptions as a guide. A subscore was computed for each dimension. To test hypotheses, scores from zero to three corresponded to the traditional setting, scores from four to six were considered transitional, and scores from seven to ten represented the electronic library. The total of subscores produced a composite score (maximum 30) reflecting the sum of technological capabilities in the reference environment. Respondents were then aligned with a particular scenario, for each of the three dimensions and for the composite. If a difference in group means indicated significance, a test of the composite measure was also conducted. Categorizing responses produced interval level data and allowed more sophisticated statistical techniques to be run.

Before mailing, the survey was subjected to three rounds of pilot tests among practicing academic reference librarians, in order to refine content and design and to assess face validity of the instrument. Two post hoc procedures were conducted to determine instrument reliability: factor analysis and a Cronbach's alpha reliability coefficient test. Reliability tests produced a low composite measure (alpha of .49) for the independent variable. This low measure indicates that other measures of technological capability in reference exist. Tests on dependent variable composites suggest that questionnaire items for planning, training, and (to a somewhat lesser degree) instruction represent consistent measures of the dependent variables, while items representing communication are not as consistently reliable.

Of the 262 questionnaires mailed, 213, or 81.2 percent, responded within eight weeks. At least one response was received from 102 libraries, (or 98.0%) of 104 libraries that were sent surveys. This represents 94.4 percent of the 108 libraries in the population. Of the 213 surveys returned, 212 were usable. These 212 were subjected to data analysis.

The SPSS-PC+ program was used to analyze data. Frequency distributions and basic descriptive statistics were generated for each variable. Analysis of variance represented the principal statistical procedure, since data were considered interval level and most hypotheses concerned the significance of difference of means. Post hoc multiple comparison tests were employed when appropriate. The final hypothesis—concerning the extent of the relationship between frequency of personal performance of each responsibility and the importance of the same responsibility—was tested using correlation procedures.

PRINCIPAL FINDINGS

The questionnaire began with a set of background items, designed to capture a demographic profile of respondents. Virtually all respondents reported that they held a master's degree in library science accredited by the American Library Association, and almost half had an additional master's degree. The typical respondent may be described as a seasoned professional; the group mean for average number of years since receiving the master's degree in library science

Table 1. Demographic Data

	N	Mean	Mode	Std. Dev.	Min.	Max.
Years post-Master's	209	16.27	17	8.23	0	42
Years current job	210	7.75	1	7.27	0	32
Reference librarians	210	9.30	10	3.89	1	26
Nonprofessionals	206	4.80	3	5.50	0	40
Organizational levels	211	1.55	2	.91	0	5
Hours at reference	209	9.45	10	4.69	0	35

was 16.3, and the average number of years in the current position was 7.7. Participants reported an average of almost twice as many reference librarians in the department as nonprofessionals. In response to a question regarding the number of people in the reporting relationship separating the respondent from the library head, scores ranged from a minimum of zero (10.4% of responses) for those who responded directly to the head to a maximum of five levels of organization (0.9% of responses) between the respondent and the head. The mean number of organizational levels was 1.5. For the group, the average number of hours per week spent performing reference duties was approximately nine and one-half. Four indicated they usually spent no hours at reference, while one reported 35 hours per week (the maximum response). Table 1 summarizes much of this information.

With regard to the first measure of the independent variable, no librarian reported traditional information content, where content consisted of only paper and microform resources. Fifty-eight responses, or 27.6 percent, represented the transitional group, and 152 responses, or 72.4 percent, were in the electronic group. The mean score was 7.3. Thus, the average respondent perceived information content in his/her reference department had moved just beyond offering limited electronic resources and was approaching a broader range of content options, such as a variety of full-text databases, electronic journals and books, Internet resources, and multimedia sources.

Ratings on assistance capability, the second measure of technological capability, produced a more varied distribution. Thirteen point seven percent of responses were in the traditional category, 66.5 percent constituted the transitional group, and 19.8 percent represented the electronic group. The mean score for assistance was 5.2, at the middle of the continuum. On average, librarians believed assistance capabilities in their department consisted of personal help from the reference staff, supplemented by computer-programmed assistance. Responses indicated that the majority of ARL reference environments did not provide online, interactive reference assistance or expert systems.

Responses for access capability resembled those for information content. Only one response fell into the traditional category, and even more scores placed respondents within the electronic scenario. Thirty-seven cases, or 17.7 percent, corresponded to the transitional environment and 172 cases, 82.3 percent, constituted the electronic group. The mean rating for access was 7.6. Data indicated a general sense that most reference departments offered at least some of the access capabilities described on the survey as part of the electronic setting: remote and gateway access, networked resources, natural language input, and hypertext searching.

Descriptive data concerning job responsibilities, the dependent variable, suggest that reference librarians are involved in a variety of activities. A majority of participants indicated that all items pertaining to instruction were performed on at least an occasional basis, with over 95 percent responding "occasionally" or "frequently" to statements dealing with individualized instruction and instructing patrons in source selection and strategy formulation. Of items in the instruction category, teaching formal courses was the least often performed, but its high standard deviation depicted considerable variation within the group.

Some planning activities were also practiced with regularity, although most subjects appeared less likely to assist with library-wide planning than with planning for their own department. Respondents indicated that they had little responsibility for budgeting (means ranged from .74 to 1.14), although variances were high and suggested some librarians were much more involved in the process than others.

Most training activities were performed on an occasional or frequent basis. Two exceptions were the training of student assistants and the evaluation of training. However, there was substantial variation in the data for both, again indicating a lack of agreement among subjects for these two items. Informal training appeared to predominate over other methods.

Communication activities as a group exhibited perhaps the widest disparity in frequency of performance. Most reference librarians reported attending reference staff meetings and library committee meetings on a frequent basis, but the majority were less involved with other activities specified in the survey. Very few reference librarians reported regular work in technical services. The analysis revealed interesting results regarding participation on university committees, as almost as many subjects reported never serving (30.9%) as did those who indicated it was an occasional duty (31.4%).

For all but three statements on the survey, means on the "How Important" index for each item exceeded those in the "How Often" index. The three pertained to instructing patrons in source selection (for which the decrease was only .02 and for which the mean was quite high in both cases), attending reference staff meetings, and serving on library committees. Nonetheless, an overwhelming majority of subjects considered all three "important" or "very important."

Both formal and informal methods of training were considered important, as was a variety of instructional approaches. As a group, items for instruction carried the highest means on "Importance." The vast majority of reference librarians did not believe work in technical services should constitute a principal job activity.

Some of the lowest means continued to be associated with budgeting. Not only did many librarians not participate in the budgeting process, but they also did not think it should be a regular part of job responsibilities.

Descriptive statistics for each dependent variable are collected in Table 2. Included for each statement are the number of respondents, the percentage that chose each item option, the mean for the item, and the standard deviation. An abbreviated description of each statement from the survey has been placed with the corresponding variable number.

To test hypotheses, the researcher identified three dimensions of reference service—information content, assistance, and access—as comprising primary types of capabilities expected to vary when comparing group means for traditional, transitional, and electronic reference settings. Thus, the testing process for each of the first eight null hypotheses involved three tests (or four when testing a composite of all three dimensions collectively). Statistical significance was indicated for tests pertaining to frequency of instruction, frequency of communication, and importance of communication. Significant

Table 2. Descriptive Data for Job Responsibilities

Variable	N	% Responses "0"	% Responses "1"	% Responses "2"	% Responses "3"	Mean	Std. Dev.
Planning Frequency							
1. Form. ref. objectives	211	6.2	17.5	43.6	32.7	2.03	.87
2. Form lib. objectives	211	20.4	32.2	38.9	8.5	1.36	.90
3. Design ref. policies	210	3.8	12.4	34.8	49.0	2.29	.83
4. Design lib. policies	211	21.8	38.9	32.7	6.6	1.24	.87
5. Plan ref. staffing	210	15.2	13.8	23.8	47.1	2.03	1.11
6. Analyze data	209	15.8	34.0	36.8	13.4	1.48	.92
7. Develop ref. budgets	211	43.1	21.3	24.2	11.4	1.04	1.06
8. Analyze expenditures	210	41.4	18.6	24.8	15.2	1.14	1.12
9. Evaluate budget	206	52.4	27.2	14.6	5.8	.74	.92
Training Frequency							
10. Assess training needs	204	8.3	16.2	36.3	39.2	2.06	.94
11. Train prof. librarians	205	9.3	26.3	46.3	18.0	1.73	.86
12. Train nonprof.	206	16.0	24.8	36.9	22.3	1.66	1.00
13. Train student asst.	203	36.9	22.2	25.1	15.8	1.20	1.10
14. Informal training	204	4.4	13.2	36.3	46.1	2.24	.85
15. Evaluate training	203	21.7	34.5	32.0	11.8	1.34	.95
Instruction Frequency							
16. Formal courses	207	17.4	14.5	23.2	44.9	1.96	1.14
17. On-demand group inst.	207	5.8	17.9	28.0	48.3	2.19	.93
18. Individualized inst.	206	.5	3.9	13.1	82.5	2.78	.53
19. Consultation by appt.	210	4.8	17.1	47.1	31.0	2.04	.82
20. Search strategy	210	1.0	3.8	17.6	77.6	2.72	.58
21. Source selection	210	.5	2.4	8.6	88.6	2.85	.45
22. Citation relevance	208	1.4	20.7	43.3	34.6	2.11	.78
Communication Frequency							
23. Ref. staff meetings	209	1.0	2.4	12.9	83.7	2.97	.52
24. Liaison with depts.	207	17.9	12.1	28.0	42.0	1.94	1.12
25. Lib. committees	208	1.9	7.2	21.6	69.2	2.58	.71
26. Univ. committees	207	30.9	23.7	31.4	14.0	1.29	1.05
27. Teams & task forces	205	8.8	15.1	36.1	40.0	2.07	.95
28. Tech. services	205	83.9	11.2	2.9	2.0	.23	.60

		N					Mean	SD
Planning Importance								
29.	Form ref. objectives	211	1.4	6.2	32.7	59.7	2.51	.68
30.	Form lib. objectives	210	4.8	13.3	45.7	36.2	2.13	.82
31.	Design ref. policies	210	1.4	5.7	29.0	63.8	2.55	.67
32.	Design lib. policies	208	5.8	21.2	47.1	26.0	1.93	.84
33.	Plan ref. staffing	210	5.7	11.0	25.2	58.1	2.36	.89
34.	Analyze data	206	7.8	12.6	48.1	31.6	2.03	.87
35.	Develop ref. budgets	208	15.9	18.8	32.7	32.7	1.82	1.06
36.	Analyze expenditures	206	19.4	17.0	33.5	30.1	1.74	1.09
37.	Evaluate budget	204	21.6	24.5	39.2	14.7	1.47	.99
Training Importance								
38.	Assess training needs	202	2.5	6.9	33.7	56.9	2.45	.73
39.	Train prof. librarians	202	4.5	10.4	40.6	44.6	2.25	.82
40.	Train nonprof.	205	4.9	12.2	41.0	42.0	2.20	.84
41.	Train student asst.	198	17.2	17.7	31.8	33.3	1.81	1.08
42.	Informal training	203	3.0	5.9	39.4	51.7	2.40	.73
43.	Evaluate training	201	9.0	10.0	43.3	37.8	2.10	.91
Instruction Importance								
44.	Formal courses	205	4.9	13.7	29.3	52.2	2.29	.88
45.	On-demand group inst.	205	4.4	12.2	30.2	53.2	2.32	.85
46.	Individualized inst.	206	1.0	1.0	17.0	81.1	2.78	.50
47.	Consultation by appt.	208	1.9	8.7	38.9	50.5	2.38	.73
48.	Search strategy	209	1.0	1.9	19.1	78.0	2.74	.54
49.	Source selection	209	.5	1.4	12.9	85.2	2.83	.45
50.	Citation relevance	206	1.0	9.7	38.8	50.5	2.39	.70
Communication Importance								
51.	Ref. staff meetings	206	.5	5.3	24.3	69.9	2.64	.61
52.	Liaison with depts.	202	8.4	8.4	37.1	46.0	2.21	.92
53.	Lib. committees	205	2.9	7.8	44.4	44.9	2.31	.74
54.	Univ. committees	205	8.8	17.6	49.3	24.4	1.89	.87
55.	Teams & task forces	203	3.4	10.3	39.4	46.8	2.30	.79
56.	Tech. services	201	59.7	25.4	12.9	2.0	.57	.79

167

differences among means occurred between the transitional and electronic groups. In all such instances, the mean for the electronic group exceeded that of the transitional group.

To test the ninth hypothesis, regarding the significance of the relationship between frequency of personal performance of each responsibility and the importance of the same responsibility, correlation techniques were utilized. Twenty-eight pairs of variables were examined, one pair per statement on the questionnaire, to assess the strength of the relationship between the two variables in each pair. One variable in each pair related to the frequency of performance of a responsibility, and the second variable corresponded to the perceived importance of the same responsibility. Statistically significant relationships were indicated for all pairs. All correlations were positive in direction.

Specific findings based upon the hypotheses tests follow:

Null Hypothesis 1. There will be no significant difference in perceived frequency of personal performance of planning and budgeting responsibilities by reference librarians in traditional, transitional, and electronic reference departments.

Results from the analysis of variance indicated no significant difference among traditional, transitional, and electronic groups regarding planning and budgeting frequency. The research failed to reject the null hypothesis. Mean scores for each responsibility suggested that on the whole, most planning responsibilities were occasionally performed by respondents whereas subjects seldom performed responsibilities of a budgeting nature. The rather high variance among many planning and budgeting responsibilities implied that they constituted a regular part of the job role for some librarians much more than others. Subsequent multiple regression procedures suggested that number of organizational levels in the reporting relationship between the respondent and the library head represented a significant negative predictor of planning and budgeting frequency. The fewer levels separating the two individuals, the more frequently it seemed that respondents performed that type of work.

Null Hypothesis 2. There will be no significant difference in perceived frequency of personal performance of training responsibilities by reference librarians in traditional, transitional, and electronic reference departments.

Results again failed to reject the null hypothesis and indicated that the frequency of ARL reference librarians performing staff training differed little from the traditional department through the electronic library. The group means in the descriptive statistics indicated that most respondents seldom or occasionally conduct training of staff. In most reference departments, informal training appeared to occur with greater frequency than did formal methods of staff training. This last finding is congruent with studies conducted by Martin Courtois and Lori Goetsch (1984), by Gerald Jahoda and Frank Bonney (1990), and by the ARL Office of Management Services (1991). Standard deviations for all items pertaining to training frequency were rather elevated, indicating a high degree of variability among respondents concerning each statement. Zero-order correlations suggested a highly significant relationship between number of organizational levels and training frequency. However, a multiple regression indicated no significance with organizational level as a predictor variable and training frequency as the criterion variable.

Null Hypothesis 3. There will be no significant difference in perceived frequency of personal performance of communication activity by reference librarians in traditional, transitional, and electronic reference departments.

Statistical significance was indicated with respect to assistance. Results suggested that reference librarians in departments with electronic assistance capabilities, such as expert systems and online reference assistance, communicated more frequently than those working with transitional capabilities such as computer-programmed assistance. Tests failed to reject the null hypothesis with respect to information content, access, and the index of total reference capabilities.

In an examination of descriptive data regarding communication frequency, attending reference staff meetings and library committee meetings were more frequently performed than other communication responsibilities. Few reference librarians worked in technical services very often. Items carrying the highest standard deviation concerned working as a liaison with instructional departments and serving on university committees.

Null Hypothesis 4. There will be no significant difference in perceived frequency of instructional responsibilities by reference librarians in traditional, transitional, and electronic reference departments.

Statistical significance was indicated in terms of access capability between electronic and transitional environments. The mean of the electronic group was higher, so the researcher could conclude that instructional responsibilities were performed more frequently in departments with electronic access capabilities, such as remote access to library resources and the capacity for hypertext and natural language searching, than in departments with transitional access, such as keyword and Boolean searching and access to resources distributed throughout a library facility. This finding appears to support the theory propounded by Joseph Rosenthal (1991) and by Mabel Shaw (1991) that increasing access to information amplifies the librarian's role as teacher and interpreter. Results also indicated statistical significance at .05 for the test involving total reference capabilities. Findings suggested that in the electronic reference environment, instructional responsibilities were more often performed than in the transitional setting. Tests involving information content and assistance capability did not result in the rejection of the null hypothesis.

Upon inspecting descriptive data associated with instructional frequency, mean scores indicated that almost all instructional responsibilities were performed with regularity. Activities pertaining to individualized instruction, source selection, and search strategy appeared to occur most often with the majority of respondents. The item concerning the teaching of formal courses exhibited a high standard deviation.

Null Hypothesis 5. There will be no significant difference in perceived importance of planning and budgeting responsibilities by reference librarians in traditional, transitional, and electronic reference departments.

No significant differences were found among group means. The researcher could conclude that ratings as to the importance of planning and budgeting were approximately the same among groups, and the tests would fail to reject the null hypothesis.

Descriptive statistics regarding planning and budgeting importance suggested that, on average, planning responsibilities were regarded as more important to reference work than were budgeting responsibilities. The item demonstrating the greatest variation in planning and budgeting importance ratings concerned the development of reference budgets.

Null Hypothesis 6. There will be no significant difference in perceived importance of training responsibilities by reference librarians in traditional, transitional, and electronic reference departments.

No significant differences were indicated among means. The research failed to reject the null hypothesis, and there was no reason to conclude that perceived importance of training would vary significantly based upon capability levels in the reference department. Descriptive data reflected that the most variation for a single item in this cluster concerned the training of student assistants.

Null Hypothesis 7. There will be no significant difference in perceived importance of communication activity by reference librarians in traditional, transitional, and electronic reference departments.

Results indicated statistical significance with access capability as the independent variable. The researcher could reject the null hypothesis in terms of access. Research could conclude with 95 percent confidence that communication was regarded as a more important responsibility among reference librarians reporting electronic access, with remote access to library resources and natural language and hypertext capabilities, than among librarians reporting transitional access, featuring keyword and Boolean searching capabilities and access to resources distributed throughout a library facility. This supports the opinion of Marilyn Moody (1992) and others in the literature that increased technological access has created a need for workers to communicate and interact differently. Other analyses of variance did not produce statistical significance at the .05 level.

> **Null Hypothesis 8.** There will be no significant difference in perceived importance of instructional responsibilities by reference librarians in traditional, transitional, and electronic reference departments.

Results indicated no statistical significance in testing of Null Hypothesis 8. Research failed to reject the null hypothesis. Even though significance was detected with access capability and instruction frequency (Null Hypothesis 4), tests between access and importance of instruction did not approach significance at the .05 level. These results may suggest that while reference librarians may perceive they are performing more instructional responsibilities in an electronic environment, they do not necessarily regard them as more important responsibilities in a highly electronic environment, in terms of their regular job role. Whatever environment in which they presently work—traditional, transitional, or electronic—mean scores suggest that instructional responsibilities are regarded as very important by the respondents.

> **Null Hypothesis 9.** There will be no significant relationship as perceived by reference librarians between frequency of personal performance of each responsibility and the importance of the same responsibility.

Significance at the .05 level was found for all 28 relationships. The research supported the rejection of the null hypothesis. Results indicated similar response patterns for variables representing the same statements on the two indexes, and prompted multiple regression procedures to assess the ability of the importance rating in predicting perceptions as to how frequently respondents perform a responsibility.

A summary of the results from the nine hypothesis tests is presented in Table 3.

Table 3.   Summary of Hypothesis Tests

Null Hypothesis 1
    There will be no significant difference in perceived frequency of personal performance of planning and budgeting responsibilities by reference librarians in traditional, transitional, and electronic reference departments.

Results:
a.   *Fail to reject* in terms of information content.
b.   *Fail to reject* in terms of assistance capability.
c.   *Fail to reject* in terms of access capability.

Null Hypothesis 2.
    There will be no significant difference in perceived frequency of personal performance of training responsibilities by reference librarians in traditional, transitional, and electronic reference departments.

Results:
a.   *Fail to reject* in terms of information content.
b.   *Fail to reject* in terms of assistance capability.
c.   *Fail to reject* in terms of access capability.

Null Hypothesis 3.
    There will be no significant difference level in perceived frequency of personal performance of communication activity by reference librarians in traditional, transitional, and electronic reference departments.

Results:
a.   *Fail to reject* in terms of information content.
b.   *Reject* in terms of assistance capability.
c.   *Fail to reject* in terms of access capability.
d.   *Fail to reject* in terms of total reference capabilities.

Null Hypothesis 4.
    There will be no significant difference in perceived frequency of instructional responsibilities by reference librarians in traditional, transitional, and electronic reference departments.

Results:
a.   *Fail to reject* in terms of information content.
b.   *Fail to reject* in terms of assistance capability.
c.   *Reject* in terms of access capability.
d.   *Reject* in terms of total reference capabilities.

Null Hypothesis 5.
    There will be no significant difference in perceived importance of planning and budgeting responsibilities by reference librarians in traditional, transitional, and electronic reference departments.

Results:
a.   *Fail to reject* in terms of information content.
b.   *Fail to reject* in terms of assistance capability.
c.   *Fail to reject* in terms of access capability.

(continued)

Table 3. (Continued)

Null Hypothesis 6.
There will be no significant difference in perceived importance of training responsibilities by reference librarians in traditional, transitional, and electronic reference departments.

Results:
a. *Fail to reject* in terms of information content.
b. *Fail to reject* in terms of assistance capability.
c. *Fail to reject* in terms of access capability.

Null Hypothesis 7.
There will be no significant difference in perceived importance of communication activity by reference librarians in traditional, transitional, and electronic reference departments.

Results:
a. *Fail to reject* in terms of information content.
b. *Fail to reject* in terms of assistance capability.
c. *Reject* in terms of access capability.
d. *Fail to reject* in terms of total reference capabilities.

Null Hypothesis 8.
There will be no significant difference in perceived importance of instructional responsibilities by reference librarians in traditional, transitional, and electronic reference departments.

Results:
a. *Fail to reject* in terms of information content.
b. *Fail to reject* in terms of assistance capability.
c. *Fail to reject* in terms of access capability.

Null Hypothesis 9.
There will be no significant relationship as perceived by reference librarians between frequency of personal performance of each responsibility and the importance of the same responsibility.

Results:
Reject

OTHER DATA ANALYSES

When assessing the dependent variable data, it was observed that certain items exhibited a high degree of variance. Moreover, when examining zero-order correlations generated as a part of the data set, it was detected that the variable dealing with levels of reporting relationship in the organization demonstrated a strong association with many of the dependent variables. Since all correlations between a "How Often" variable and its "How Important" counterpart were also found to be significant, it was determined as a final analysis to perform a series of four multiple regression procedures. For each, a composite measure of the dependent variables dealing with frequency—planning frequency, training frequency, instruction frequency, and communication frequency—would serve as the criterion variable. The importance measure of the same responsibility would represent one predictor variable, and the organizational levels variable mentioned above would be a second predictor variable. A regression with data for part and partial correlation coefficients was conducted to assess the relative contribution of each predictor variable to the variation in the criterion variable while holding constant the second predictor variable.

In each case, the importance of a responsibility was significant in predicting the frequency of the same responsibility. Organizational level was a significant predictor of frequency for three types of responsibilities: planning, instruction, and communication. In the case of planning, organizational level was a stronger predictor than planning importance, but not when other variables were held constant. In other cases, the importance of the activity emerged as the stronger predictor variable.

The importance of each responsibility was positively associated with the frequency of the same responsibility. The number of organizational levels was positively associated with frequency of instruction, so reference librarians at lower levels of the organization performed more instruction. In other cases, the number of organizational levels was negatively related. For example, heads of reference would be expected to perform more planning than other reference librarians based upon the results of the analysis.

CONCLUSIONS

The findings of this study support the following conclusions:

1. ARL reference librarians working in environments with electronic access capabilities, comprising such features as remote access to library resources and hypertext and natural language methods of searching, more frequently perform instructional responsibilities than do ARL reference librarians working in environments with transitional access capabilities instead, such as Boolean and keyword searching and access to library resources limited to service points distributed throughout the library facility.

2. ARL reference librarians working in environments with electronic reference capabilities based upon measures of information content, assistance, and access more frequently perform instructional responsibilities than do ARL reference librarians working in environments with transitional reference capabilities based upon measures of information content, assistance, and access.

3. No evidence was found to support the notion that ARL reference librarians working in environments with varying degrees of information content or assistance capability differed significantly as to frequency of performance of instructional responsibilities.

4. ARL reference librarians working in environments with electronic access capabilities, comprising such features as remote access to library resources and hypertext and natural language methods of researching, rate the importance of communication more highly than do ARL reference librarians working in environments with transitional access capabilities instead, such as Boolean and keyword methods of researching and access to library resources limited to service points distributed throughout the library facility.

5. No evidence was found to support that ARL reference librarians working in environments with varying degrees of information content or assistance differed significantly as to assessing the importance of communication in terms of regular job responsibilities.

6. ARL reference librarians working in environments with electronic assistance capabilities, such as online, interactive reference assistance and expert systems, communicate with greater frequency than do ARL reference librarians working with transitional assistance capabilities, such as computer-programmed assistance and onscreen help features.

7. No evidence was found to support that ARL reference librarians working in environments with varying degrees of information content or access differed significantly as to frequency of communication.

8. No evidence was found that ARL reference librarians working in departments representing varying degrees of capability associated with traditional, transitional, and electronic environments differ in frequency of performing

planning and budgeting, frequency of performing training, assessing the importance of planning and budgeting, assessing the importance of training, or assessing the importance of instruction.

9. With respect to the measures of information content, assistance, and access on the survey instrument, the majority of respondents indicated that ARL libraries were not as technologically advanced regarding assistance as for information content and access.

10. Reliability tests indicated that dimensions other than information content, assistance, and access are likely to exist in assessing variation in reference capabilities.

11. The number of levels of reporting relationship separating the respondent from the library head was a significant predictor in the frequency with which ARL reference librarians performed planning and budgeting responsibilities, and the frequency with which they performed instructional responsibilities and communication activity. Reference librarians in a reporting relationship most proximate to the library head reported more frequent performance of communication activity and planning and budgeting responsibilities, and less frequent performance of instructional responsibilities than did other reference librarians.

12. In analyzing responses, each score on the "Frequency" index was determined to be significantly related to its counterpart on the "Importance" index. This indicated that respondents more frequently performed responsibilities that they regarded as most important. Of course, it may also suggest that respondents were assigning importance to responsibilities they more often performed.

IMPLICATIONS AND CONTRIBUTIONS OF THE STUDY

An examination of findings following data analysis produced the following set of implications:

1. The indication of an association between measures of increasing technology and frequency of instruction may lend credence to the position of numerous authors (Loomis, 1989;

Cornick, 1989; Stewart, Chiang, and Coons, 1990) that changes or advances in technology appear to demand additional time of the reference librarian. Results appear to counter the theory held by others (Mood, 1994; Ewing and Hauptman, 1995) that as technology is used to its potential, a diminished need for user instruction will result.

2. The overall high mean scores associated with items pertaining to frequency of instruction and to importance of instruction tend to support the earlier findings of Danuta Nitecki (1976), and of Nancy Emmick and Luella Davis (1984), that instruction is viewed as a central responsibility by reference librarians. However, the study was unable to conclude that an association exists between measures of increasing technology and assessment of the importance of instruction. This indicates that although instruction appears to be regarded as a primary activity and even though electronic capabilities may contribute to the frequency of performing instruction, it is not necessarily a consequence that instruction is regarded by reference librarians as a more important responsibility in the electronic library.

3. The indication of an association between access capabilities and communication importance supports the research of Rosabeth Kanter (1983), who viewed decentralization of resources and open communication systems as necessary tools in the innovative organization. For Kanter, distributing access to information contributed to the involvement of those from throughout the work force in problem solving and decision making.

4. The indication of an association between electronic assistance capabilities and communication frequency appears plausible in that interactive reference assistance, by definition, should be a more communicative activity than programmed assistance. This research may also support Dana Smith (1989), who suggested the collaboration often needed in designing expert systems and in interpreting the findings to management.

5. Descriptive statistics regarding the importance of communication revealed that the mean score was highest for attending reference staff meetings, a rather traditional responsibility. A less traditional responsibility, serving on interdepartmental

teams and task forces, placed somewhat high as well, and could indicate that traditional hierarchical structures are adapting to accommodate temporary and flexible structures, as suggested in recent surveys conducted by Lois Buttlar and Rajinder Garcha (1992), and by ARL (1992).

6. Results indicate that when significant differences among means existed, they always occurred between the transitional group and the electronic group. This suggests either that more change occurs in work responsibilities at that point in the continuum rather than as capabilities migrate from traditional to transitional, or it may reflect the paucity of cases in the traditional category.

7. Published literature (Lewis, 1994; Kong, 1995) indicated that managerial responsibilities such as planning and staff training should be more frequently performed and more highly regarded by reference librarians as technology increases. This study found no significant support for that opinion. When regarded in relation to the first implication above, one could conclude that as technology increases in quantity in libraries and as it diversifies, instruction is more frequently performed but no extra attention is given to training those providing the instruction, or to more often involving reference personnel in planning to meet needs of the users they serve. This could pose serious consequences for the quality of instruction users receive, the success of their research, and the choice of the library as the organization to serve their informational needs.

8. Most respondents indicated that assistance capabilities lagged behind capabilities for information content and for access. If this information can be assumed as valid, this may suggest that technological development and diversification have moved beyond the capacity of the library to provide guidance and direction, and could have consequences for levels of frustration and stress in the reference department.

9. Reliability tests indicate that the index of total reference capabilities is an incomplete measure of a reliable composite and may not reflect the summed capabilities that it is intended to represent.

10. Of the 28 responsibilities addressed in the survey, over half of the respondents reported that they performed nineteen of

them on at least an occasional basis. This could present difficulties with time management, especially since the scope of this study did not include collection development, interlibrary loan, and other activities often associated with reference work. Library managers should monitor the workload expected of reference personnel, and consider the range of responsibilities and hierarchies when designing and evaluating jobs.

This study aimed to contribute to previous research concerning the effects of technology in reference work by

1. Organizing and describing much of the rather copious literature associated with technology and its possible consequences for reference, especially related to the specific job responsibilities of planning and budgeting, training, instruction, and communication.
2. Designing a measuring scale for reference capabilities in changing technological environments.
3. Testing the association between varying degrees of reference capability and certain responsibilities assumed to comprise part of the job role of reference librarians.

A special strength of the study is that current perceptions regarding technology and responsibilities in the workplace were collected and represent 94 percent of academic libraries holding membership in the Association of Research Libraries. Therefore, data should represent a rather comprehensive assessment of ARL reference departments based upon the views of many of the employees.

RECOMMENDATIONS FOR FURTHER STUDY

1. This study represented an initial and formative endeavor to test the association between level of reference capabilities and responsibilities in reference work. A survey was designed to explore the subject in an identifiable, appropriate population and gather data for possible subsequent research. Further study could utilize the data to identify a small number of ARL libraries representing each of the three scenarios—traditional,

transitional, and electronic—and conduct case studies to reduce biases inherent in self-reporting. As an example, an in-depth investigation could examine the validity of the respondents' perceptions that more frequent instruction is performed when electronic access is available. Site visits would also provide an opportunity to investigate possible causes for this increased frequency: whether a function of an additional quantity of queries from users, a result of more in-depth user questions, or other factors.

2. ARL libraries exhibited less variation in the population than anticipated in regard to levels of information content and access. Consideration could be given to performing a similar study among members of the College Libraries Section of the Association of College and Research Libraries or another appropriate group, with the expectation that a greater variance in capabilities would result. A more equitable distribution of cases among traditional, transitional, and electronic environments could yield more significance when comparing differences in means, especially when multiple comparison procedures are required.

3. Reliability tests suggest that consideration should be given to identifying and measuring categories of reference capabilities, other than information content, assistance and access, that may influence the work of reference librarians.

4. In reliability tests, some clusters of dependent variables demonstrated little internal consistency. Items pertaining to communication appeared especially diffuse. Consideration should be given to combining or removing variables to improve the reliability of the measure.

5. Consideration should be given to examining the frequency of performance of reference responsibilities in relation to an accepted valid, reliable measure of stress in the work environment, such as the Maslach Burnout Inventory.

6. In the data analysis the number of reporting relationships separating the respondent from the library head emerged as a significant predictor variable. Future study related to the subject should include this item as a variable for further analysis.

7. In further research consideration should be given to differentiating responses of reference heads from those of

nonheads, since the former group would be expected to assume different responsibilities and greater involvement in administrative activity.

REFERENCES

American Library Association, Reference and Adult Services Division. 1979. *A Commitment to Information Services: Developmental Guidelines 1979*. Chicago: American Library Association.

American library directory, 1994-1995. 1994. 2 vols. New Providence, NJ: R.R. Bowker.

Anderson, B., and S.T. Huang. 1993. "Impact of New Library Technology on Training Paraprofessional Staff." *Reference Librarian* (39): 21-30.

Andrews, V.L., and C.M. Kelley. 1988. "Changing Staffing Patterns in Technical Services Since the 1970s: A Study in Change." *Journal of Library Administration* 9: 55-70.

Association of Research Libraries. 1985. *Automation and Reorganization of Technical and Public Services*. (SPEC Flyer 112). Washington, DC: ARL.

————. 1991. *Information Desks in Libraries* (SPEC Flyer 172). Washington, DC: ARL.

————. 1992. *The Emerging Virtual Research Library* (SPEC Flyer 196). Washington, DC: ARL.

————. 1993. *Providing Public Services to Remote Users* (SPEC Flyer 191). Washington, DC: ARL.

Battin, P. 1984. "The Electronic Library—A Vision for the Future." *EDUCOM Bulletin* 19: 13-15.

Bednar, M. 1988. "Automation of Cataloging: Effects on Use of Staff, Efficiency, and Service to Patrons." *Journal of Academic Librarianship* 14: 145-149.

Benson, J.A. 1987. "Reference Planning and Budgeting in the New Technological Era." *Reference Librarian* 19: 5-14.

Bichteler, J. 1986. "Human Aspects of High Tech in Special Libraries." *Special Libraries* 77: 121-128.

————. 1987. "Technostress in Libraries: Causes, Effects and Solutions." *The Electronic Library* 5: 282-283.

Birch, N., M.P. Marchant, and N.M. Smith. 1986. "Perceived Role Conflict, Role Ambiguity, and Reference Librarian Burnout in Public Libraries." *Library and Information Science Research* 8: 53-65.

Blauner, R. 1964. *Alienation and Freedom: The Factory Worker and His Industry*. Chicago: The University of Chicago Press.

Bonta, B., and S. Kallin. 1989. "CD-ROM Implementation: A Reference Staff Takes Charge." *Reference Services Review* 17 (summer): 7-11, 93.

Boyer, L.M., and W.C. Theimer. 1975. "The Use and Training of Nonprofessional Personnel at Reference Desks in Selected College and University Libraries." *College and Research Libraries* 36: 193-199.

Braverman, H. 1974. *Labor and Monopoly Capital: The Degradation of Work in the Twentieth Century*. New York: Monthly Review Press.

Brod, C. 1982. "Managing Technostress: Optimizing the Use of Computertechnology." *Personnel Journal* 61: 753-757.

Buckland, M.K. 1988. "Library Materials: Paper, Microform, Database." *College and Research Libraries* 49: 117-122.

————. 1992. *Redesigning Library Services: A Manifesto*. Chicago: American Library Association.

Bunge, C.A. 1984. "Potential and Reality at the Reference Desk: Reflections on a "Return to the Field." *Journal of Academic Librarianship* 10 (3): 128-133.

————. 1986. "Reference Desk Staffing Patterns: Report of a Survey." *RQ* 26: 171-179.

Burns, T., and G.M. Stalker. 1961. *The Management of Innovation*. London: Tavistock.

Buttlar, L.J., and R. Garcha. 1992. "Organizational Structuring in Academic Libraries." *Journal of Library Administration* 17 (3): 1-21.

Caputo, J.S. 1991. *Stress and Burnout in Library Service*. Phoenix, AZ: Oryx Press.

Carande, R. 1992. *Automation in Library Reference Services: A Handbook*. Wesport, CT: Greenwood.

Cargill, J., and G.M. Webb. 1988. *Managing Libraries in Transition*. Phoenix, AZ: Oryx Press.

Childress, B., and J.L. Boosinger. 1990. "Staff and User Training for CD-ROM at Auburn University." Pp. 73-88 in *Public access CD-ROMs in Libraries: Case Studies*, edited by L. Stewart, K.S. Chiang, and B. Coons. Westport, CT: Meckler.

Clay, E.S. 1987. "Changes in Attitudes, Changes in Latitudes: Reference/ Information Services Management in a Time of Transition." *Reference Librarian* 19: 27-38.

Cline, G.S. 1987. "Budgeting for Reference Services in the Academic Library: A Tutorial." *Reference Librarian* 19: 53-73.

Cline, H.F., and L.T. Sinnott. 1983. *The Electronic Library: The Impact of Automation on Academic Libraries*. Lexington, MA: Lexington Books.

Cline, N.M., and S.M. Meringolo. 1991. "A Strategic Planning Imperative: The Penn State Experience." Pp. 201-221 in *Strategic Planning in Higher Education*, edited by J.F. Williams. New York: Haworth Press.

Cole, D.E. 1946. "Some Characteristics of Reference Work." *College and Research Libraries* 7: 45-51.

Collier, M.W., A. Ramsden, and Z. Wu. 1993. "The Electronic Library: Virtually a Reality?" In *Opportunity 2000: Understanding and serving users in an electronic library,* edited by A.H. Helal and J.W. Weiss. Essen: Essen University Library.

Collins, K.L.K., and S.N. Takacs. 1993. "Information Technology and the Teaching Role of the College Librarian." *The Reference Librarian* 39: 41-51.

Cornick, D. 1989. "Automated Reference Service: Pressing F1 for Help." *North Carolina Libraries* 47: 145-150.

Corrall, S. 1993. "Management Development in the Networked Library." Pp. 68-82 in *Opportunity 2000: Understanding and serving users in an electronic library*, edited by A.H. Helal and J.W. Weiss. Essen: Essen University Library.

Courtois, M.P. and L.A. Goetsch. 1984. "Use of Nonprofessionals at Reference Desks." *College and Research Libraries* 45: 385-391.

Craghill, D., C. Neale, and T.D. Wilson. 1989. *The Impact of IT on Staff Development in UK Public Libraries*. Wetherly, UK: British Library.

Crawford, W., and M. Gorman. 1995. *Future Libraries: Dreams, Madness, and Reality*. Chicago: American Library Association.

Creth, S.D. 1986. *Effective On-the-Job Training*. Chicago: American Library Association.

_____. 1989. "Beyond Technical Issues: The Impact of Automation on Library Organization." Pp. 4-13 in *Questions and Answers: Strategies for Using the Electronic Reference Collection*, edited by L.C. Smith. Urbana, IL: University of Illinois Graduate School of Library and Information Science.

Daval, N., and P. Brennan. Comps. 1994. *ARL Statistics, 1992-1993*. Washington, DC: Association of Research Libraries.

DeSirey, J., C. Dodge, N. Hargrave, R. Larson, and S. Nesbitt. 1988. "The Quality Circle: Catalyst for Library Change." *Library Journal* 113 (April 15): 52-53.

Dillon, M. 1993. "Measuring the Impact of Technology on Libraries." Pp. 14-20 in *Library and Information Services Policy: A Forum Report*. Washington, DC: U.S. National Commission on Libraries and Information Science.

Dowlin, K.E. 1984. *The Electronic Library*. New York: Neal-Schuman.

Drucker, P.F. 1988. "The Coming of the New Organization." *Harvard Business Review* 66 (January-February): 45-53.

Duncan, C.B. 1973. *An Analysis of Tasks Performed by Reference Personnel in College and in University Libraries in Indiana*. Doctoral dissertation, Indiana University.

Eadie, T. 1992. "Beyond Immodesty: Questioning the Benefits for BI." *Research Strategies* 10: 105-110.

Eaton, N.L., and N.B. Crane. 1987. "Integrating Electronic Information Systems Into the Reference Services Budget." *Reference Librarian* 19: 161-177.

Emmick, N.J., and L.B. Davis. 1984. "A Survey of Academic Library Reference Service Practices: Preliminary Results." *RQ* 24: 67-81.

Euster, J.R. 1990. "The New Hierarchy: Where's the Boss?" *Library Journal* 115 (May 1): 41-44.

Evans, A.J. 1992. "Information Services in a University Library—Will the 21st Century Bring Us Anything Different or Will it be More of the Same?" *IFLA Journal* 18: 345-350.

Evans, G.E., A.J. Amodeo, and T.L. Carter. 1992. *Introduction to Library Public Services* (5th ed.). Englewood, CO: Libraries Unlimited.

Ewing, K., and R. Hauptman. 1995. "Is Traditional Reference Service Obsolete?" *Journal of Academic Librarianship* 21: 3-6.

Farah, B. 1989. "Academic Reference Librarians: A Case for Self-Evaluation." *Reference Librarian* 25-26: 495-505.

Farber, E.I. 1995. "Bibliographic Instruction, Briefly." Pp. 23-34 in *Information for a New Age: Redefining the Librarian*. Englewood, CO: Libraries Unlimited.

Freudenberger, H.J. 1974. "Staff Burn-Out." *Journal of Social Issues* 30 (1): 159-165.

Frick, E. 1984. "Humanizing Technology Through Instruction." *Canadian Library Journal* 41: 263-267.

Galbraith, J.R. 1974. "Organization Design: An Information Processing View." *Interfaces* 4 (May): 28-39.

Gardner, J.J. 1989. *Strategic Plans in ARL Libraries.* Washington, DC: ARL.

Gater, H.L. 1991. "The Price of Partnership." In *Creative Planning for Library Administration,* edited by K. Hendrickson. New York: Haworth Press.

Goettler, E., M. Hawthorn, and S. McCaskill. 1990. "CD-ROM End User Searching: Implementation Issues in Ontario." in *Public Access CD-ROMs in Libraries: Case Studies,* edited by L. Stewart, C.S. Chiang, and B. Coons. Westport, CT: Meckler.

Goodyear, M.L. 1985. "Are We Losing Control at the Reference Desk?: A Re-examination." *RQ 24*: 85-88.

Gorman, M. 1983. "Reorganization at the University of Illinois—Urbana/Champaign Library: A Case Study." *Journal of Academic Librarianship* 9: 223-225.

Gossen, E., F. Reynolds, K. Ricker, and H. Smirensky. 1990. "Forging New Communication Links in an Academic Library: A Cross-Training Experiment." *Journal of Academic Librarianship* 16: 18-21.

Green, S. 1876. "Personal Relations Between Librarians and Readers." *American Library Journal* 1 (November 30): 74-81.

Haack, M., J.W. Jones, and T. Roose. 1984. "Occupational Burnout Among Librarians." *Drexel Library Quarterly* 20: 46-72.

Hafter, R. 1986. "Born-Again Cataloging in the Online Networks." *College and Research Libraries* 47: 360-364.

Hammond, C. 1992. "Information and Research Support Services: The Reference Librarian and the Information Paraprofessional." *Reference Librarian* 37: 91-104.

Heinlen, W.F. 1976. "Using Student Assistants in Academic Reference." *RQ* 15: 323-325.

Henshaw, R. 1986. "Library to Library." *Wilson Library Bulletin* 60 (April): 44-45.

Hobrock, B.G. 1991. "Creating Your Library's Future Through Effective Strategic Planning." Pp. 37-57 in *Creative planning for library administration,* edited by K. Hendrickson. New York: Haworth Press.

Holley, R.P. 1981. "The Future of Catalogers and Cataloging." *Journal of Academic Librarianship* 7: 90-93.

Horny, K.L. 1987. "Fifteen Years of Automation: Evolution of Technical Services Staffing." *Library Resources and Technical Services* 31: 69-76.

Huang, S. 1990. "The Impact of New Library Technology on Reference Services." *Illinois Libraries* 72: 600-603.

————. 1993. "Introduction: Modern Library Technology and Reference Services." *Reference Librarian* 39: 1-3.

Hudson, J. 1986. "Copy Cataloging Activities: Report of a Survey." *Cataloging and Classification Quarterly* 7: 63-67.

Hurt, C.S. 1991. "A Vision of the Library of the 21st Century." *Journal of Library Administration 15* (3-4): 7-19.

Hutchins, M. 1994. *Introduction to Reference Work.* Chicago: American Library Association.

Intner, S.S., and J.R. Fong. 1991. *Technical Services in the Medium-Sized Library: An Investigation of Current Practices.* Hamden, CT: Library Professional Publications.

Jahoda, G., and F. Bonney. 1990. "The Use of Paraprofessionals in Public Libraries for Answering Reference Queries." *RQ 29:* 328-331.

Johnson, P. 1991. *Automation and Organizational Change in Libraries.* Boston: G.K. Hall.

Johnston, W.K., and J.S. Clarke. 1992. "Bibliographic Instruction and Information Technologies." Pp. 223-247 in *Community College Reference Services: A Working Guide for and by Librarians,* edited by B. Katz. Metuchen, NJ: Scarecrow.

Jones, D. 1989. "Library Support Staff and Technology: Perceptions and Opinions." *Library Trends 37:* 432-456.

Kanter, R.M. 1983. *The Change Masters: Innovation and Entrepreneurship in the American Corporation.* New York: Simon and Schuster.

Keller, G. 1983. *Academic Strategy: The Management Revolution in Higher Education.* Baltimore, MD: The Johns Hopkins University Press.

King, J. 1987. "Builders of the Future: Reference Influence on Library Automation." Pp. 195-210 in *Reference Services Today: From Interview to Burnout,* edited by B. Katz and R.A. Fraley. New York: Haworth Press.

Kissane, E., and D.J. Mollner. 1993. "Critical Thinking at the Reference Desk: Teaching Students to Manage Technology." *RQ 32:* 485-489.

Klassen, R. 1983. "Standards for Reference Services." *Library Trends 31:* 421-428.

Kong, L.M. 1995. "Reference Service Evolved." *Journal of Academic Librarianship 21:* 13-14.

Kupersmith, J. 1992. "Technostress and the Reference Librarian." *Reference Services Review 20* (Summer): 7-8.

Lancaster, F.W. 1983. "Future Librarianship: Preparing for an Unconventional Career." *Wilson Library Bulletin 57* (May): 747-753.

_____. 1993. "Librarians, Technology and Mediocrity." Pp. 100-113 in *Opportunity 2000: Understanding and Serving Users in an Electronic Library,* edited by A.H. Helal and J.W. Weiss. Essen: Essen University Library.

Landoni, M., N. Catenazzi, and F. Gibb. 1993. "Hyper-Books and Visual Books in an Electronic Library." *The Electronic Library 11:* 175-177.

Lawrence, G.S. 1986. "Online Catalogs and System Designers." Pp. 1-14 in *The Impact of Online Catalogs,* edited by J.R. Matthews. New York: Neal-Schuman.

Lawson, A.V. 1969. *Reference Service in University Libraries: Two Case Studies.* Doctoral dissertation, Columbia University.

Lewis, D.W. 1994. "Making Academic Reference Services Work." *College and Research Libraries 55:* 445-456.

_____. 1995. "Traditional Reference is Dead; Now Let's Move on to Important Questions." *Journal of Academic Librarianship 21:* 10-12.

Lin, P.Y. 1992. *Analyzing Library Literature on Academic Library Automation: Authorship and Subject Coverage.* Masters thesis, Kent State University.

Littlejohn, A.C. 1987. "End-User Searching in an Academic Library—The Students' View." *RQ 26:* 460-465.

Loomis, R., J. Jaros, K. Jackson, and C. Gilreath. 1987. "Electronic Versus Printed Access to Reference Tools: Two Approaches." *Reference Services Review* 13 (Fall): 49-53.

Lowry, C.B. 1992. "Management Issues in The "Informated" Library." Pp. 100-131 in *Information Management and Organizational Change in Higher Education: The Impact on Academic Libraries,* edited by G.M. Pitkin. Westport, CT: Meckler.

Lyle, G.R. 1974. *The Administration of the College Library* (4th ed.). New York: H.W. Wilson.

Lynch, B. 1979. "Libraries As Bureaucracies." *Library Trends* 27: 259-267.

Macdonald, M., C. Marshall, and J. Aver. 1990. "CD-ROM at Brock University: Introduction, Integration, Adaptation." Pp. 23-38 in *Public Access CD-ROMs in Libraries: Case Studies,* edited by L. Stewart, K.S. Chiang, and B. Coons. Westport, CT: Meckler.

Malinconico, S.M. 1983. "Listening to the Resistance." *Library Journal* 108 (February 15): 353-355.

———. 1984. "Planning For Obsolescence." *Library Journal* 109 (February 15): 333-335.

Markey, K. 1986. "Users and The Online Catalog: Subject Access Problems." Pp. 35-69 in *The Impact of Online Catalogs,* edited by J.R. Matthews. New York: Neal-Schuman.

Maslach, C. 1982. *Burnout, the Cost of Caring.* Englewood Cliffs, NJ: Prentice-Hall.

Maslach, C., and S.E. Jackson. 1981. "The Measurement of Experienced Burnout." *Journal of Occupational Behavior* 2: 99-113.

McClure, C.R., and A.R. Samuels. 1985. "Factors Affecting the Use of Information for Academic Library Decision Making." *College and Research Libraries* 46: 483-497.

McCombs, C.F. 1929. *The Reference Department.* Chicago: American Library Association.

McCombs, G. 1986. "Public and Technical Services: Disappearing Barriers." *Wilson Library Bulletin* 61 (November): 25-28.

———. 1988. "Public and Technical Services: The Hidden Dialectic." *RQ* 27: 141-145.

Mech, T. 1988. "The Realities of College Reference Service: A Case Study in Personnel Utilization." *The Reference Librarian* 19: 285-308.

Meyer, R.W. 1993. "Selecting Electronic Alternatives." *Information Technology and Libraries* 12: 173-180.

Miller, R. 1986. "The Tradition of Reference Service in the Liberal Arts College Library." *RQ* 25: 460-467.

Miller, W. 1984. "What's Wrong With Reference: Coping With Success and Failure at The Reference Desk." *American Libraries* 15 (May): 303-306, 321-322.

Montanelli, D.S. 1987. "What Reference Librarians Should Know About Library Finances." *Reference Librarian* 19: 15-25.

Mood, T.A. 1994. "Of Sundials and Digital Watches: A Further Step Toward The New Paradigm of Reference." *Reference Services Review* 22: 27-32.

Moody, M.K. 1992. "Reference Librarians and Technical Services Librarians: Who's Accountable?" *The Reference Librarian* 24: 191-200.

Murfin, M.E., and C.A. Bunge. 1988. "Paraprofessionals at the Reference Desk." *Journal of Academic Librarianship* 14: 10-14.

Mulhare, E.M. 1991. "The Library Long-Range Planning Process at Wayne State." Pp. 113-129 in *Strategic Planning in Higher Education*, edited by J.F. Williams. New York: Haworth Press.

Neal, J.G. 1987. "Reflections On The Organizational Environment." *Journal of Academic Librarianship* 13: 348-349.

Nielsen, B. 1980. "Online Bibliographic Searching and The Deprofessionalization of Librarianship." *Online Review* 4: 215-224.

_____. 1982. "Teacher or Intermediary: Alternative Profession Models in the Information Age." *College and Research Libraries* 43: 183-191.

Nitecki, D.A. 1976. "Attitudes Toward Automated Information Retrieval Services Among RASD Members." *RQ* 16: 133-141.

Oberg, L.R., M.E. Mentges, P.N. McDermott, and V. Harusadangkul. 1992. "The Role, Status, and Working Conditions of Paraprofessionals: A National Survey of Academic Libraries." *College and Research Libraries* 53: 215-238.

Oberman, C. 1991. "Avoiding the Cereal Syndrome, or, Critical Thinking in the Electronic Environment." *Library Trends* 39: 189-202.

Palmini, C.C. 1994. "The Impact of Computerization on Library Support Staff: A Study of Support Staff in Academic Libraries in Wisconsin." *College and Research Libraries* 55: 119-127.

Pankake, M. 1986. "Reaction to "Funding Online Services From the Materials Budget." *College and Research Libraries* 47: 236.

Penhale, S.J., and N. Taylor. 1986. "Integrating End-User Searching into a Bibliographic Instruction Programs." *RQ* 27: 212-220.

Peters, T. 1987. *Thriving on Chaos: Handbook For a Management Revolution*. New York: Harper & Row.

Rader, M.H. 1981. "Dealing with Information Overload." *Personnel Journal* 60: 373-375.

Reese, J. 1990. "CD-ROM: A Successful Format in The Education Library." Pp. 39-58 in *Public Access CD-ROMs in Libraries: Case Studies*, edited by L. Stewart, C.S. Chiang, and B. Coons. Westport, CT: Meckler.

Reeves, E.B., B.J. Howell, and J. Van Willigen. 1977. "Before The Looking Glass: A Method to Obtain Self-Evaluation of Roles in Library Reference Service." *RQ* 17: 25-32.

Riggs, D. 1984. *Strategic Planning for Library Managers*. Phoenix, AZ: Oryx Press.

Rockman, I.F. 1993. "Teaching About the Internet: The Formal Course Option." *The Reference Librarian* 39: 65-75.

Rogers, R.D., and D.C. Weber. 1971. *University Library Administration*. New York: H.W. Wilson.

Rosenthal, J.A. 1991. "Crumbling Walls: The Impact Of The Electronic Age On Libraries and Their Clientele." *Journal of Library Administration* 14: 9-17.

Rothstein, S. 1955. *The Development of Reference Services Through Academic Traditions, Public Library Practice and Special Librarianship.* Chicago: Association of College and Reference Libraries.

_____. 1989. "The Measurement and Evaluation of Reference Service." *Reference Librarian* 25-26: 173-190.

St. Clair, J.W., and R. Aluri. 1977. "Staffing the Reference Desk: Professionals or Nonprofessionals?" *Journal of Academic Librarianship* 3: 149-153.

Schloman, B.F. 1993. "Managing Reference Services in An Electronic Environment." *Reference Librarian* 39: 99-109.

Schreiner-Robles, R., and M. Germann. 1989. "Workload of Reference-Bibliographers in Medium-Sized Academic Libraries." *RQ* 29: 82-91.

Shaw, M.W. 1991. "Technology and Service: Reference Librarians Have a Place In The '90s." *The Reference Librarian* 23: 51-58.

Shepard, J. 1971. *Automation and Alienation: A Study of Office and Factory Workers.* Cambridge, MA: MIT Press.

Smith, D.E. 1989. "Reference Expert Systems: Humanizing Depersonalized Service." *The Reference Librarian* 29: 186-188.

Smith, N.M. and V.C. Nelson. 1983. "Burnout: A Survey of Academic Reference Librarians." *College and Research Libraries* 44: 245-251.

Smith, N.M., and Nielsen, L.F. 1984. "Burnout: A Survey of Corporate Librarians." *Special Libraries* 75: 221-227.

Spyers-Duran, P. 1979. "The Effects of Automation on Organizational Change, Staffing, and Human Relations in Catalog Department" Pp. 24-39 in *Requiem For The Card Catalog*, edited by D. Gore, J. Kimbrough, and P. Spyers-Duran. Westport, CT: Greenwood.

Stafford, C.D., and W.M. Servan. 1990. "Core Competencies: Recruiting, Training, and Evaluating In The Automated Reference Environment." *Reference Librarian* 14: 81-97.

Stewart, L., C.S. Chiang, and B. Coons. (Eds.) 1990. *Public Access CD-ROMs In Libraries: Case Studies.* Westport, CT: Meckler.

Stieg, M.F. 1990. "Technology and The Concept of Reference; Or, What Will Happen to The Milkman's Cow?" *Library Journal* 115 (April 15): 45-49.

Sullivan, M. 1991. "A New Leadership Paradigm: Empowering Library Staff and Improving Performance." Pp. 73-85 in *Creative Planning for Library Administration*, edited by K. Hendrickson. New York: Haworth Press.

Taylor, B., E.B. Mann, and R.J. Munro. 1988. *The Twenty-First Century: Technology's Impact On Academic Research and Law Libraries.* Boston: G.K. Hall.

Taylor, M.E. 1984. "Participative Management and The New Librarian Model." *Journal of Academic Librarianship* 10: 201-203.

Tenopir, C., and R. Neufang. 1992. "The Impact of Electronic Reference on Reference Librarians." *Online* 16 (May): 54-60.

Tobin, C. 1984. "Online Computer Bibliographic Searching As An Instructional Tool." *Reference Services Review* 12:71-73.

Turner, J.A. 1990. "Earlham College Tests Value of Mass Use of "Dialog" Database." *Chronicle of Higher Education* 37 (September 26): A 15, A 20-21.

Veaner, A.B. 1984. "Librarians: The Next Generation." *Library Journal* 109 (April 1): 623-625.

_____. 1985a. "1985 to 1995: The Next Decade in Academic Librarianship, Part I." *College and Research Libraries* 46: 209-229.

_____. 1985b. "1985 to 1995: The Next Decade in Academic Librarianship, Part II." *College and Research Libraries* 46: 295-308.

Vedder, R.G. 1990. "An Overview of Expert Systems." In *Expert Systems in Libraries*, edited by R. Aluri, and D.E. Riggs. Norwood, NJ: Ablex.

Von Wahlde, B. 1993. "The Impact of the Virtual Library on Library Management and Organization." Pp. 28-41 in *Opportunity 2000: Understanding and Serving Users in an Electronic Library*, edited by A.H. Helal and J.W. Weiss. Essen: Essen University Library.

Von Wahlde, B., and N. Schiller. 1993. "Creating The Virtual Library: Strategic Issues." Pp. 15-46 in *The Virtual Library: Visions and Realities*, edited by L.M. Saunders. Westport, CT: Meckler.

Walbridge, S.L. 1991. "New Partnerships Within the Library." *Journal of Library Administration* 15: 61-72.

Wallace, P.M. 1993. "How Do Patrons Search the Online Catalog When No One's Looking?: Transaction Log Analysis and Implications for Bibliographic Instruction and System Design." *RQ* 33: 239-252.

Watson, P.D. 1986. *Reference Services in Academic Research Libraries*. Chicago: American Library Association.

Watstein, S.B. 1979. *Burnout: From a Librarian's Perspective*. (ERIC Document Reproduction Service No. ED 195 232).

Welch, J.M. 1988. "Are All Reference Jobs Created Equal?: A Comparison of Public and Academic Libraries." *RQ* 28: 396-403.

Westerhouse, M.A. 1979. *The Effects of Tenure, Role Conflict, and Role Conflict Resolution on the Work Orientation and Burnout of Teachers*. Doctoral dissertation, University of California—Berkeley.

Whitlatch, J.B. 1990. *The Role Of The Academic Reference Librarian*. Westport, CT: Greenwood.

Wilson, T.C. 1989. "Training Reference Staff For Automation In A Transitional Environment." *Library Hi Tech* 7 (4): 67-70.

Winstead, E.B. 1994. "Staff Reactions to Automation." *Computers in Libraries* 14(April): 18-21.

Wood, R.J. 1989. *Stress Among Academic Librarians and Library Directors*. (ERIC Document Reproduction Service No. ED 330 350).

Wyer, J.I. 1930. *Reference Work*. Chicago: American Library Association.

Youngkin, M.E., K.M. McCloskey, N.E. Dougherty, and W.J. Peay. 1990. "CD-ROM Utilization In a Health Sciences Setting." Pp. 123-134 in *Public Access CD-ROMs in Libraries: Case Studies*, edited by L. Stewart, K.S. Chiang, and B. Coons. Westport, CT: Meckler.

Zuboff, S. 1982. "New Worlds of Computer-Mediated Work." *Harvard Business Review* 60 (Sept. - Oct.): 142-152.

_____. 1991. "Informate The Enterprise: An Agenda For The Twenty-First Century." *National Forum: The Phi Kappa Phi Journal* 71: 6.

ACADEMIC REFERENCE STAFFING
FOR THE TWENTY-FIRST CENTURY

Marilyn Searson Lary

After a history of hundreds of years, the library profession has finally "grown up." The information age with its identification, acquisition, description, storage, access and retrieval of data has arrived. For survival, libraries must respond to these escalating changes. As Richard DeGennaro says of his tenure at Harvard: "what I wanted to do and what was needed—was just that: to position the library to face coming changes" (Berry, 1995, p. 30).

Librarianship, in all its many facets, must respond to this changing information environment, must define its place in the information age, and must describe the expectations which the information profession has of its employees. It is no longer possible (and, certainly, was never desirable) to label librarians as the only "professionals" who are employed in libraries (Estabrook, 1992). To value individuals and reward them with respect, higher salaries, continuing education opportunities, and internal mobility based on specific degrees has

Advances in Library Administration and Organization,
Volume 14, pages 191-205.
Copyright © 1996 by JAI Press Inc.
All rights of reproduction in any form reserved.
ISBN: 0-7623-0098-1

never served the profession well and should be relegated to mistakes of the past. A "professional" defines one who reflects a mature, service-oriented attitude; who responds appropriately to change and respects each individual's contributions. A sense of professionalism does evolve, grow, and develop and, as a result, improves the working environment for each employee. With continuous change within the information arena and with static levels of support for library/information agencies, it is critical that academic library administrators define the role of various types of information workers in their particular organizations, that contributions of each employee be evaluated and that these contributions be rewarded appropriately.

"PROFESSIONALS" VERSUS OTHER STAFF

No longer is it permissible to divide library employees into two categories: librarians and support staff. The skills and knowledge needed by information professionals may be obtained through various educational and experiential routes. Increasing expectations of academic library staffs are so diverse and encompassing that individuals with widely different skills are needed to provide responsible service (St. Lifer, 1995). Many of these skills are found in education and training that does not include graduate library/information studies programs. Educational technologists, information mangers, computer support gurus, grants persons, publicists, educators and bibliographers have made and continue to make substantial contributions to academic libraries. In fact, without their expertise and commitment to information access, academic libraries would have been much less successful. In American libraries in the 1990s such employees are busily engaged in activities previously performed primarily by librarians. Because of changing demands, primarily technological ones, librarians' responsibilities have changed; their interaction with instructional faculty, with students' introduction to online services and with researchers has been redefined. The new technology has influenced library staff responsibilities as well (Voelck, 1995). Despite these changes, however, libraries must still function and provide services; the primary support for these daily operations comes from non-librarians. In the words of a library staff member: "Many of us bring extensive training, broad experience, and special skills to our positions" (Farynk, 1995, p. 11) and libraries are finding that these skills, commitment and service must be recognized and valued.

Suggesting that only "librarians" are "professionals" is onerous, indeed (Farynk, 1995). At some time in library history, trained librarians may have provided the primary expertise in management and services; but that has not been true for many years. The financial support provided in the heady days of Lyndon Johnson's Great Society expanded library collections immeasurably, in established academic libraries and in those completely new collections built to support new or expanded universities that developed. Librarians with graduate degrees were not readily available, but libraries increased in size and strengthened their collections, nonetheless.

A professional library employee is not necessarily produced by a formal program of study. A professional is an evolving practitioner, one dedicated to the underlying principles of a profession and one who is committed to improving his or her knowledge and expertise. Such an employee is always valued. The routes by which employees comes into academic librarianship may be quite varied. Employee contributions must be evaluated in light of skills and abilities brought to the workplace and the subsequent growth in those attributes, as well as the development of new strengths. Thus, rewards— promotion, remuneration, development opportunities, and so forth—should be based on contributions and service, not on degrees or graduate-level coursework.

As many librarians graphically discover, academic library users do not distinguish among library personnel or request service only from librarians. The values which librarians themselves espouse— academic status or instructional opportunities, for example—are of little or no concern to users and, in reality, they have little influence on the quality of academic library services. Why, then, do academic librarians denigrate the very persons who maintain the library's functions, who provide the time, support, and opportunity for librarians to enhance or restructure their own contributions?

REFERENCE SERVICES AND STAFFING

One does not often hear debate on the place and value of support/ clerical staff in academic technical services. But voices are often raised against using nongraduate trained employees in reference services.

This debate is continuing, despite the prevalent usage of non-M.L.S. staff in reference services. In 1990 Larry Oberg (1992) found that "...88 percent of the Association of Research Libraries and 66 percent of the smaller college and universities libraries nationally regularly assign paraprofessionals to work at their reference desks" (p. 106). Why is employee support in reference services perceived so differently from support in technical services? Why has the professional felt that only librarians must respond to the public's informational needs? A staff of three of four reference librarians who serve the public daily, often in alternating hours, cannot be consistently responsive to the different demands from the public. In order to provide positive staff support for reference services, academic libraries need to engage as many effective staff members as possible in that area.

Traditional Organization

For many years library personnel characterized by heterogeneous working experience, education, and training have been forced into artificial homogeneous staffing patterns. Many libraries have had no more than three staff classifications: managers, librarians, and support staff. Managers have most often been librarians who were promoted into administrative positions. Librarians supervised support staff, defined services, and generally were involved in overseeing operations. Support staff were responsible for daily operation of the library.

As reference services have expanded in terms of both the depth and breadth of services, libraries have needed people with more diverse skills. One's knowing the individual idiosyncrasies of the H.W. Wilson's Indexes [for example: *moving pictures* as a subject heading for current motion picture reviews] does not necessarily guarantee effective searching strategies on a CD-ROM based periodical index. To be effective, a staff needs the technological-electronic skills required to maintain or to access computerized data. Knowledge of employment law or employer responsibilities in personnel management have become critical to library administrators. The patience, language skills, and ability to communicate with diverse groups have demanded new, sometimes evolving, skills as libraries provide services to the physically challenged, the foreign student, the minority student or the uninitiated community user.

Response to these user demands for reference services have been provided by a variety of employees in reference: librarians, clerks, instructors, assistants, technicians, and students.

But, as noted earlier, the library's organizational plan and its deployment of personnel has been static, defined by a limited structure that allowed little flexibility in job assignment, limited mobility, and totally inadequate salaries for nonlibrarians. To overcome this, it is critical that academic reference service define itself; identify abilities and skills needed by reference providers; and carefully delineate the levels of service each staff member is expected to provide. More appropriate job descriptions, titles, responsibilities, and salaries must be developed without regard to academic qualifications. These can then be used to determine the appropriate mix of M.L.S. and non-M.L.S. personnel. The services offered academic library users, the expertise necessary to provide these services and the effectiveness of the employees in reference services should be the determinants for future staffing in reference services with academic credentials being used only when a specific skill set or mix of skills is required.

Service Levels, Staff Contributions

In the late 1960s Lester Asheim developed a career ladder for library personnel which provided for many routes into the library/ information profession (Asheim, 1968). The traditional masters degree in library science was not perceived as the only method of entering this field. Dr. Asheim advocated the acceptance of alternate career paths into librarianship—backgrounds which, while not including a degree in library/information studies, would serve libraries and library users effectively. In times which demand different services supported by less funding, library directors already rely on a variety of staff to serve and even to espouse the basic tenets of historical librarianship, and Asheim's model reflected this reality. When a service commitment or a concern for users' searching methods becomes a part of the working ethic of a media technician or of a computer technician, that employee has embraced the basic principle of effective library service and such an internalization of values has helped to create an effective information worker. Today's library organization lacks the capacity to recognize this level of commitment, to promote it and to compensate for it.

CHANGING USER EXPECTATIONS

Changing needs of library users and changing expectations themselves are also influencing the structure and services provided by reference units (Millson-Martula and Menon, 1995). Academic librarians are finding that their users are generally more interested in acquiring data than in learning to identify and retrieve it themselves. As Herbert White (1992) indicates, the most important need of a library user is the need she or he has today. The appropriate response to any question addresses that specific need (p. 28). Thomas Childers (1994) also notes that the immediate need for specific data is more important than the need to learn to retrieve that information. "With the popular emergence of electronic access, more people expect simple delivery of the answer, rather than guidance or instruction" (p. 32). This expectation, while demanding staff to retrieve information for the same patron repeatedly, has profound implications for the teaching function so often defended in many circles of academic librarianship. Perhaps, the effort required to teach people the research process may best be directed at those who really have an interest in learning it, not to those who have no interest in the process at all. In many libraries, fewer and fewer users want to learn to do research; this is as true of teaching faculty and students as it is of the general public (White, 1992). While interest in undertaking traditional library research may be shrinking, interest in accessing the Internet, in becoming familiar with e-mail, in subscribing to appropriate listserves and in using other electronic resources is increasing. There is not less interest in information per se, just less interest in the traditional information strategies which reference services have provided.

There exists, then, a burgeoning opportunity for reference service units to become even more critical to and supportive of information seekers in responding to different demands (Mendelsohn, 1994). Yet, reference services still must provide support for those who need basic help: a jammed copy machine, today's paper, directions to the rest room, steps in printing an Internet guide, providing bibliographic information which is incomplete, or locating the address of a publisher. As there are different levels of reference needs, so it is appropriate to provide different levels of reference personnel. When those answering the basic questions relieve others who can then respond to more in-depth, complicated, time consuming needs, library administrators and librarians must appreciate each staff member's contribution. There is much to be said for a consistently polite, dedicated, approachable reference staff member, librarian or not (Dewdney and Ross, 1994).

Reference services units face another equally demanding challenge: the wide variation in the knowledge level of academic users. Despite the promise of technological advances and information availability, large segments of our academic population have underdeveloped information-seeking skills. These include administrators who have used only the telephone for networking and keeping up; faculty who have relied on classic data which has been superseded; bright students with learning difficulties who, nevertheless, must compete; older students returning to school; administrative staff who need to upgrade information seeking strategies via online resources and immigrants who must think in a language other than their native tongue. At the same time, there are students and employees who are technical gurus who have little patience with basic information retrieval processing and elementary instructions and who expect specialized assistance.

To serve all these people effectively, it is even more critical than ever to provide all library employees with a working knowledge of their public. No longer do academic libraries service homogeneous communities where basic assumptions of searching competence, information awareness, and so forth can be made. Reference services staffers must interact with library users to determine the information the user is seeking, the level of information that is needed and the ability of the user both to identify needs and to retrieve data. This plethora of needs combined with widely varying abilities among users vividly supports the wisdom of a reference unit with different levels and abilities in personnel. Staff members with limited training can provide basic help, information or instruction and are then able to refer users to other staff who can give them more specialized attention and personalized service when needed.

Users, staff, and the library all benefit from such an arrangement. The user has a much higher likelihood of being understood and satisfied; the staffer's success in meeting the user's need is much more likely to be assured, and the library is able to meet those needs promptly at a reasonable cost. Good service produces better service; satisfied users contribute substantially to the reputation of the library and its personnel; and efficiency allows for an optimum use of resources.

PROFESSIONAL DEVELOPMENT OPPORTUNITIES

Information providers must assume that continuing technological developments and the public's increasing awareness of information's power will escalate demand for data and, consequently, create a greater demand for reference services. As technological expansion provides more and more access to data, information professionals must remember that technology does not provide data as uniformly as does print; does not gather, retrieve, or provide the same type of access as does print; and is much less consistent in the information supplied. As efforts are undertaken to create virtual libraries, library or information people must be involved and consulted. They are the professionals who understand the vast complexity involved in creating these libraries, as well as the means necessary to retrieve the data contained therein (Cage, 1994). This knowledge of both information, of interfaces to that information and of the needs of users must be harnessed if workable systems are to be developed (Cage, 1994, p. A17).

A base of knowledge about users and the information they seek must be internalized by every library employee. Each employee's awareness of user abilities, employees' individual skills, and their diverse information interests add to the total service endeavor of the library. That reality must be acknowledged in libraries today, not just by administrators, but by those professionals who hold graduate degrees in librarianship and other disciplines, who wield power and authority over staff employees and who are responsible for evaluating them. Library schools, administrators and the librarians themselves must reflect the conviction that all manner of training, work experience, and personalities contribute to successful library service. This acceptance of each employee's contributions must be followed by an appropriate evaluative system and, finally, by reasonable levels of compensation.

REDESIGN OF PERSONNEL NEEDS

Library administrators' failure to assess and acknowledge staff competencies based on the needs of library users rather than on graduate library degrees has produced a stalemate in many academic libraries. The contributions, dedication, and importance of the library support staff has gone unacknowledged so long that staffers have begun to organize, attend professional meetings, and fight for recognition. The recent controversy in Virginia related to membership in the Virginia Library Association highlights the bitterness of many library support employees and the arrogance of some who have M.L.S. degrees (Farynk, 1995). Fortunately, most associations at the state as well as the national level welcome all library employees into their ranks.

The recognition afforded these employees is now and has generally been inadequate, and the resulting lack of inclusion of library employees in the profession continues to be devisive in library organizations. When status, salaries, recognition, and opportunities for growth are based on a degree regardless of the quality of the school or of the educational experience, those without the degree but with comparable education, competence, and interest have reason for resentment. False values and flagrant (and often unwarranted) attitudes of superiority from librarians combined with significant salary differentials between librarians and other employees often undermine mutually supportive work environments.

INDIVIDUAL MISSIONS, UNIQUE STAFFS

Although most academic libraries provide many of the same services and many of the same resources in the same formats, academic libraries today are still unique institutions. Every academic library differs from every other academic library in some aspect of its mission; and because the institutions they serve and the clients who use them differ, that mission certainly should define both the resources and the services of the library and the specific contributions expected from individual staff members. Typical academic library missions require staff members who reflect a conscientious concern for information needs; who have appropriate and, often, additional communicative skills (multilingual staffers); who are approachable and have responsive interpersonal skills; and who have obtained educational/experiential backgrounds which prepare them to fulfill the duties of their positions. However, one academic library may support a strong program in religious studies which primarily requires historical/theoretical support through printed sources while another academic library with a large enrollment in early childhood education may provide collections in various media formats. Such formats allow for variations in learning among the heterogeneous students of today: the disabled, the immigrant, the disadvantaged, the gifted, and so forth. The former library may provide very limited mediated titles and little media support; the second library may produce slide, tape, and video-based programs. In such cases, there will obviously be differences in staff talents and interests. However, the individual strengths of staff members may also influence the methods used to carry out the library's mission. Imagine a reference staffer who is fascinated by *learning theory*, excited about the implications of responding to different learning styles, and who implements this interest and enthusiasm into bibliographic instruction/library usage sessions. Those unique skills and interests are not to be ignored but are to be recognized and nurtured to support the library's mission. Educational experiences, skills, even personality characteristics are the issues, not that each employee or each librarian has had the same course exposure in Reference 101.

REDESIGN OF WORKPLACE RESPONSIBILITIES

As academic libraries redesign reference services to provide for or expand technological support, to rearrange physical resources, and to integrate services with daily providers library administrators must redefine staff responsibilities as well. Such an effort is best undertaken by administrators and staff working in common. The redesign should be undertaken in discrete steps that begin with an effort to define common values and expectations clearly and then proceed to build structures based on those values and expectations. Redefining these premises is critical to developing both organizations and work assignments that make sense.

Academic reference services basically consist of at least two fairly definitive areas: daily tasks which maintain a consistent level of service and supportive attitudes, both toward the information which people need and toward the manner in which these needs are provided. Each reference staff member should identify his or her own individual responsibilities and attitudes; later, some common agreement must define the responsibilities of reference staff as a whole. For example, responsibilities for the first two hours of reference service operations on a weekday morning consist of a wide array of duties and functions. These duties must be enumerated and those responsible for them identified. In such a process, all library staff can, then, be made aware of the contributions necessary for the efficient functioning of the unit. That degree of awareness should engender a greater respect for the unit's wide array of services and for the cooperation necessary for effective functioning.

This analysis of work and duties must be applied to daily operations and the necessary activities must be included in specific job responsibilities. The functions and those responsible for them must be clearly defined and understood by each employee. Educational requirements for each position should be considered at the end of the process, rather than at the beginning. Such an understanding of the parts of a process and of the contributions of particular employees in the operation should enhance appreciation of each staff member's contributions. The most severe criticism of supervisors arises when employees believe that supervisors have no appreciation of the responsibilities, accomplishments or demands of the employees' positions. As suggested, including employees in the process of defining duties can do much to alleviate these concerns.

INFORMATION MANAGERS' EVOLVING RESPONSIBILITIES

Redesigning and restructuring library services require that the responsibilities and duties of librarians also be redesigned and restructured. This restructuring must be based on the individual library's unique mission and the information services that it provides. Services, programs, activities, and tasks necessary to provide full reference services must be delineated and each task must be included in some staff member's job responsibilities. Librarians, having been relieved of many traditional tasks, must be redeployed in keeping with their institution's mission. Librarians in reference services must continue to provide guidance to some library users. However, rather than providing similar instruction to individuals, classes, and groups, they must use their knowledge of resources, their organizational abilities, and their understanding of presentation methods to produce learning experiences. A librarian with database expertise will plan, and perhaps execute, an instructional experience for graduate students in online searching techniques. The delivering format may actually be produced by a multimedia librarian with assistance in scripting, illustrating or layout from a graphic designer. In a smaller institution, a librarian and a staffer may design, create, and produce an entire product.

While it may not be possible for professional library/information programs to produce "leaders," they surely should produce problem solvers: information managers who recognize a problem or identify a need; who determine the resources needed to respond; and who oversee the effort. This does not guarantee a successful product or project. It does, however, encourage experimentation, a constructive response to change and flexibility. An effective conductor brings temperamental, gifted individuals together to produce a satisfying whole. So should information professionals. They must through natural aptitude, learned behavior, or evolving maturity provide a vision; and must be able to shape that vision through organization, management, and direction of its component parts.

A currently under served public which academic libraries might well serve are users who are not physically located within the academic campus. Consider references service in such areas as: position papers or status reports for local businesses on current financial information about their competitors; data on market trends, developing trade partners, hostile take overs; innovative programs to address specific educational problems or weaknesses in local school systems; breakthrough medical information for those health professionals with inadequate access to current medical research; provision of ecological data, demographics, and economic trends to local planning boards.

As graduate trained information managers utilize their particular expertise, library administrators' expectations of these professionals must increase. One with graduate education must embrace a *holistic view* of information, must subscribe to and help develop within the organization a *service philosophy* which responds to all levels of users from the knowledgeable to the uninformed, and must help mold disparate employees into *functioning teams*. This will require excellent "professionals." Those are the only ones who will survive in the lean, down-sized, technologically-based, responsive library/ information center of the twenty-first century.

The expectations of library users and those of employers toward information professionals will continue to be greater than ever before. Today's and tomorrow's information staffers will serve a greater number of individuals who reflect a wider variety of information needs. Old assumptions related to ability of users, shared backgrounds, common experience, and previous educational exposure must be forgotten. Even the physical presence of those seeking information in the library itself will cease to be necessary. As a result, administrators must seek information managers trained in professional library/information schools who possess the following abilities:

- organizational aptitude: in designing work teams; in identifying, defining, and staffing services; in planning and evaluating programs and personnel
- conceptual ability: in defining service goals, objectives, and parameters; in project development and guidance; in supporting professional development experiences for staff
- knowledge of technological applications: in choosing methods needed for information access; in communicating with technical support personnel; in awareness of limitations and opportunities of such applications
- leadership skills: in communicative abilities with internal and external constituencies; in advocacy commitment; in awareness of political considerations and opportunities; in operating within a political organization; in valuing individual contributions which support team endeavors
- collegial orientation to solving common problems, cooperative endeavors, and sharing solutions.

INFORMATION PROFESSIONALS OF THE TWENTY-FIRST CENTURY

In information organizations of the future substantial knowledge of an academic discipline may be just as critical to an effective (and respected) information professional as it now is to an instructional employee. Every information manager trained in a professional school does not need to be a scholar. But to interact with academicians, the professional *must* have discipline-based knowledge. In its concern for developing generalists, librarians have often forsaken the specialist-driven values of the academic community. Academic background has always been a factor in being accepted among college faculty; librarians must reflect greater specialization in their educational attainments, as well as more interest in continuing to obtain specialized expertise. The increasing availability of all kinds of information makes this specialized knowledge more necessary. Academic libraries need librarians who are not only experts in searching and accessing information but who are also experts in particular disciplines or in interdisciplinary knowledge. Basic to using this specialized knowledge are also communication skills, adaptability (to "fit in" an organization), and flexibility in responding to change.

Library organizations of the future are very likely to be submerged within larger organizations of wider scope. For example, some academic campuses are organizing units or divisions of information services or information support services. Information support services often *include* library services, instructional support/faculty development, media services, and academic computing within one organizational framework. The dean or director of such a unit may be a librarian; but that person may just as likely be an information manager, a computing guru, or an educational technologist. Flexibility is paramount in such an evolving environment, as well as a clear sense of the worth and purpose of specific library services and the employees who provide them.

Information management in the twenty-first century is surely not a field for the fainthearted, the uncommitted, or the casual worker. From the 1990s onward the information arena will be a place of continuous change and challenge. Library employees' orientation to their work must be characterized by *flexibility*, an *eagerness* to develop new avenues for information access, and a commitment to mutual support in a *team environment*. Anything less will condemn employees to dissatisfaction and failure and the library to unresponsive service.

REFERENCES

Asheim, L.E. 1968. "Education and Manpower for Librarianship." *ALA Bulletin* 62: 1096-1106.
Berry, J. 1995. "Departing Shots from Richard De Gennaro." *Library Journal* 120(19): 30-31.
Cage, M.C. 1994. "The Virtual Library." *The Chronicle of Higher Education* 41(4): A23+.

Childers, T.A. 1994. "California's Reference Crisis." *Library Journal* 119(7): 32-35.
Dewdney, P., and C.S. Ross. 1994. "Flying a Light Aircraft: Reference Service Evaluation From a User's Viewpoint." *RQ* 34(2): 217-230.
Estabrook, L. 1992. "Managing the Work of Support Staff." *Library Trends* 41(2): 231-249.
Farynk, L. 1995. "The Golden Rule Revisited: Paraprofessionals and Professionals Working Together as Members of a Team." *The Southeastern Librarian* 45(1): 10-13.
Mendelsohn, J. 1994. "Human Help at OPAC Terminals Is User Friendly." *RQ* 34(2): 173.
Millson-Martula, C., and V. Menon. 1995. "Customer Expectations: Concepts and Reality for Academic Library Services." *College and Research Libraries* 56: 33-47.
Oberg, L.R. 1992. "Response to Hammond: Paraprofessionals at the Reference Desk: The End of the Debate." *Library Trends* 37: 105-107.
St. Lifer, E. 1995. "We *ARE* the Library! Support Staff Speak Out." *Library Journal* 120(18): 33-34.
Voelck, J. 1995. "Job Satisfaction among Support Staff in Michigan Academic Libraries." *College and Research Libraries* 56: 157-170.
White, H. 1992. "The Reference Librarian as Information Intermediary: The Correct Approach Is The One That Today's Client Needs Today." *The Reference Librarian* 37: 28.

ACADEMIC LIBRARIES, ACADEMIC COMPUTER CENTERS, AND INFORMATION TECHNOLOGY

Onadell Bly

For the last 30 years academic libraries and academic computing centers, two traditionally independent campus departments, have been moving along two seemingly parallel paths: the computing center developing and using technology to produce information; the library collecting information and organizing and storing it to permit access by any user in pursuit of knowledge. In the last decade this parallelism began to disappear as these paths began to merge into one. The merging of the paths began slowly, but in very recent years it began to accelerate, and the necessity for a blending of the units took on an increasing urgency. Librarians foresaw the merger of the paths for many years and began to study the make-up of the organizations supporting computing and library operations. They suggested models that would integrate the functions of libraries with

Advances in Library Administration and Organization,
Volume 14, pages 207-225.
Copyright © 1996 by JAI Press Inc.
All rights of reproduction in any form reserved.
ISBN: 0-7623-0098-1

computing centers and other information providers in an attempt to produce viable organizations that could serve users to the best advantage in the new world of Information Technology (IT). But traditional definitions of the library, the computer center, and technology frequently muddied these discussions and slowed the process of bringing libraries and computer centers and their methods of information delivery together. It was clear that new definitions were required. This paper is designed to explore past explorations and suggest new paths for IT operations in the university setting.

Technology has always been a part of libraries. The monk with his quill in the thirteenth century was employing the best technology of the time to achieve his goal of preserving and sharing information. Both libraries and computer centers have had "information" in their vocabularies, but their approaches to it have traditionally come from very different perspectives. The computer center has been a place where raw data was collected and, through the use of computers, meaningful information was produced and distributed, usually in paper form, to the end user. Computer personnel seldom made use of the end product. In contrast, the library has been a place in which books, manuscripts, musical scores, or other literary and artistic materials were kept for use by patrons and distributed to them on demand. In most cases, libraries maintained collections that included some raw data, but most often their collections focused on data that had been processed and interpreted by scholars.

Information Technology (IT), the technical method employed to communicate knowledge, has come to encompass both of these concepts. Though technology has always been a part of libraries, more emphasis has been placed on the storage and retrieval of processed information since printing and book production came under the auspices of publishers and printers in the Renaissance libraries. This separation between the book trade and the maintenance of the human record clearly defined roles in the distribution of information, and this separation remained valid through the 1970s. Libraries have employed other technologies in support of their operations like the production of standardized cards and card catalogs and indexing devices to organize the contents of their collections and to make it easier for the users to find information. In the last 25 years these technologies have been enhanced by bibliographic utilities using computers like OCLC, RLIN, and CD-ROMs. But generally, due to the stability of the technologies that were employed and the limitations of emerging technologies, basic change in libraries has been slow. On the other hand, computer centers have by definition always employed technologies that were quickly dated and that required updating based primarily on technological innovation. Only recently has the pace of this change begun to outstrip the capacity of these organizations to change.

Computers are not new to libraries. Libraries began to take advantage of some of their programming and production needs by employing capabilities provided by computers in the late 1960s when bibliographic utilities like OCLC and RLIN were formed. These were followed by information brokerage services such as DIALOG in the 1970s, and librarians began to offer these services to patrons very soon after this kind of access became available. The 1980s brought microcomputers to the desks of many library staff and CD-ROMs, mounted on independent workstations, to the public sector of the library. But even then, the growing impact of computing and computer centers on libraries was not consciously appreciated by most librarians, and, if it was, the intrusion of these experts was often resented. At the same time, computer center personnel seemed to have given little thought to the impact that librarians might have on the management of computer center operations except in those cases when they expressed their conviction that they would soon take over the traditional role of libraries.

With the advent of online local library systems, campus networking, desktop computing, and the ever growing demands of the user to have information available from the desktop, the real issues presented by IT began to emerge. By the late 1970s IT was beginning to creep into every activity of the academic library and, through the 1980s, IT began to affect every department on campus. The widespread use of microcomputers changed the traditional roles of libraries and computer centers. Librarians began to ask questions like, what will become of libraries and librarians; what will the organizational structure of the library be; and will the computer center replace the library? At the same time, computer personnel made subtle changes to incorporate the added responsibilities of networking, supporting PC hardware and software support into their operations. However, they seemed unaware of other implications, such as information organization and retrieval that were emerging as the "real" issues presented by IT.

With the advent of networking all librarians were and are suddenly faced with problems and concerns that were foreseen by some, ignored by others, and generally swept aside by most as everyday work continued to occupy their time. As IT grew and expanded into new areas, librarians developed a compelling urge to independently conquer all the problems and answer all the questions posed by automation. However, it eventually became apparent to most that academic libraries and librarians had neither the resources nor the education needed to incorporate the library and its staff into the world of IT. More recently, computer centers have also experienced similar difficulties.

The identity of the "computer center" has changed from one that focused primarily on research and business to one that must concern itself with teaching and word processing. Computer personnel are faced with a need to cope with academic users whose sophistication and knowledge of personal computers and desktop computing are increasing steadily. They are faced with developing an effective public service program to support hardware and software located in dozens, if not hundreds, of locations on campus, not just in the computer center and a few computer labs. They are also being challenged by the development of instructional delivery for multimedia. The distributed environment in which computer centers find themselves, an environment in which multiple small machines are either supplementing or replacing main frames and where the network is becoming the center of IT, is requiring computer personnel to change the way they define themselves and the way they look at information.

Today, libraries and computer centers share, to a greater or lesser extent, many of the responsibilities presented by the surge of IT. All of academia is being challenged in this area, and only now is the question of how to manage IT beginning to be asked by a wide array of users. The answer is not easy. Many librarians and others have published their thoughts on what they believe to be the best ways to bring academic libraries and librarians into the world of IT and at the same time to insure that users will have the best possible support as they enter the IT world. This discussion is becoming increasingly sophisticated. Recently, many have addressed the issue in a more realistic manner: they are investigating how librarians and computer personnel can combine the skills traditionally attributed to each group to successfully cope with IT and provide the best service to academic users.

This discussion began years ago. As early as 1979, Joe B. Wyatt (1979) wrote that, "Every librarian should be computer-literate—to be able to read and write computer programs for a variety of information applications. To avoid doing so will, over time, result in a growing lack of understanding for both the new material that you will find in your collections and the computer-literate clients who wish to use it" (p. 124). IT has developed rapidly since 1979, and Wyatt's statement has proven to be only partially true: librarians have been forced to become computer-literate, but the need for every librarian, or even every computer person, to be able to read and write computer programs has proven unnecessary by advances in software and technology. Wyatt could not foresee the paths IT would take, and perhaps more important, he did not consider that on every university campus there was a computing center that had a pool of computer experts who could and should be expected to assist in the integration of computers and technology in libraries.

Since Wyatt, many writers have advocated the merger of the library and the computer center into a single information agency. While mergers may have been implemented on some university campuses, the need seemed only to be based on the perception that librarians needed computer centers. Few computer center personnel believed that they needed librarians or libraries, except, perhaps, to justify the purchase of larger machines. Computer personnel did not, and have not, recognized the skills that librarians possess relating to the development of databases, the interpretation of data for novice users, and the training and education of users.

Even so, there are many examples of cooperative efforts between librarians and computer center personnel beginning in the late 1970s and early 1980s and extending through the mid-1990s. Library systems, such as NOTIS, VTLS, and Mankato State's PALS, were developed in-house through cooperative efforts that included library and computer personnel. Some of these eventually were spun off as commercial enterprises, and the systems were sold to libraries across the United States and throughout the world.

Other smaller cooperative efforts have also gained attention. Laine Ruus (1982) described the unique organization of the British Columbia Data Library which was jointly operated by the library and computing center of the university. A description of the California State University at Chico's integration of information systems and services appeared in *CAUSE-EFFECT* in 1986. In many of these cooperative efforts the libraries' patrons frequently became the largest computer users, and the libraries' need and rationale for larger machines and additional equipment grew rapidly. Misic (1995) tells about the successful collaborative effort at Northern Illinois University between the College of Business and the University's Computer Network Department and with support from outside enterprises. Misic addresses both the benefits and problems of the installation issues about which librarians have been concerned (p. 17). While the library was not directly involved in this project, the article does give credence to the idea that cooperative efforts can and do work to the benefit of all involved.

As libraries began to install online catalogs, cooperative efforts were sometimes initiated between libraries and computer centers. Some libraries relied on computer center personnel to assist in the installation, wiring, and programming for the new systems. Other libraries struck out on their own, purchasing computers, terminals, and software for use with vendor-supported turnkey systems, and hiring their own systems personnel. In both cases, the library's involvement with the computer center was strictly project-oriented, and seldom was long term involvement or cooperation anticipated by either group.

However, stand-alone library systems were destined not to 'stand alone' for long. As networked systems came into existence, users demanded the ability to access library catalogs from remote locations. Those libraries which had mounted their catalogs on central mainframes pressured computer centers to add their library catalogs to the campus network; those libraries which had installed stand-alone systems on dedicated machines turned to the computer centers to make their systems compatible with and available over campus networks. Libraries were also asking computer centers to provide networks and software that would enable both library and campus-wide access to CD-ROM towers and other database installations located within the libraries as these resources became critical components of their service programs.

In describing a project at the University of Minnesota to integrate the support and delivery of information services to faculty and staff, Joseph Branin (1993) identified and described the problems confronted on that campus that mirror those that have been and are being faced on many university campuses today:

In the mid-1980s...advances in information technology were creating multiple options for information services at the university. Mainframe computer applications were available from four computer services on campus to support various academic and administrative needs. The University Libraries had just introduced its online catalog of collection holdings and was also offering access to remote online databases for indexing and abstracting services. Faculty were beginning to use microcomputers at their desks for word processing and spreadsheet applications, and the Libraries' CD-ROM databases were becoming available for access from stand-alone microcomputer workstations.... There was not much integration of this new information technology, and it was difficult to move from one type of information system to another (pp. 75-76).

As noted earlier, librarians began to realize fairly early that they could not fulfill all the demands being placed upon them. They began to look for common ground between libraries and computer centers. Hugh Standifer and others (1979) presented five brief papers which described the role of the computer center in the library. These early discussions on merger/cooperation warned of problems in communication, expectations, ability, and reliability. Others also wrote of merger and cooperation, but many seemed to be unable to overcome the perception that irreconcilable differences existed between the approaches taken by the two groups. Paul Zurkowski (1981) wrote, "Many computer experts come at information with a machine-oriented attitude. Many don't have the vaguest [ideas] about the discipline of information, ideas they need that librarians have" (p. 1384). Cimbala (1987) described one difference between the two information units. She said that, "a major difference between the library's and the university computing center's use of computing is that, with the exception of functional activities, the library's electronic services largely reflect access to externally generated information, while computing centers are concerned primarily with internally produced data" (p. 394). An issue of *Libraries and Computing Centers: Issues of Mutual Concern* ("Ingredients...," 1988) defined in more detail the differences between the two units. Differing philosophies of service, methods of support, and organizational differences were all cited as major differences that might prevent a successful merger of these units.

Anne Woodsworth (1988) identified additional characteristics of librarians and computer personnel which may interfere with a merger process. She noted that, "[Their] academic credentials are different, [their] salaries are different, [and their] status and stature in the academic community differ" (p. 30).

In 1994, a group of librarians and computer center personnel meeting together in Chicago for the Third Library Solutions Institute (Lipow and Creth, 1995) contributed some observations which confirmed that the perceived differences between the two groups are still prevalent today. Computer personnel said that librarians do not understand technology, are inflexible and resist change, and deliberate over issues and problems forever. Librarians perceived computer personnel as lacking a set of common values, being inconsiderate of users, and not being service oriented.

In spite of all the differences that were and continue to be identified between librarians and computer professionals, the literature indicates an increasing understanding of the need for a cooperative interface between the two units. Richard W. McCoy (1987) remarked, "It is time we recognize that our research libraries and our computer centers are in the same business" (p. 39). Pat Molholt (1987) commented further that, "Within the university, the library and computer center affect more people more directly and frequently than do any other service units or departments" (p. 33a). Referring specifically to academic libraries, Woodsworth (1988a) wrote:

> Despite territorial instinct and tradition, the boundary lines are blurring around library services. What was once a fairly autonomous operation must increasingly rely on other campus units to function. The campus data network is needed to access the library's online catalog and other information databases.... We are dependent on the computer center for hardware, software, and network operation... (p. 48).

The American Library Association also addressed the issue of mergers/partnerships. James M. Rosser and James I. Penrod (1990) reported on ALA concerns:

> ...at the 1988 mid-winter meeting of the American Library Association, a task force of the Association of College & Research Libraries presented a draft document aimed at providing "unbiased" guidelines for campuses considering convergence of libraries and computer centers. After discussion, the tone of the document was changed to focus on cooperation between units rather than convergence. This change and the fact that the library community feels that guidelines are needed suggests that librarians may have some feeling of insecurity in forging new partnerships (p. 22).

Recognizing the importance of cooperative efforts between the two groups, librarians worked on identifying commonalities between themselves and computer personnel. Pat Molholt (1985) identified many characteristics of the two groups which are highly complementary and desired by both groups. Both groups would like to be able to offer all of the listed services, but in most academic settings the services are limited to the specific department. Computer centers offer twenty four-hour access, unlimited and cost-effective storage, direct access to both local and remote data, easily manipulatable files, and a high degree of technical expertise. Libraries are able to offer a user-friendly orientation, highly structured files and collections, relative uniformity of access which generally obviates extensive user training, and a high degree of subject expertise (p. 286).

An editorial in *Journal of Academic Librarianship* in 1988 called "The Ingredients of a Good Relationship" pointed to similarities that bond the units. Both units deliver services throughout campus. They are frequently organized along similar lines. The technical services departments in libraries are similar to both systems programming and operations in computer centers. Library public service is akin to user services in a computing center. Both units rely on a corps of highly organized professionals. And, perhaps most important, both units deal with the same commodity: information.

Woodsworth and others (1992) identify other commonalities between the units. They point out that both units develop training tools and systems documentation; both units design, operate, and use local and wide area networks; both units plan, select, and operate systems hardware and software; both collect and organize information in various forms and formats; both create, maintain, query, and manage databases; both analyze users, services, and system needs; both provide consulting and technical assistance; and both instruct faculty, students, and staff in all of the above (p. 253). They went on to say, "Goals of both units in these functions are much the same: helping users to access, manipulate, or use information through the optimum use of hardware, software, and communications systems" (p. 253). Anne G. Lipow and Sheila D. Creth (1995) reported that academic librarians and computer professionals recognize that they share these goals.

Cooperation between the units would save much replication of effort and, in many cases, much frustration for both the staffs of the library and computer center, as well as for the user. In many cases, the user does not know whom to ask when confronting a "computer" problem or is put off by the answer received. At the same time, there are many times when the academic staff member who is asked does not know who is responsible for answering the question or solving the problem. A single coherent and predictable set of channels for dealing with questions and triage techniques must be developed among all information providers to meet this need.

Anne Woodsworth (1988) also identified several practical reasons for merging, or at least developing a high level of cooperation between the library and academic computing. She pointed to such issues as staving off declining levels of support, developing user oriented services, sustaining the growth and development of information and network services, getting and sharing resources to equip libraries and computing labs, coordinating the management of various units responsible for the information technologies on campus, finding space on campus for workstations for faculty and students, and measuring the effectiveness of computing and information services (p. 29).

Marilyn J. Sharrow (1995) offered some good advice for those librarians and computer personnel who are involved in collaborative efforts. She cited nine challenges that must be recognized and addressed for partnerships to be successful: priority setting, funding, staffing, areas of responsibility, awareness of effort, levels of authority, communication, personalities (trust and respect), and campus politics and climate.

And so, the "merger debate," as it has come to be called, goes on and on. Librarians have talked and thought, and have written long and hard about it; few, if any, computer center leaders have given much attention to the issue beyond commenting that paper based information was declining in importance. At the same time, university administrators have begun to recognize the changing role of computing in the world of IT and its impact on the university campus. But whether or not organizational change has taken or will take place on campuses, staff of libraries and computing centers have been adjusting their activities to fill the needs brought on by the converging needs of information users.

Librarians began to recognize this change in communication levels in the late 1980s. From the library perspective, Pat Molholt (1989) wrote, "Instead of merging, libraries and computer centers have evolved into a functional cooperation" (p. 96a). She goes on to remark that one indicator of the change in the attitude that was taking place was the degree to which the computer centers have begun to use and identify themselves with words that have been traditionally associated with the library. Words like information and end-user are a standard part of the computing vocabulary. Many computer centers have begun to call themselves Information Centers or Information Services rather than computer centers.

Maurice Mitchell and James Williams (1993) presented a perspective from the computing side. They recognized that computer centers have a need for cooperation with libraries and that computer center personnel are no longer capable of filling all the needs of the users in today's networked environments. They wrote that, "We have a plethora of new challenges to meet.... Those of us from the computing center have a piece of the puzzle. We have networking expertise..., but historically librarians understand how to organize and present the material and know how to help the researcher in his quest" (p. 133).

In spite of the arguments, both pro and con, that librarians and computer personnel presented on the merger issue, university administrations did not jump on a merger bandwagon (p. 17). While the merger issue was being debated at lower levels, some universities began to approach the organizational problem from another angle. A position generically called the Chief Information Officer (CIO) began to be established on some campuses. Anne Woodsworth, Kaye Gapen, and Kenneth Pollock (1987) noted that in the early 1980s there were many "information-management positions." "These included library directors, media-center directors, telecommunications directors, computer center directors, and networking directors" (p. 2). In some cases there was redundancy in these positions, but more importantly, every director was, for their own purposes, moving in a similar direction with little coordination in planning and much replication in effort. As these authors noted:

> One of the major reasons for creating a CIO position in academic institutions is that information services and technologies are increasingly viewed as a utility, providing "power" to a broad spectrum of the academic community. This utility must be developed effectively and efficiently, and plans must be made to cope with the inevitable changes in information technology, so that an institution can incorporate them in a cost-effective manner (p. 2).

Anne Woodsworth (1988a) added other reasons for the creation of the CIO position:

> [The decision to establish a CIO position was driven by] the fear that decentralized hardware and software purchases would result in chaos and incompatibility... A more publicly acknowledged and more noble reason was the improvement that could be derived in information services if all components worked more closely and intelligently in applying the converging technologies that underpinned all their operations (p. 38).

As the concept of the CIO became more prevalent, librarians began to anticipate better communication and cooperation between themselves and computing personnel; the hope of librarians was that the CIO would either be a librarian, or that the CIO would encourage the inclusion of libraries in campus networking and information decisions. However, these changes did not always occur as librarians had believed and hoped that they would.

Anne Woodsworth, Kaye Gapen, and Kenneth Pollock (1987) conducted a survey in 1986 on the position of CIO at institutions who were members of the Association of Research Libraries. Library directors of 91 institutions were polled. Their survey revealed that the position titles assigned to CIOs varied widely. Woodsworth and colleagues reported that:

> Of ... 30 [identified] CIO positions, 10 carried the title of vice president or vice chancellor. The others had such titles as associate or assistant vice president or vice chancellor, or associate or vice provost. The descriptive part of the title also varied considerably. The most commonly used terms on descending order of frequency were: information systems, information services, telecommunications, and information resources. Often, some combination of terms was used—e.g., vice president for information systems and computing (p. 3).

Interviews were conducted with 11 CIOs and 11 Library Directors from the universities which had a CIO position. Based on these interviews, the surveyors were able to report that CIO positions were viewed very differently by the library directors and CIOs themselves.

> Library directors saw the CIO as having little or no involvement in the formulation of policies and determination of long-range goals, while the CIOs said they exercised some responsibility for these activities. The CIOs also reported a higher level of involvement in budgeting and in decisions about

major hardware and software purchases than the library directors attributed to them (p. 3).

The early surveys conducted by Fleit (1986) and Woodsworth, Gapen, and Pollock (1987) indicated that few of the early CIOs had any input or control over library activity, and more recent research by James Penrod and Wilder, as cited by Woodsworth (1992), "has found that 90 percent of colleges and universities in the United States...manage their information functions without a CIO" (p. 252).

Recent library literature supplies little information about current CIO positions, and it is clear from the literature that most institutions have not, until very recently, realized the need for a CIO. However, as technology develops across campuses, it does appear that the original rationale for a CIO as a campus-wide coordinator of networking, hardware, and software will likely change. Woodsworth, Gapen, and Pollock (1987) pointed out that, "the position of CIO as it exists today will be obsolete in five to 10 years, at least in those institutions that are on the leading edge of information technology. (The kind of CIO needed) is likely to focus more on the content and service aspects of information resources than on the technology" (p. 4).

Woodsworth (1988a) went on to say that, "Current developments in the technology itself point to the elimination of the need for central policies and controls.... The role and responsibility [of the CIO] will shift as the strategic vision focuses less on the technology itself and more on the provision of information resources and services in support of research and scholarship.... It is in this arena that the library director has the opportunity to emerge as tomorrow's CIO" (p. 43).

David C. Weber (1988) described four approaches to solving the organizational dilemma now presenting itself to the information manager:

1. The Columbia University model: the library director has a good background in information technology and is given responsibility for both the library and the computer service organization.
2. The Carnegie Mellon University model: the information technology service organization director may be skilled and knowledgeable of the traditional library and is given the responsibility of coordinating both organizations.

3. Both organizations may be kept separate with the heads of the two reporting to a senior academic officer.
4. The library director may report to the senior academic officer and the computer service director to a business vice-president, a vice provost for computing or an officer for information technology reporting to a vice-president or the president (p. 8).

These four models represent very broad definitions for the IT organization on university campuses, and they rely upon maintaining, more or less, the same departments that have traditionally existed on most campuses. The existing model may not be the important issue, however, particularly since organizational structures are likely to be changing. What is important is the level of cooperation and dedication to the goal of each individual making up the groups within the model.

This kind of cooperation can be illustrated by Ann Koopman's (1995) recent study of two successful library Web implementations. The organizational models under which the two described implementations were completed are quite different and help to illustrate that various models can be successful in reaching similar goals. Other recent articles indicate that merger and cooperative efforts between libraries and computer centers are taking place and seem to be successful using very different organizational models. Kenneth Flowers and Andrea Martin (1994) described the history of collaboration, the current status of RiceInfo, and plans for future information technology developments at Rice University. Lowry (1994) described the development and success of the University of Iowa Libraries' Information Arcade. Haaland (1994) described the plan to merge the library and the computing services department into one unit at Gettysburg College.

Marilyn Sharrow (1995) emphasized that, "The motivation for creating all of this electronic access is the fact that without it one cannot be an active player within, or beyond, the campus of today" (p. 56). With this thought in mind, the following questions emerge and must be put into perspective. Where are academic libraries and computing centers in 1996? Has IT made any differences in library services and computer center development? Will the influence of IT increase and continue to change organizational structures in the future?

To date, library and computer center mergers have not generally taken place. A review of the job ads in the *Chronicle of Higher Education* for the last half of 1995 reveals many listings for what are apparently "CIO" positions. Each is different in scope, and it is still not clear if there is a pattern in how these positions relate to libraries and how libraries are being incorporated into IT developments on campuses. Does this mean libraries are being left further and further behind in IT development, that computer centers are not responding to and supporting the needs of the library, or that libraries are leading the change? The author believes the answer to all of these questions is, "No."

While administratively-organized cooperative efforts have generally not yet occurred, and while the impact of campus CIOs is still not clear, what Kenneth Flowers (1987) called "an advanced level of interaction" (p. 99) has and is taking place almost universally between librarians and computer center personnel. This interaction involves the computer center assisting the library with its computer(s), the library becoming involved in both local and wide area networks, and an informal link of cooperation being developed between programmers and technical staff from the computer center and librarians involved with systems support for library services. Librarians are becoming involved in Internet and other user training activities. The author believes this advanced level of interaction will continue to grow as academic libraries become more involved in the development of access to networked resources and as computer centers become more aware of the necessity and challenge of organizing those resources that are located in the library, at other locations on campus, and around the world.

The most urgent need for continued and increased cooperation between libraries and computer centers lies in the ever growing influence and presence of the World Wide Web. It is the belief of the author that the Web has created the largest impact of any technology on the university campus to date and that it is the epitome, to date, of Information Technology. As universities, academic libraries, and academic departments build home pages, set up links to resources, and create their own resource databases, it is immensely important that each university's primary Web site and every subordinate site be well planned, consistently organized, well maintained, and appropriately indexed to serve the needs of the population on that campus.

Computer center personnel and librarians are the best qualified people on campus to oversee these activities. The technical and programming skills of computer personnel and the organizational skills of librarians must all be used to develop these resources fully and to adapt them to local needs. While no one should be prohibited from accessing anything they might wish to retrieve, it is imperative that the Web be a useful and approachable tool that will meet the needs of a given university's clientele. Just as libraries collected materials that supported the curricula of their universities, and just as computer centers provided support and services for their universities based on the needs of the faculty, staff, and students, local Web sites must be carefully built to give the same support.

Anne Woodsworth and Ellen Hoffman (1988), wrote, "Libraries are not the only information resources nor are they the only source of access to information" (p. 92). If this was true in 1988, then it is a fact that cannot be argued in 1996. By the same token, the author believes that academic computing centers are neither the only technical resources nor the only source for technical support. If academic libraries and computing centers do not work in a cooperative effort to support the clientele of their universities, then that clientele will go elsewhere to find the information and support they need. Independent search services, network carriers/suppliers, and Web development services are becoming more and more numerous in the for-profit business world. These companies are willing to offer service and support to all levels of users. If libraries and computer centers are not able to coordinate and broaden their services to fill the needs of academia, libraries will become archives and repositories to retain records of the past, and computing centers will be limited to their old role as data processing units serving campus administrative needs, if these needs are not also contracted to an outside firm.

There is little doubt that the library, as it has existed since Dewey developed his first classification system, and that the computer center, as it has existed since the manipulation of data using machines began fifty years ago, will continue to exist for many years. It is likely that libraries will never disappear: the total contents of libraries may never be totally replaced by computer access, and libraries will need people to preserve, organize, and service these collections for years to come. It is likely, however, that the traditional computer center will disappear or at least change dramatically. As desktop computing becomes more and more powerful and as client-server installations become more sophisticated, it is likely that many of the labor intensive activities on campus that require a "mainframe" and central support will be transferred to distributed systems that run purchased software packages. Future librarians and computer personnel will work in much different ways than they do today...and they will either be working together, or many may not be working at all.

The challenges and changes we face are exciting. Today's definition of *Information Technology*, the access and retrieval of information using electronic devices, requires that organizational examination, cooperation, and change occur. The only constant in the future is human kind's need for information and knowledge, and it is likely that future attempts to delineate between IT and more traditional systems for the delivery of information will be increasingly difficult.

The days of universal organizational models are gone. Each university will pursue the organizational track that best suits its needs. The roles of librarians and computer personnel within that track will be very similar to each other, perhaps in some cases even identical. Whatever the model: the library and computer center acting as single departmental unit, as dual departments under a common administrative head, or as separate units working together in an advanced level of interaction, librarians and computer personnel will continue to need each other and rely on each other: *both library service programs and IT* demand it.

REFERENCES

Branin, J.J., G. D'Elia, and D. Lund. 1993. "Integrating Information Services in an Academic Setting: The Organization and Technical Challenge." *Library Hi Tech* 11 (4) (Issue 44): 75-83.

"California State University, Chico: College and University Computing Environment." 1986. *CAUSE/EFFECT* 9 (July): 18-20.

Cimbala, D.J. 1987. "The Scholarly Information Center: An Organizational Model." *College and Research Libraries* 48 (5): 393-398.

Fleit, L. 1986. "Choosing a Chief Information Officer: The Myth of the Computer Czar." *CAUSE/EFFECT* 9 (3): 26-30.

Flowers, K.E. 1987. "Academic Libraries on the Periphery: How Telecommunications Information Policy Is Determined in Universities." *Journal of Library Administration* 8 (2): 93-114.

Flowers, K., and A. Martin. 1994. "Enhancing User Services through Collaboration at Rice University." *CAUSE/EFFECT* 17 (3) (Fall): 19-25.

Haaland, G.A. 1994. "Strategic Information Resources: A New Organization."
    *CAUSE 94: New Opportunities for Partnering. Proceedings of the 1994
    CAUSE Annual Conference*, November 29-December 2, 1994, Walt Disney
    Dolphin, Orlando, Florida. III-2-1—III-2-9.
"The Ingredients of a Good Relationship: The Library's Point of View." 1988.
    Libraries and Computer Centers: Issues of Mutual Concern. *Journal of
    Academic Librarianship* 13 (6): 364a-364d.
Koopman, A. 1995. "Library Web Implementation: A Tale of Two Sites." *CAUSE/
    EFFECT* 18 (4): 15-21, 29.
Lipow, A.G., and S.D. Creth. (ed). 1995. *Building Partnerships: Computing and
    Library Professionals. Proceedings of Library Solutions Institute.* Number
    3, Chicago, Illinois, May 12-14, 1994. Berkeley: Library Solutions Press.
Lowry, A.K. 1994. "The Information Arcade at the University of Iowa." *CAUSE/
    EFFECT* 17 (3): 38-44.
McCoy, R.W. 1985. "The Electronic Scholar: Essential Tasks for the Scholarly
    Community." *Library Journal* 110 (16): 39-42.
Misic, M. 1995. "Collaborative Management of Technological Resources at
    Northern Illinois University." *Techtrends* (November/December): 15-18.
Mitchell, M.C., and J.E. Williams. 1993. "The Virtual Library: The Computing
    Center Perspective." Pp. 131-444 in *The Virtual Library: Visions and Realities*,
    edited by L.M. Saunders. Westport, CT: Meckler Press.
Molholt, P. 1985. "On Converging Paths: The Computing Center and the Library."
    Journal of Academic Librarianship 11 (5): 284-288.
————. 1987. "On Converging Paths: the Computing Center and the Library."
    Libraries and Computer Centers: Issues of Mutual Concern. *Journal of
    Academic Librarianship* 13 (1): 32a-32d.
Rosser, J.M., and J.I. Penrod. 1990. "Computing and Libraries: a Partnership Past
    Due." *CAUSE/EFFECT* 13 (2): 21-24.
Ruus, L.G.M. 1982. "The University of British Columbia Data Library: An
    Overview." *Library Trends* 30 (Winter): 397-406.
Sharrow, M.J. 1995. "Library and IT Collaboration."*CAUSE/EFFECT* 18 (4): 55-
    56.
Standifer, H., M.J. Young, K. Bierman, B. Markuson, and W.D. Mathews. 1979.
    "The Library and the Computer Center." *Journal of Library Automation* 12
    (1): 362-378.
Weber, D.C. 1988. "University Libraries and Campus Information Technology
    Organization: Who Is in Charge Here?" *Journal of Library Administration*
    9 (4): 5-19.
Woodsworth, A. 1988. "Computing Centers and Libraries as Cohorts: Exploiting
    Mutual Strengths." *Journal of Library Administration* 9 (4): 21-34.
————. 1988a. "Libraries and the Chief Information Officer: Implications and
    Trends." *Library Hi Tech* 6 (1): 37-44.
————. 1992. "The Information Job Family: Results of an Exploratory Study."
    Library Trends 41 (2): 250-268.
Woodsworth, A., D.K. Gapen, and K.Pollock. 1987. "Chief Information Officers
    on Campus." *EDUCOM Bulletin Summer*: 2-4.

Woodsworth, A., and E. Hoffman. 1988. "Information Technology: New Opportunities—New Problems." *Journal of Library Administration* 9 (2): 91-104.

Wyatt, J.B. 1979. "Technology and the Library." *College and Research Libraries* 40 (2): 120-124.

Zurkowski, P.G. 1981. "The Library Context and the Information Context: Bridging the Theoretical Gap." *Library Journal* 106 (13): 1381-1384.

THE LITERATURE OF JOINT-USE LIBRARIES

Rashelle S. Karp

INTRODUCTION

The concept of joint-use libraries dates back at least to the 1800s (Fitzgibbons, 1989), and has at its roots many different catalysts. The literature over the past 30 years indicates that these may include:

1. Initiatives for "total community library services" (Garrison, 1973; Kitchens, 1973a; Fenwick, 1979), which have been variously referred to as "community schools," "community education" ("School Library...," 1975b; Fonstad, 1976; Aaron, 1978b; Waters and Mashinic, 1983), "free schools," (Petrino, 1972), neighborhood research centers (Martin, 1973; Willis, 1980), "therapeutic communities" (Shirk, 1978), and community education centers (Baker and Radoff, 1983).
2. Recognition that all people have the right to read (Izard, 1974).

Advances in Library Administration and Organization,
Volume 14, pages 227-271.
Copyright © 1996 by JAI Press Inc.
All rights of reproduction in any form reserved.
ISBN: 0-7623-0098-1

3. Belief in the rights of all people to have access to information (Dougherty, 1989) and research materials ("Pioneer...," 1973).
4. Initiatives to coordinate all of the cultural institutions in a state or region (Denis, 1972), to provide a range of cultural outlets at one library facility ("Texas...," 1974), or to provide a cultural outlet for specific populations (Sayre, 1976).
5. Needs of a community's citizens for free quality learning support services such as nonprint media and equipment ("Utah...," 1976).
6. Mandated rehabilitative services ("Seattle...," 1972; "School/ Public...," 1974) and vocational education services ("Cooperating...," 1975) for all who require them.
7. Commitment to lifelong learning ("School/library...," 1979b; Del Vecchio, 1993; Sunseri, 1994), adult education ("School...," 1974), adult basic education such as GED and ABE ("School/library...," 1974b), college entrance assistance for those who need it ("New...," 1976), and continuing education ("Library...," 1972).
8. Enthusiasm for the "open university" concept ("Andover...," 1973; "Open...," 1973; Simpson, 1973; Wyesinghe, 1988).
9. Pressures to make better use of decreasing financial resources (Woolard, 1978) and to make libraries more cost-efficient (Gerhardt, 1992).

Official reports from education and library agencies also have, since the late 1800s (Broderick, 1967), been catalysts for cooperation and joint-use (Fletcher, 1876; National Education Association, 1899; Joint Committee..., 1941; American Library Association Committee..., 1945; Public Library Association, 1960, 1964, 1979; National Commission..., 1975, 1980, 1983, 1984).

In spite of this support from many sectors, the concept of joint-use is debated, and surveys indicate a lack of agreement within the profession regarding its advantages and disadvantages (Amey and Smith, 1976; Quinn, 1979; Craver, 1987; Dedrick, 1994).

DEFINITION OF A JOINT-USE LIBRARY

A strict definition for joint-use might be "a single library facility serving the informational, educational, cultural, and recreational needs of an entire community" (Graham and Travillian, 1978, p. 97). Using this definition, the most frequently described categories of joint-use include:

1. joint school/public libraries ("Suffolk...," 1973; Junkin, 1975; Opatow, 1976; Dwyer, 1981; Taylor, 1989; Reading, 1992), especially joint school/public branch libraries ("DC Branch...," 1974; Johnson, 1977; Kitchens and Bodart, 1980; Enochs, 1991);
2. joint school/community college libraries (Baker and Radoff, 1983);
3. joint college or university/public libraries ("Waniassia...," 1977; "University...," 1979; "Public/School...," 1985; Ralston and Oldenburg, 1992); and
4. joint-use community college/school, community college/university ("Public Library-Community...," 1977; Anderson, 1990; Conley, 1994), community college/public libraries (Wintersteen, 1980; Connole, 1991; "Learning center...," 1994).

A less strict definition of joint-use might be more appropriately referenced as "modified joint-use." A modified joint-use library is one in which two or more libraries cooperate in specific and limited areas in order to provide on-site access to informational, educational, cultural, and recreational materials and services. The difference between a modified joint-use library and a network (or multitype network) is that in a network, access to materials and services is more often electronic and remote (e.g., through online catalogs, networked CD-ROM workstations, and online cooperative acquisitions) rather than personal and on-site. The most frequently described modified joint-use libraries include all of the above mentioned joint-use combinations, as well as joint special/university libraries and joint college or university/school libraries, including the use of academic and other libraries to promote economic development within a region through information use (O'Keefe, 1975; Fiscella and Ringel, 1988; Breivik, 1992).

Regardless of the definition used, the literature seems to focus on three main areas: discussions of the pros and cons of joint-use libraries, descriptions of cooperative efforts, and suggestions regarding methods to ensure success. Each type of literature since 1970 (when the majority of literature on the topic began to be written) and through 1994 (see Stenstrom, 1978) is summarized following.

THE PROS AND CONS

Opponents of joint-use libraries cite many reasons for their condemnations, including general negative attitudes ("Iowa...," 1982), a general reluctance on the part of librarians to speak out on the topic (Sullivan, 1970), and the high priority that librarians place on self preservation and protection of territory and autonomy (Dyer, 1977, 1978; Bender, 1979). It is also indicated in the literature that some librarians consider their colleagues rivals (Paton, 1971), and hold a philosophy that professionals from different libraries should not "work in a comingled atmosphere" ("Rocky...," 1973, p. 594). Other reasons include the following perceptions:

1. The roles and management (White, 1963; Woolls, 1985/1986) of school and public libraries are different enough (Minnesota..., 1980; Laughlin, 1990) that they should cooperate (Clubb, 1988) rather than combine (Pammett, 1973). This contention is supported, at least in part, by a survey (Doll, 1982, 1984) in which the overlap between children's collections in public and school libraries was found to be small. In this case, the author used the results to conclude that school and public libraries should cooperate rather than merge. This conclusion is also supported by others, who indicate that public libraries serve individual students in ways which the school library cannot (Morris, 1973; Stone, 1980) and that schools exist to support formal curricula (Trait, 1977), while public libraries support informal education (Haycock, 1975).
2. Adults are reluctant to use a joint school/public library which is located in a school (Amey, 1976; Mynatt, 1981; Lemerande and Sturzl, 1983) because entering a public school is psychologically unappealing for adults.
3. Public librarians are not colleagues, but rather supplemental personnel for the school library (Vincent, 1983).
4. A public library housed in a school will develop an anonymity that is detrimental to its ability to fulfill its mission ("School-Library...," 1973; Teahan and Huska, 1990), and to provide even minimal public library service (Minnesota..., 1966).
5. Joint public/school libraries thwart the growth of each entity rather than facilitating it (Weir, 1975).

6. In a joint library situation, both libraries are forced to compromise to the point that neither can completely fulfill its mission (Douglas, 1990).

7. There is too much noise when school students are in the public library (Czopek, 1990) and too much labor intensive work for librarians when school students are in the academic library (Miller and Russell, 1987).

8. Academic librarians are too insular and their collections too scholarly to be able to combine with public libraries ("Educators...," 1975; Terland and Terland, 1979).

9. Legal barriers (Pettem, 1978) and governance questions (Bell, 1979) work against joint-use libraries, especially when a branch public/school library is sited in an urban school, thus leaving suburban residents without library service ("Va. School...," 1973) or when school taxes are used to support the public part of a joint school/public library (Miller, 1971).

10. Joint school/public library facilities deplete the public library's collections (Creech, 1982).

11. A public library situated in a school library becomes a "babysitting" service ("Librarian...," 1976).

12. Joint school/public libraries force public librarians to censor their collections (Royal, 1986).

13. Because of their use, public libraries must be situated in busy locations in order to facilitate use ("Public Library Use...," 1977); school libraries must be located in less busy locations in order to conform to school districting and in order to ensure the safety of students (Hegarty, 1971; Whitney and Burgess, 1974). These conflicts indicate that joint-use libraries cannot work.

14. Joint-use academic/special libraries infringe on academic freedom and commercialize the academic environment (McDonald, 1985).

15. Joint-use academic/public libraries seriously drain the resources of the academic library (Russell, 1979; Venkateswarlu, 1980).

16. Students become distracted when their parents come in to use a joint school/public library (Ontario, 1973).

17. Public libraries which are housed in school libraries are perceived as school libraries ("New...," 1973).

18. Joint-use libraries may result in staff reductions (Lemerande and Sturzl, 1983) and burn-out among librarians who are filling dual roles (Mitson, 1982).

19. Conflicts of interest among diverse patron groups using a joint-use library cause irritation for everyone (Jones, 1977).

20. Structures in which more than one academic library share one facility are costly and possibly inadequate for the schools' needs ("Library co-op...,"1993).

In spite of the seemingly overwhelmingly negative literature (Amey, 1989), proponents of joint-use libraries are very committed to the concept. Two articles in the literature even suggest doing away with public libraries and merging them into academic and school libraries (Olivera, 1974; Bloomfield, 1986); another suggests doing away with school libraries and merging them into the public library (Freiser, 1967). Some cited advantages of joint-use libraries are listed following.

1. Joint-use libraries are especially helpful in rural ("Sheldon...," 1972; "Public...," 1973; Jones, 1989) or smaller (Nelson, 1972) communities, and in poorer (Aaron, 1978) communities which cannot afford separate libraries (Dwyer, 1989); which cannot afford any library (Miller, 1976; Savage, 1988); which cannot afford quality library service at more than one location (Haycock, 1973; Kitchens, 1980); which are just beginning to provide library services ("School...," 1975a), or which are geographically isolated from metropolitan centers (Gauld, 1988).

2. Since school and public libraries share similar concerns (Bingham, 1982), educational roles (Baker, 1977a), and overall goals (Moon, 1970; Nettleford, 1976), they, as the two educational forces in the community (Hill, 1992), are natural choices for the joint-use concept.

3. A joint-use library at a convenient location will be more used than two separate libraries in inconvenient locations (Piternick and McInnes, 1975).

4. Joint-use libraries make better use of available money ("Combined...," 1975; Berry, 1979; "California...," 1981; Zavortnik, 1987; Burns, 1988; Koldenius and Nilsan, 1992; "Two Ohio...," 1994) because selection tools, audio visual materials (O'Connell and Thurner, 1982), specialized

services, personnel ("Wisconsin Drafts...," 1976; Bennett, 1989), and equipment (Gee, 1983) can be shared, and costly duplication avoided ("California...," 1980).

5. Since both public and school libraries are supported by local taxes, it makes sense that they be combined (Everett, 1980) or that they cooperate (Williams, 1975).

6. Surveys indicate that when the public library and the school library are in close proximity, patrons physically use the collections of both, rather than relying on interlibrary loan (Barron, 1977). This phenomenon supports the joint-use concept.

7. A joint school/public library allows two collections, which do not have significant overlap, and each of which separately satisfies only one-third of its patrons' information resource needs ("Philadelphia...," 1973), to be easily accessed by more people ("Cooperation...," 1982; "Fairbanks...," 1982).

8. Joint-use libraries facilitate local and regional (Major, 1990) development since they can provide a broader range of information to people working in corporations (Brodribb, 1972; Pautz, 1972; Soltow, 1976), can better support home-schooling (LaRue and LaRue, 1991), can provide a broader range of professional materials for teachers (Downes, 1975), and can better support lifelong learning (Ray, 1991).

9. Summer reading opportunities are the single most strongly related activity to children's summer learning (Heyns, 1978). Joint-use public/school libraries increase the amount of reading that a child does (Proseus, 1989) and that a child is capable of (Howes, 1986).

10. The perceived differences between school libraries as learning and instruction centers, and public libraries as cultural centers are artificial and ungrounded; their goals are the same (Baker, 1977b).

11. Shared staffing in joint-use libraries fosters better knowledge and utilization of both libraries (Weiss, 1980).

12. Joint school/public libraries allow students to avoid being isolated from the broader intellectual and cultural environment around them ("Interim...," 1973).

13. Joint-use libraries allow a library to increase the number of hours (Christopher, 1972; "Interlibrary...," 1977) and the number of days per week ("Cooperation...," 1982) that it is open.

14. Legislation such as laws mandating library cooperation (Horn, 1987; Kauppinen, 1987; Sorensen, 1987; Olsson, 1991) and laws stipulating that government depository libraries must serve the entire community (Prince and Nelson, 1985) support the joint-use concept.

15. Joint-use libraries are less threatening to economically and culturally disadvantaged adults (Barron, 1978).

16. Multitype libraries which are housed in a school library allow children to use the public library without having to deal with parental restraints regarding leaving a "safe" location and travelling to another location (Bates, 1972).

17. Joint-use academic/public libraries help to ameliorate town/gown hostilities (Simon, 1992), help to increase the amount of public funding provided for academic libraries (Judd and Scheele, 1984), and help to build bridges between high school and college for students ("Where...," 1971; Nofsinger, 1989).

18. Introducing public school children to the academic library helps to ensure that they behave when they do use the academic library (Hammond, 1989).

19. Joint-use ventures between academic and public libraries are good recruitment tools for talented and gifted students (LeClerq, 1989).

20. Joint-use libraries increase the accuracy of information provided for patrons (French, 1979).

21. Joint-use libraries increase the library's visibility within the community (Young, 1985) and maximize resources from which students, teachers, and the public benefit (Kinsey and Honig-Bear, 1994).

TYPES OF JOINT-USE

The types of joint-use that occur range from simple information exchanges ("School/Public...," 1979), outreach programs ("New York...," 1992), publicity programs (Woolls, 1974), and coordination of hours of service (Whitelock, 1975), to complicated joint facilities (Young, 1979) with joint funding and legislative arrangements (Horowitz, 1979; "UC-Santa Cruz...," 1985) and with formal standards and agreements ("North Dakota...," 1972, 1973, 1976). They also range from models for library cooperation which comprise only informal communication (Billman and Owens, 1985/

1986) to models in which the participants communicate in strictly formalized (Shannon, 1991) and supportive (Cooprider, 1972) ways. There are school libraries which are run by public libraries (Ellis, 1984); college library branches which are staffed by the public librarians ("Community and...," 1972); school libraries staffed and administered by the public library (Sliney, 1988); public libraries located on college campuses and jointly funded by the county library and the college (Beach, 1989); public libraries which are the designated college library for nontraditional (Johnson, 1980) and extension (Power and Keenan, 1991) students; college libraries staffed, in part, by corporate librarians who primarily serve the needs of their parent corporations ("Industry...," 1973); and public/school library branches of the public library (Hirsch, 1973; Cherry, 1982; Vulturo, 1985). There are even public academic libraries which are administered by library science education programs (Alafiatayo and Aleraiye, 1987) and combined public/school/community college libraries (Brown and Mashinic, 1983). The combinations are as varied as people's commitments to them; some librarians merely tolerate outside use of their libraries (Wiseman, 1975), some recognize it as a necessity (Craver, 1989), others accept it as a legal mandate (Landwirth, Wilson, and Dorsch, 1988), and others actively encourage it (Thompson and Rhodes, 1986). Regardless of the level of cooperation, the most frequent combinations are those in which two or more libraries cooperate for specific purposes (Heck, 1973; Shoup and Tadin, 1979) such as multicultural awareness (Mahoney, 1991), National Library Week (Varley, 1973), library open houses (McCombs, 1991), or special programs such as author series ("Home...," 1975; McCormick, 1986) and humanities programming (Drake and Lynch, 1978), but primarily in order to share resources ("School/Library...," 1980; Doll, 1983). Following is a summary of the types of joint-use cooperation that the literature discusses.

JOINT-USE BETWEEN ACADEMIC AND PUBLIC LIBRARIES

This category includes the following activities:

1. University classes which require research (Holloway, 1983) and bibliographic instruction at the public library (Raedeke and Meyers, 1982)

2. Borrowing privileges and library cards for all community residents ("North Point...," 1972; "University...," 1972; "Connecticut Community...," 1973; Tolliver, 1976; Bortz, 1981; Process, 1983; "Columbus...," 1989) or for selected community residents who are not affiliated with the university (Cone, 1982), or for public library card-holders (Hules, 1982).

3. Provision of curriculum materials by the public library for university extension courses (Cowser, 1978) and for distance learning students ("Public...," 1976; Barnett, 1986; Coatney, 1993).

4. Provision, by the academic library, of research (Willis, 1980; Lesh and Geeman, 1987) and business (Barrie, 1988) materials for the public library's local community ("Ohio...," 1989) and vice versa (Mittelman, 1975).

5. Joint oral history projects (Reid, 1976)

6. Provision of resources by the public library to support university independent study and correspondence courses ("Enoch...," 1982)

7. Use of the public library facility to offer academic coursework (Little and Gilliland, 1977a, 1977b)

8. Reserve shelves maintained at the public library for use by university students (Grundt, 1972; "Minnesota County...," 1976)

9. Provision of information and referral services for the general public at the academic library (Wheeler, 1985; Leavy and Moore, 1988; Dougherty, 1989)

10. Provision of job and career information for the general community at the academic library (Josephine and Reneker, 1989)

11. Provision of health related information by university health sciences libraries (Marshall, 1982)

12. Use of the public library as the library service provider for university extension (see, Latham, 1991) classes (Soules, 1979)

13. Contracts between academic and public libraries in which the public libraries provide extension services (Dollerschell, 1991) for university extension programs

JOINT-USE BETWEEN ACADEMIC
AND SCHOOL LIBRARIES

Here, the following activities are cited in the literature:

1. Special instructional modules provided for high school honors and advanced students at the university library and staffed by the academic librarians (McAndrew, 1989; Nopenger, 1989; Campbell and McCully, 1992)
2. Special bibliographic instruction programs provided for high school minority students at the academic library (Egbers and Giesecke, 1989)
3. Literacy seminars (Hollifield and Lawrence, 1986), bibliographic instruction (Canelas and Westbrook, 1990), and critical thinking instruction (Kennedy and Wilson, 1986) provided for local high school and junior high school students at the academic library and staffed by academic librarians
4. Use of the university library facility during times when the school library is unavailable (Petty, 1976)
5. Distribution of university library cards to advanced high school students (LeClercq, 1986)
6. Special collections, for example, international studies (Cochrane, 1989), housed at the academic library for use by public school students
7. Offerings of special bibliography courses, for example, medical bibliography (Chu and Shellhase, 1983), at the university library for high school students
8. Provision, by academic librarians, of bibliographic and research instruction for high school students to ensure that entering freshmen acquire necessary library skills before they come to college (Kemp, Nofsinger, and Spitzer, 1986)
9. Development and maintenance of an "audiovisual study center" at the university library for use by public school students (Ascroft, 1988).

JOINT-USE BETWEEN ACADEMIC AND SPECIAL LIBRARIES

The most predominant cooperative activity in this category involves academic librarians' provision of services to business and industry. Among the services provided are:

1. Translation services (Domotor, 1985, 1988), selective dissemination of information and current awareness services (Sundquist, 1976), document delivery (Martins, 1988), information and referral services (O'Keefe, 1975), and reference services (Cody and Richards, 1982)
2. Fee-based information services (Hornbeck, 1983; Richards and Widdicombe, 1985; Caren and Somerville, 1988; Allen and Corley, 1990; Nicholson, 1992) which are cost recovery (Grant and Ungarelli, 1987) or profit making (Marvin, 1988).
3. Business and industry use of CD-ROM products at the academic library (Simons and Garten, 1992)
4. Use of the university's patent collections by special library patrons (Fellmann and Wehefritz, 1985)
5. Development of profit-making companies within the university library which provide services to business and industry, and whose profits are turned back to the university (Forsey and Lamble, 1985)
6. Education and training provided by academic librarians for special library patrons in the area of management information systems (Nosek and Yaverbaum, 1991)
7. Document delivery and various information services provided by academic librarians for information brokers (Ballard, 1988; Brauch, 1988; Dunn, 1988; Maxwell and Reinheimer, 1988).

JOINT-USE BETWEEN SCHOOL AND PUBLIC LIBRARIES

Surveys (Aaron, 1980) indicate that students most frequently use the public library for reference purposes (Mancall and Drott, 1983; Razzano, 1983). It is therefore not surprising that the most frequently cited cooperative activities in this category comprise efforts aimed at educational coordination (Conrad, 1985; Edwards, 1990), especially the development of term paper clinics (Good, 1990), homework centers (Black, 1990; "N.C. Homework...," 1982; "Buffalo...," 1983; "Homework...," 1983; Brewer, 1992), "assignment alerts," (Kreigh, 1980; McWilliam and Fatzer, 1988; Callison, Fink, and Hager, 1989), branch libraries whose purpose is to serve as homework libraries ("Birmingham...," 1990; Wallace, 1990), and other homework related services (Nylin, 1970; Shapiro, 1975; Hyland, 1983; Boldt, 1987) or adult education services ("School...," 1974a, 1974b). Among the many activities represented in the literature are:

1. Joint ventures to provide services for immigrant populations ("Toronto...," 1972; Messineo, 1991), troubled youth (MacWilliams, 1976), homeschoolers (Madden, 1991; Morley and Wooten, 1993), at-risk children (Welborn, 1992); and underserved rural populations (Kerns, 1991).

2. Visits by preschoolers to the public library (Davis, 1985), especially for story hours ("Unique...," 1977) and deposit collections from public libraries to preschools (Lambert, 1985).

3. Promotional visits and promotional materials provided by public librarians for school libraries (Griffith, 1974; McShane, 1975; Katz, 1978; Huntoon, 1979; Bonham, 1987).

4. Internships at the public library for high school students who earn high school credits from the work experience ("Students...," 1974).

5. Publication of student writing by the public library (Leitle, 1985; Vernerder, 1988).

6. Deposit collections provided by the public library (Marchand and DeVinney, 1972; Solberg, 1974) for school libraries and vocational educational school libraries (Peterson, 1973), especially for specific curricular areas (Treweek, 1977) and for parenting materials (Sager, 1992).

7. Public library deposit collections provided by the school library during the summers ("Arizona...," 1974; Wolford, 1975; Zizis, 1977).

8. Reserve shelves ("School/Library...," 1977), expanded reference service (Kerns, 1991), and provision of materials on reading lists (Cornford, 1980) for public school students, provided by the public library.

9. Public library staffing for the school library throughout the entire school year (Roeder, 1983), during the summers (Downen, 1978), at night (Fales and Olsen, 1972; McFadden, 1977; "School/Public...," 1981), during teachers' strikes ("Chicago...," 1980), and during school shut-downs ("School/Library...," 1978).

10. Joint staffing of two libraries' paraprofessional services (Zipsie, 1977), including joint ordering of materials (Middleton and Scott, 1976).

11. Joint video production ventures ("Connecticut...," 1984) and joint borrowing privileges for commercially produced videos

(Van Orsdel, 1975) and audio visual equipment (Dresang and Unger, 1981).

12. School library staffing of the public library for special programs ("Timberland...," 1979).

13. Joint continuing education efforts for professionals ("School/ Library...," 1979a).

14. Literacy programs which are jointly sponsored and jointly resourced ("Thirteen...," 1973; Persell, 1980; Rinzenberg and Currie, 1988).

15. Microcomputers which are provided by the school library for use by school students in the public library ("School...," 1982), and microcomputers provided by the public library but housed in the school library (DeMarco, 1979).

16. Shared summer reading programs (O'Neal, 1976; "School/ Library...," 1980; Markey and Moore, 1983; Volz, 1986).

17. Provision by the public library of Laubach literacy training (Stump, 1982) and other support services (Andres, 1989) for disabled students (Ahlen, 1989).

18. Homework (Black, 1986; Smith, 1988; Arent, 1989) and tutoring (Mamimski, 1982; Mashinic 1984) services for reluctant readers (Dombey, 1988) and immigrant students (Dunmore and Hardiman, 1987) provided at the public library for public school students.

19. Joint efforts to alert public librarians to upcoming homework assignments (Scarpellino, 1979), to recruit volunteer (Adamec, 1990) "homework helpers" (Winslow, 1979), and to provide supplemental materials and services for use during after-school hours (Rollock, 1978).

20. Public library bookmobile services which are provided to local school libraries (Amis, 1974; "Bookmobile...," 1990), especially to provide resources for summer school offerings (Will, 1970), and to provide paperback materials (Vonko, 1971).

21. Joint compilations of community resource guides (Nelson and Wagnitz, 1980; "Cooperation...," 1981).

22. Storytelling (Bull, 1973; Good, 1988), booktalking (Sterling, 1980; Tuccillo, 1986; Weenstein and Thwing, 1989; Barban, 1991; Pierce, 1991), videotaped booktalks (Clement, 1989) read aloud sessions (Rovenger, 1986), special reading programs (Brady and Heroy, 1989; Olson, 1994b), general library programming (Davis, 1989), enrichment programming

(Calisch and Steiner, 1979; Rader, 1990; Caruthers, 1991; Bloom, 1992), young adult services (Bessant, 1983; Tyson, 1989), career counselling ("Chicago...," 1982a), and bibliographic instruction (Flentge, 1973; Dearman and Meyers, 1974; "Minneapolis...," 1980; Rowbottom, 1982; Hart, 1986; Kinney, 1988; Eaton, 1989; "Linking...," 1989; Van Puleo, 1989; Paramore, 1992), provided at the public library for local school children.

23. Family game nights and family film nights for school children and their parents ("A Joint Venture...," 1993).

24. Home schooling resources provided at the public library as a supplement to those provided at the school library (Robbers, 1991).

25. Joint library cards ("Pupil...," 1990).

26. Public library preservation of local and oral history collections (Lagerbloom, 1980) from the region's schools ("High...,." 1988-1989) for use in school assignments (York, 1992).

27. Maintenance of audio visual (Emrich, 1973) and instructional materials centers at the school or public library for use by people involved in individualized teaching structures (Williams, 1970; Aaron, 1981; Dubber, 1989).

28. Joint faculty/public library staff meetings (Grote, 1970), especially for purposes of curriculum support from the public library (Donahoe, 1971).

29. Implementation and maintenance of vertical file collections at the public library for use by school students (Davis, 1970).

30. Use of Adult Basic Education materials in the school library by adult patrons (Young, 1972; Swarm, 1975).

31. Science materials and experiments provided by school librarians for use in the public library (Sullivan, 1974).

32. Reading laboratory workshops provided at the public library and by public librarians for parents of school children ("Reading...," 1976).

33. "Adopt-a-school" programs from public libraries in which the school library is helped with resources and expertise provided by the public librarians ("Chicago...," 1982b).

34. Prepackaged portable collections of professional materials on specific topics provided by the public librarians for use by public school professionals (Wroblewski, 1987).

35. Provision of school textbooks in the public library (Davis, 1987).
36. Babysitter's clinics provided at the public library for public school students (Shoup and Tadin, 1979).
37. Tutoring services provided at the public library by young adults for public school students (Maminski, 1990).
38. Use of the public library as a "magnet" school for public high school students interested in information technology (Olson, 1994a).

JOINT-USE BETWEEN ACADEMIC, SCHOOL, PUBLIC, AND SPECIAL LIBRARIES

This category includes the following activities:

1. Provision of information services for local business, industry and government (Schwartz, 1976; Venett, 1981; Flanders, 1984; Webber, 1989; Rogers, 1992), especially fee-based services (Dodd, 1974; Richards, 1991), cost-recovery based services ("Northwestern...," 1988), and selective dissemination of information services (Tell, 1972).
2. Provision of resources for adult independent learning (i.e., for job retraining) by all the libraries in a region (Claussen, 1992).
3. Distribution of city-wide library cards (Clark and Eisnaugle, 1989; Cage, 1990) and city-wide check-out privileges (Hill, 1992).
4. Religious libraries housed in the public library (Karp, 1990-1991).
5. Provision of literacy training (Fisher, 1990).
6. Workshops on the evaluation of art presented for the public at a museum library (Sigala, 1990).
7. Provision of special collections materials for use by the general public, especially for leisure time activities (Toyne, 1987).
8. Job tutoring provided by the public library for government supported employment plans (Beckerman, 1976).
9. Special education classes held at the public library and jointly staffed by teachers and librarians (Mallette, 1981).
10. Use of public and special libraries to provide resources for college students (Hewitt, 1975).

11. National initiatives to link all types of libraries together in information networks (Cook, 1981).

INGREDIENTS FOR SUCCESS

Almost all of the literature which describes successful efforts at joint-use cites some commonalities:

1. Each joint venture must be considered individually ("Community Library...," 1972). Although there is no blanket policy that can be established (Sheen, 1974), the texts of joint-venture contracts from other libraries (Amey, 1979, 1987; Woolard, 1980a) can be helpful.
2. Joint ventures should begin with a local request for the service (Dwyer, 1989), with a justification of need (LaBrake, 1991), a definition of each library's role and function (Nickel, 1970; Wisconsin, 1976; Haycock, 1990), and with an exploration of whether a joint-use library is appropriate (Aaron, 1980) and which types are most advantageous (Haycock, 1989). The planning process must include representatives from all segments of the community (Legg, 1970; Calkins, 1977; Vulturo, 1985), must establish formal terms of governance (Jaffe, 1985/1986) and financing (Fleming, 1978), must base planning on community information needs rather than desires to cut costs (Warncke, 1973; Henington, 1986), and must culminate in a formal program (Hiebring, 1970).
3. Joint bibliographic instruction programs should be implemented in conjunction with formal educational programs at the school ("Pa. Public...," 1973) and with classroom assignments (Spinella and Hicks, 1988).
4. All joint ventures must be preceded by a survey in which all exigencies and patron groups (Louie, 1985) are identified (Amey, 1976; Shuman, 1983; Dobbs, 1988).
5. In a joint venture, the librarians must differentiate between types of materials and services which can and cannot be used by non-primary clientele (Ford and Likness, 1988-1989).
6. In joint ventures, the extent of services and borrowing privileges that will be provided for nonprimary clientele must be spelled out (Eshelman, 1977; Reilly, 1978; "Homework...,"

1985; Cooke, 1992; Heath, 1992; Russell, 1992; Tilles, 1992). Limits should also be placed on who qualifies as a legitimate nonprimary user (McNamara and Williams, 1992), as well as on the types of requests that will be honored from nonprimary user groups (Boylan, 1984; Sutton, 1987). Guidelines on the use of academic libraries by persons other than primary clientele may serve as models for such identification (American Library Association, 1975a, 1975b).

7. If several libraries will be cooperating rather than merging, a liaison person (Drescher, 1976; Tevis, 1979) or liaison committee (Hendley, 1991) is necessary.

8. Rather than being a source of income, charges for specific services provided in a joint-venture may be a source of control over large volume user groups (Piternick, 1979).

9. Formal instruction for all participants (Crowe and Shaeval, 1980) and discussions regarding linkages between library educational programs (Sullivan, 1984) are necessary at the beginning of a joint-venture program.

10. Charges for certain services from one publicly supported library to another are not necessarily illegal ("Missouri...," 1974).

11. Facilities planning for a new joint-use library must parallel planning for the whole venture ("Long...," 1973) and must allow for library use during times when the rest of a larger facility is not in use ("Experiment...," 1972).

12. Successful joint-use ventures include incentives to encourage libraries to participate (Tameem, 1988) and must be backed by committed librarians (Piersa, 1981).

13. Cooperative ventures must be planned at local, regional (Weech, 1979), and state or provincial levels (Sones, 1981; Amey, 1987), and must include all library administrators in order to avoid crisis management (Lindauer, 1975).

14. Administrators must be involved early in the planning stages for a joint-venture (Shockey, 1978), but librarians "in the trenches" must be the actual planners (Sullivan, 1979).

15. Planning for joint-use ventures should include recognition and use of electronic networks (Chambers, 1990).

16. Joint-use libraries tend to be most successful in sparsely populated (Ramachandran, 1974; Woolard, 1980; Jaffe, 1982) or rural (Stevens and Wright, 1990) areas.

17. Successful joint-use libraries are those whose planners do not enter the process thinking in terms of merging, but rather in terms of the development of a totally new library program (Kitchens, 1973b).

18. A joint-use library must be sited at a central (Horncastle, 1973) location which is convenient (Shaw, 1990) to all groups who will be using the facility (Woolard, 1978; Mansbridge, 1991), which provides accessible (Wallace, 1983) entrances appropriate (Ganst and Ugland, 1975) for diverse various patron groups, ("Chicago...," 1972; Doidge, 1984), and which provides security for younger patron groups (Miller, 1991).

19. Although joint-use patterns should evolve slowly (Reckenback, 1977), their initial stages should be completely planned (Kuhn, 1977).

20. A joint-use library initiative must aggressively develop and participate in formalized resource sharing (Jaffe 1985/1986).

21. Partners in joint use ventures must be sensitive to each others' needs, decisions must accommodate all parties' needs, and each joint-use venture must be approached as a totally unique experience (Call, 1993).

CONCLUSIONS

Although the literature debates the merits of joint-use libraries, a preponderance of writers seem to agree that cooperation in some form is necessary in order for libraries to meet the increasingly complex demands of their patrons. It would seem that the future of libraries is inextricably linked with carefully managed formal cooperation.

REFERENCES

Aaron, S.L. 1978a. "Combined School Public Library Programs: An Abstract of a National Study." *School Media Quarterly* 7 (Fall): 31-32; 49-53.

————. 1978b. "Community Education: New Directions for School Media and Public Library Programs." *School Media Quarterly* 7 (Fall): 9-32.

————. 1980a. *School/Public Library Cooperation; a State of the Art Review.* ERIC Clearinghouse on Information Resources, 130 Huntington Hall, Syracuse University, Syracuse, N.Y. 13210. 1980.

_____. 1981. "School/Public Library Cooperation-The Way It Is." *Catholic Library World* 52 (February): 280-285.

_____. 1980. *Study of Combined School-Public Libraries*. Chicago: American Library Association, American Association of School Librarians.

Adamec, J. 1990. "Homework Helpers: Making Study Time Quality Time." *Wilson Library Bulletin* 65 (September): 31-32.

Ahlen, B. 1989. "The Library and Dyslectics." *Scandinavian Public Library Quarterly* 22 (2): 18-20.

Alafiayatayo, B.O., and J.T. Aleraiye. 1987. "Samaru Public Library: an Example of a University Public Library Service in Nigeria." *Information Development* 3 (January): 36-39.

Allen, B.L., and K. Corley. 1990. "Information Brokers in Illinois Academic Libraries." *Illinois Libraries* 72 (November): 596-600.

American Library Association. Association of College and Research Libraries. 1975a."Committee on Community Policy Guidelines." *College & Research Libraries News* 5 (May): 167-169.

_____. 1975b. Committee on Community Use of Academic Libraries. "Access Policy Guidelines; Approved as Policy by the Board of Directors of the Association of College and Research Libraries, July 3, 1975." *College & Research Libraries News* 10 (November): 322-323.

American Library Association. Committee On Post War Planning. 1945. *School Libraries for Today and Tomorrow*. Chicago: American Library Association.

Amey, L.J. 1979. *Canadian School-Housed Public Library*. London: Dalhousie University, School of Library Service.

_____. 1976. "Combination School and Public Library: A Bibliography with Special Emphasis on the Canadian Experience." *Canadian Library Journal* 33 (June): 263-265.

_____. 1987. *Combining Libraries: The Canadian and Australian Experience*. Metuchen, NJ: Scarecrow Press.

_____. 1989. "Success in the Outback: The Case for School-Housed Public Libraries." *School Library Journal* 35 (March): 109-114.

Amey, L.J., and R.J. Smith. 1976. "Combination School and Public Libraries: An Attitudinal Study." *Canadian Library Journal* 33 (June): 251-261.

Amis, T.K. 1974. "Extension Librarian in a New Brunswick Library Region." *APLA Bulletin* 38 (Spring): 11-15.

Anderson, S. 1990. "Shared Libraries: Focus on Florida." *Community and Junior Colleges* 7 (1): 3-16.

"Andover Library Becomes College 'Campus'." 1973. *American Libraries* 4 (September): 466.

Andres, J. 1989. "A Special Outreach." *Indiana Libraries* 8 (2): 31-32.

Arent, J. 1989. "Homework Assignments-We Can Help!" *Ohio Media Spectrum* 41 (Fall): 43-48.

"Arizona School and PL Share Reading Materials." 1974. *Library Journal* 99 (December 15): 3234.

Ascroft, S. 1988. "AVM in the University." *Audiovisual Librarian* 14 (May): 87-89.

Baker, D.P. 1977a. *School and Public Library Media Programs for Children and Young Adults*. Syracuse, NY: Gaylord Professional Publications.

————. 1977b. "School and Public Library Programs and Information Dissemination." *School Media Quarterly* 5 (Winter): 119-127.

Baker, J., and L.I. Radoff. 1983. "Carnegie Branch Library and Community Education Center: an Experiment in Cooperation." *Public Library Quarterly* 4 (Fall): 71-83.

Ballard, R.M. 1988. "The Effect of Information Brokers on Reference Services: Reference Librarians Express Their Opinions." *The Reference Librarian* 22: 81-91.

Barban, L. 1991. "Booktalking: the Art of the Deal." *School Library Journal* 37 (August): 106.

Barnett, C. 1986. "Public Libraries, Students, and the Provision of Academic Reading Materials."Pp. 108-119 in *Student Reading Needs and Higher Education*, edited by D. Baker. London: Library Association.

Barrie, J. 1988. "Can Small College Libraries Serve the Business Community? Should They?" *The Bookmark* 47 (Fall): 33-35.

Barron, D.D. 1978. "Role of the School Media Program and Specialists in Community Education." *School Media Quarterly* 7 (Fall): 12-18.

Barron, R.E. 1977. "Public Library Systems Report on Interlibrary Loans to School Libraries." *The Bookmark* 36 (Summer): 106-109.

Bates, H.E. 1972. "Jitney Library Service." *Illinois Libraries* 54 (April): 279-283.

Beach, C. 1989. "The Public Library as Provider of Library Services to Educational Institutions." *Journal of Library Administration* 11 (1-2): 173-187.

Beckerman, E.P. 1976. "Woodbridge Tutorial Program." *School Library Journal* (February): 22-25.

Bell, M. 1979. "School Library-Public Library Cooperation Reviewed." *Texas Libraries* 41 (Fall): 129-139.

Bender, D.R. 1979. "Networking and School Library Media Programs." *School Library Journal* 26 (November): 29-32.

Bennett, P. 1989. "An ANGEL in the Southeast: Private Small School Networking." *Southeastern Librarian* 39 (Summer): 55-56.

Berry, J.N. 1979. "School/Public Library Service." *Library Journal* 104 (May 1): 989.

Bessant, D.L. 1983. "What a School Librarian Would Like to Say to a Public Librarian About Young Adult Services." *Illinois Libraries* 65 (September): 449-452.

Biehl, M.J. 1985. "Cooperation Plus." *Illinois Libraries* 67 (January): 35-36.

Billman, B.V., and P. Owens. 1985/1986. "School and Public Library Cooperation: a Prerequisite for Cooperative Collection Development." *Collection Management* 7 (Fall/Winter): 183-195.

Bingham, R.T. 1982. "Values and Where We Stand as Private School and Public Librarians." *Catholic Library World* 54 (July): 25-28.

"Birmingham Library Retargets Audience; Alabama Branch Gets New Mission as Homework Center in Response to Neighborhood Changes." 1990. *Library Journal* 115 (March 15): 16.

Black, N.E. 1986. "School Assignments: A Public Library Responsibility." *Emergency Librarian* 13 (May/June): 25-26.

_____. 1990. "School Assignments: A Public Library Responsibility." In *The School Library Program in the Curriculum*, edited by K. Haycock. Englewood, CO: Libraries Unlimited.

Bloom, L. 1992. "The Math and Science Enrichment Center at East Cleveland Public Library; Public School-Public Library Cooperation." *Ohio Libraries* 5 (March/April): 16.

Bloomfield, M.A. 1986. "A Modest Experiment for Columbus, Ohio." *Unabashed Librarian* (59): 29.

Boldt, C.H. 1987. "Homework Assignments and the Library." *Unabashed Librarian* 65: 11-12.

Bonham, C. 1987. "Lodestar." *Voice of Youth Advocates* 10 (June): 68-70.

"Bookmobile Serves Tornado-Damaged Schools." 1990. *Wilson Library Bulletin* 64 (March): 12.

Bortz, B. 1981. "Not Squabbling." *Library Journal* 106 (June 15): 1256.

Boylan, P. 1984. "Young Adult Reference Services in the Public Library." *Top of the News* 40 (Summer): 415-417.

Brady, D., and P. Heroy. 1989. "Working Together to Serve Youth; School and Public Library Cooperation." *Louisiana Library Association Bulletin* 51 (Winter): 131-133.

Brauch, P.O. 1988. "Working Together-the Librarian and the Broker." *The Reference Librarian* 22: 93-103.

Breivik, P.S. 1992. "Building an Information Infrastructure." *AGB Reports* 34(September/October): 30-34.

Brewer, R. 1992. "Help Youth at Risk: a Case For Starting Public Library Homework Centers." *Public Libraries* 31 (July/August): 208-212.

Broderick, D.M. 1967. "Plus CA Change: Classic Patterns in Public/School Library Relations." *Library Journal* 92 (May 15): 1995-1997.

Brodribb, M. 1972. "Information Needs of Smaller Firms: Some Comments on Two Recent Australian Surveys." *Australian Academic and Research Libraries* 3 (September): 170-172.

Brown, F., and A. Mashinic. 1983. "Public, School and Community College Library Services Combine in Houston Public Library Branch." *Public Libraries* 22 (Fall): 91-92.

"Buffalo Schools and Libraries Offer Teens Help With Homework." 1983. *Library Journal* 108 (March 15): 540.

Bull, R.P. 1973. "Top Priority: Service to Children." *Illinois Libraries* 55 (January): 34-36.

Burns, G.E. 1988. "The School Based Public Library: Perspectives and Suggestions for Improving the Delivery of Library Programs and Services." *School Libraries in Canada* 8 (Winter): 35-40.

Cage, A.C. 1990. "Multitype Library Cooperation in a Small College Town." *Texas Library Journal* 66 (Winter): 119-121.

"California Escalates Drive for School/Library Co-Op." 1981. *Library Journal* 106 (June 15): 1264.

"California Puts LSCA into School/Library Co-Op." 1980. *Library Journal* 105 (September 1): 1694.

Calisch, R., and J. Steiner. 1979. "School/Community Arts Guild." *English Journal* 68 (March): 45-47.

Calkins, A. 1977. "How to Develop T.L.C. [Tender, Loving Care] Between the T's, L's, and C [Teachers, Librarians, and Children]." *Ohio Library Association Bulletin* 47 (October): 10-12.

Call, I.S. 1993. "Joint-use Libraries: Just How Good Are They?" *College and Research Libraries News* 10 (November): 551-552.

Callison, D., J. Fink, and G. Hager. 1989. "A Survey of Cooperation and Communication Between Public School Librarians in Indiana and Beyond." *Indiana Libraries* 8 (2): 78-86.

Campbell, C., and L. McCulley. 1992. "A Model for College Library Visits." *Book Report* 10 (January/February): 32-33.

Canelas, C., and L. Westbrook. 1990. "BI in the Local High School." *College & Research Libraries News* 3 (March): 217-220.

Caren, L., and A.N. Somerville. 1988. "Issues Facing Private Academic Libraries Considering Fee-Based Programs." *The Reference Librarian* 22: 37-49.

Caruthers, T. 1991. "The Literature Enrichment Program: a Cooperative Effort." *Tennessee Librarian* 43 (Winter): 24-32.

Chambers, J.L. 1990. "Academic Libraries: an Unrecognized National Strength?" *College & Research Library News* 11 (December): 1086.

Cherry, S.S. 1982. "Public Library Branches in Schools: The Kansas City Experience." *American Libraries* 13 (January): 24-25.

"Chicago Cooperation: Joint School-Public Library." 1972. *Library Journal* 97 (December 15): 4020.

"Chicago Public Library Adopts a High School." 1982. *Library Journal* 107 (March 1): 498.

"Chicago Public Library Will Adopt a School." 1982. *School Library Journal* 28 (February): 12.

"Chicago Teacher's Strike Spurs CPL Into Action." 1980. *Library Journal* 107 (March 15): 666-667.

Christopher, S.J. 1972. "Suggestion for Increasing Co-ordination of Library Services Within the Community." *PNLA Quarterly* 36 (April): 22-24.

Chu, S.C., and J. Shellhase. 1983. "Special Health Sciences Library Skills Program for High School Students." *Show Me-Libraries* 34 (February): 12-15.

Clark, M., and J. Eisnaugle. 1989. "Toledo and Dayton go for 'Library Cards for All'." *Ohio Libraries* 2 (March/April): 6-7.

Claussen, F. 1992. "The Future is Here: Distance Learning Expands Our Horizons." *Colorado Libraries* 18 (March): 19-21.

Clement, P.G. 1989. "Videotapes: a Rosy Answer to Budget Cut Blues." *Voice of Youth Advocates* 12 (December): 260-261.

Clubb, B. 1988. "The School-Housed Public Library Revisited." *School Libraries in Canada* 8 (Summer): 10

Coatney, L. 1993. "A New Library Patron: The Systemwide User." *Illinois Libraries* 75 (May): 240-242.

Cochrane, K. 1989. "University of Missouri-St. Louis and Missouri: Partners in Global Education." *Show-Me Libraries* 41 (Fall): 7-10.

Cody, S.A., and B.G. Richards. 1982. "One Thousand-Dollar Alternative: How One University Structures a Fee-Based Information Service for Local Industry." *American Libraries* 13 (March): 175-176.

"Columbus Area Libraries to Share Resources." 1989. *Wilson Library Bulletin* 63 (February): 11.

"Combined School/Public Library Reduces cost by $500,000." 1975. *American School and University* 47 (July): 10-12.

"Community and its College Share Library Facilities: Memphis Public Library and Information Center to Serve Shelby State Community College." 1972. *Library Journal* 97 (November 15): 3669.

"Community Library Service is Focus of ALA-NEA Meet." 1972. *Library Journal* 97 (July): 2328-2330.

Cone, L.B. 1982. "Community Access to a State College Library." *Bay State Librarian* 71 (Spring): 13-16.

Conley, K.M. 1994. "The Milner/Heartland Connection." *Illinois Libraries* 76 (Winter): 18.

"Connecticut Community College Opens Doors to P.L. Patrons." 1973. *Library Journal* 98 (April 1): 1075.

"Connecticut Mini-Grants Foster School/PL Cooperation." 1984. *Library Journal* 109 (October 15): 1886.

Connole, T. 1991. "Providing Library Services in a Non-Traditional Mode at the Community College of Aurora." *Colorado Libraries* 17 (September): 9-11.

Conrad, R. 1985. "The Asking of Questions and the Offering of Services." *Illinois Libraries* 67 (January): 32-34.

Cook, J. 1981. "School Library's Place in the Community's Information Network." Pp. 167-179 in *School Librarianship*, edited by J. Cook. New York: Pergamon Press.

Cooke, G.W. 1992. "What Are All These College Students Doing in the Public Library." *New Jersey Libraries* 25 (Spring): 25-26.

"Cooperation and Planning in School Librarianship." 1981. Pp. 55-100 in *Recent Advances in School Librarianship*, edited by F.L. Carroll. London, New York: Pergamon Press.

"Cooperation in Arizona: School/Library Merger." 1982. *Library Journal* 107 (July): 1280.

"Cooperating in Cicero." 1975. *American Libraries* 6 (February): 81-82.

Cooprider, D. 1972. "Library Cooperation: School Libraries in Illinois." *Illinois Libraries* 54 (May): 334-341

Cornford, M. 1980. "Let's Make Reading Lists Readable." *Library Association Record* 82 (March): 123.

Cowser, R.L. 1978. "Cooperative Activity Links Colleges and Public Library." *Texas Libraries* 40 (Winter): 179-181.

Craver, K.W. 1989. "The Imact on the School Library of Online Access to Academic Libraries: Implications for the Future." *Catholic Library World* 60 (January/February): 164-168.

_____. 1987. "Use of Academic Libraries by High School Students: Implications for Research." *RQ* 27 (Fall): 53-66.

Creech, H.E. 1982. "Function and Form in Public Library/Academic Library Co-operation." *Canadian Library Journal* 39 (October): 293-296.

Crowe L., and E. Shaevel. 1980. *Cooperative Seminar for School and Public Librarians Working with YAs.* Springfield, IL: State Library.

Czopek, V. 1990. "Terra Incognita: Public Library Tours for Students." *Emergency Librarian* 18 (November/December): 18.

Davis, C. 1970. "And What Would They Do in the Summer?" *Illinois Libraries* 52 (April): 363-366.

Davis, E. 1985. "Once Around the World: Inviting the Preschools Into the Library." *Emergency Librarian* 13 (November/December): 17-18.

Davis, V. 1987. "Homework Center-Textbooks in the Library." *School Library Journal* 33 (April): 52.

————. 1989. "After a Full Day at School, Let Us G.A.S.P." *Unabashed Librarian* 70: 11-12.

"DC Branch Library Set Up in School Building." 1974. *Library Journal* 99 (December 1): 3086.

Dearman, M., and R. Meyers. 1974. "Just Like Having Two Stores." *Louisiana Library Association Bulletin* 37 (Summer): 55-57.

Dedrick, A.J. 1994. "Shared Academic Library Facilities: The Unknown Form of Library Cooperation." *College and Research Libraries* 55 (September): 437-443.

Del Vecchio, S. 1993. "Connecting Libraries and Schools With C.L.A.S.P." *Wilson Library Bulletin* 68 (1): 38-40.

DeMarco, E. 1979. "School and Library Cooperation: A Road to the Future." *Bay State Librarian* 68 (Fall): 16-17.

Denis, L.G. 1972. "Library Service Unlimited: Jotting on the Draft Report of the Commission on Post-Secondary Education in Ontario." *Canadian Library Journal* 29 (March): 141-143.

Dobbs, B. 1988. "Cooperative Partnerships for Kids." *Colorado Libraries* 14 (September): 32.

Dodd, J.B. 1974. "Pay-As-You-Go Plan for Satellite Libraries Using Academic Facilities." *Special Libraries* 65 (February): 66-72.

Doidge, S. 1984. "Restoration Comedy." *New Library World* 85 (January): 9-10.

Doll, C.A. 1984. "Study of the Overlap and Duplication Among Children's Collections in Selected Public and Elementary School Libraries." *The Library Quarterly* 54 (July): 277-289.

————. 1982. "Overlap Studies of Library Collections in School and Public Libraries." *Public Libraries* 21 (Spring): 33-34.

————. 1983. "School and Public Library Collection Overlap and the Implications for Networking." *School Library Media Quarterly* 11 (Spring): 193-199.

Dollerschell, A. 1991. "Contracting with Local Libraries for Off-Campus Library Services." In *The Fifth Off Campus Library Services Conference Proceedings*, edited by C.J. Jacob. Albuquerque, NM. October 30-November 1, 1991. Mt. Pleasant, Michigan: Central Michigan University.

Dombey, K.W. 1988. "Cross-Age Tutoring Works Wonders; Enthusiasm Proves Contagious to Poor Readers." *American Libraries* 19 (September): 726-727.

Domotor, A. 1985. "The Industrial Use of University Resources." Pp. 73-76 in International Association of Technological University Libraries Meeting [11th: 1985: Oxford, England]. *The Future of Information Resources for Science and Technology and the Role of Libraries*. London: International Association of Technological Libraries.

_____. 1988. "Information Services to Industry by the Central Library of Veszprem University." *IATUL Quarterly* 2 (September): 165-170.

Donahoe, B. 1971. "Cooperation: Public Library Systems-School Libraries." *Illinois Libraries* 53 (September): 467-470.

Dougherty, R.M. 1989. "Building Bridges." *Catholic Library World* 60 (March/ April): 222-225.

Douglas, J. 1990. "The Public Library and the School System: Partners in Lifelong Education." *Emergency Librarian* 18 (November/December): 9-11.

Downen, T.W. 1978. "Cooperation is Alive and Ongoing in the State of Michigan." *Michigan Librarian* 44 (Summer): 11-13.

Downes, V.J. 1975. "Complimenting and Cooperating! Total Library Service to Children Through Maximum Use of the Children's Room and the Media Center." *Illinois Libraries* 57 (January): 31-34.

Drake, S.L., and M.J. Lynch. 1978. *Community Colleges, Public Libraries, and the Humanities; a Study of Cooperative Programs*. Washington, DC: American Association of Community and Junior Colleges.

Dresang, E.T., and B. Unger. 1981. "Bucket Brigade: a School-Public Library Cooperative Audio-Visual Repair Project." *Wisconsin Library Bulletin* 77 (Summer): 53-54.

Drescher, R.A. 1976. "Children's Services/School Services Liaison." *Illinois Libraries* 58 (December): 821-823.

Dubber, G. 1989. "Teachers and Librarians-Working Together with Resource Based Learning-the Challenges and the Difficulties." *Public Library Journal* 4 (September/October): 111-116.

Dunmore, A.J., and K.C. Hardiman. 1987. "'My Turn' Boosts Teen Self-Esteem." *American Libraries* 18 (October): 786.

Dunn, E.B. 1988. "The Attitudes of Academic Reference Librarians Toward Information Brokers." *The Reference Librarian* 22: 51-79.

Dwyer, J.G. 1989. "The Joint-Use Phenomenon: A Positive Approach." Pp. 166-180 in *Voices From Around the World*, edited by P. Hauck. Metuchen, NJ: Scarecrow Press.

_____. 1981. "School/Community Library." Pp. 215-226 in *School Librarianship*, edited by J. Cook. London: Pergamon Press.

_____. 1989. "South Australia's School-Housed Public Libraries: an Alternative in the Rural Area." *Emergency Librarian* 16 (January/February): 19-26.

Dyer, E.R. 1978. *Cooperation in Library Service to Children*. Metchuen, NJ: Scarecrow Press.

_____. 1977. "New Perspective on Cooperation in Library Services to Children." *School Media Quarterly* 5 (Summer): 261-270.

Eaton, E.G. 1989. "What the Public Children's Librarian Needs to Know About Locational Skills Instruction in Elementary Schools." *Journal of Youth Services in Libraries* 2 (Summer): 357-366.

Edwards, L. 1990. "Go for the Card: a School and Public Library Partnership Put to the Test." *Ohio Media Spectrum* 42 (Winter): 34-36.

"Educators and Practitioners: Is Cooperation Possible?" 1975. *Bay State Librarian* 64 (October): 9-10.

Egbers, G., and J. Giesecke. 1989. "SPICE [Summer Pre-College Instruction and Career Experience] Programs in Nebraska." *College & Research Libraries News* 9 (October): 840.

Ellis, A.C.O. 1984. "From Caretaking to Caring: 100 Years of Development in Schools." *Library Association Record* 86 (February): 69-70.

Emrich, M. 1973. "School Audiovisual Department Located in Library." *Wyoming Library Roundup* 28 (December): 40.

"Enoch Pratt and University of Maryland Join in Open University Project." 1982. *Library Journal* 107 (September 15): 1705.

Enochs, J.C. 1991. "Booking the Future." *CMLEA Journal* 14 (Spring): 33-36.

Eshelman, W.R. 1977. "Research Library Borrows Leaf From PL Book: Limit Outside Users to 50 Transactions a Month." *Wilson Library Bulletin* 51 (February): 465-466.

Everett, K. 1980. "The Squabbles of Librarians: A Lay Person's Views." *Library Journal* 105 (December 15): 2552-2553.

"Experiment in Joint City-School Use." 1972. *PNLA Quarterly* 36 (January): 31-32.

"Fairbanks Library and School Share a CLSI Circ System." 1982. *Library Journal* 107 (May 1): 846.

Fales, S.L., and R. Olsen. 1972. "They're Reaching for a Full Service Library." *Utah Libraries* 15 (Spring): 11-14.

Fellmann, U., and V. Wehefritz. 1985. "Library Services to Industry in Aachen and Dortmund." Pp. 65-71 in International Association of Technological University Libraries Meeting [11th: 1985: Oxford, England]. *The Future of Information Resources for Science and Technology and the Role of Libraries.* London: International Association of Technological University Libraries.

Fenwick, S.I. 1979. "Schools and Public Libraries: Frontiers in the Seventies." Pp. 93-104 in *Frontiers of Library Service for Youth.* NY: Columbia University, School of Library Service.

Fiscella, J.B., and J.D. Ringel. 1988. "Academic Libraries and Regional Economic Development." Pp. 127-136 in *Libraries and the Search for Academic Excellence.* Metuchen, NJ: Scarecrow Press.

Fisher, D.R. 1990. "Families Reading Together: Sharing the Joy." *Texas Library Journal* 66 (Fall): 84-88.

Fitzgibbons, S. 1989. "Cooperation Between Teachers, School Librarians, and Public Librarians: Improving Library Services for Children and Young Adults." *Indiana Libraries* 8 (1): 57-69.

Flanders, D. 1984. "Wanted: A Librarian in Seven League Boots." *Illinois Libraries* 66 (February): 101-102.

Fleming, L. 1978. "Public and School Libraries: Partners in the 'Big' Picture." *School Media Quarterly* 7 (Fall): 25-30.

Flentge, M.E. 1973. "Communication and Cooperation for Better Service." *Illinois Libraries* 55 (January): 28-30.

Fletcher, W. 1876. *Public Libraries in the USA*. Urbana, IL: University Illinois.

Fonstad, C. 1976. "Everyone is Welcome to Learn; Bridging the Gap Between School and Community." *Wisconsin Library Bulletin* 72 (July): 165-166.

Ford, B.J., and G.S. Likness. 1988-1989. "Varied Clientele, Service Objectives and Limited Resources: the Academic Library in Transition." *Urban Academic Librarian* 6-7 (Fall-Spring): 20-24.

Forsey, M.R., and J.H. Lamble. 1985. "Bath University Library and the SWIRL [South Western Industrial Research Ltd.] Business and Technical Information Service." Pp. 127-131 in International Association of Technological University Libraries Meeting [11th: 1985: Oxford, England]. *The Future of Information Resources for Science and Technology and the Role of Libraries*. London: International Association of Technological University Libraries.

Freiser, L. 1967. "The Civilized Network." *Library Journal* (September 15): 3001-3003.

French, B.A. 1979. "Fourth Generation: Research Libraries and Community Information." Pp. 284-290 in *New Horizons for Academic Libraries*, edited by R.D. Stueart and R.D. Johnson. London: Saur Verlag.

Ganst, I., and L. Ugland. 1975. "The Combination Library; a Norwegian Specialty?" *Scandinavian Public Library Quarterly* 8 (1): 12-16.

Garrison, G. (ed.). 1973. *Total Community Library Service; Report of a Conference Sponsored by the Joint Committee of the American Library Association and the National Education Association*. Chicago: American Library Association.

Gauld, V. 1988. "School Community Libraries in South Australia." *International Review of Children's Literature and Librarianship* 3 (Winter): 156-166.

Gee, P. 1983. "Building Bridges: School/Public Library Cooperation." *Mississippi Libraries* 47 (Fall): 68-69.

Gerhardt, L.N. 1992. "Philistines in the Inner City." *School Library Journal* 38 (June 15): 4.

Good, J.M. 1988. "St. Louis Public Library-Public School Cooperation." *Show-Me Libraries* 40 (Fall): 17-18.

_____. 1990. "Term Papers: Where to Turn." *School Library Journal* 36 (August): 102.

Graham, M., and J.M. Travillian. 1978. "Merged Facilities: Potential and Constraints." Pp. 97-102 in *Media Centers Facilities Design*, edited by J.A. Hannigan and G. Estes. Chicago: American Library Association.

Grant, M.M., and D.L. Ungarelli. 1987. "Fee-Based Business Research in an Academic Library." *The Reference Librarian* 19: 239-255.

Griffith, R.L. 1974. "Library Sampling: Program to Inform Young Patrons About the Services in the Children's and Junior High Departments." *Library Journal* 99 (November 15): 3024.

Grote, D.V. 1970. "Extending the Public Library and Public School Partnership." *Illinois Libraries* 52 (April): 343-344.

Grundt, L. 1972. "College Reserve Room Reaches Out." *Unabashed Librarian* 5 (Fall): 5.

Hammond, C.B. 1989. "Kids, the Academic Library and the Schools." *College & Research Libraries News* 4 (April): 264-266.

Hart, K. 1986. "Using Each Other—A Necessity: School-Public Library Cooperation." *Colorado Libraries* 12 (December): 12-13.

Haycock, K. 1989. "Beyond Courtesy: School and Public Library Relationships." *Emergency Librarian* 16 (May/June): 27-30.

————. 1973. "Community Involvement in School Libraries: A Public Relations Approach." *Canadian Library Journal* 30 (March): 110-115.

————. 1990. "The School Housed Public Library ." *Emergency Librarian* 17 (March/April): 33-34.

————. 1975. "To Combine or not to Combine: The School Media Center and the Public Library." *NASSP Bulletin* 59 (September): 67-73.

Heath, F.M. 1992. "Conflict of Mission: the Mid-size Private University in an Urban Environment." Pp. 15-23 in *Academic Libraries in Urban and Metropolitan Areas*, edited by G.B. McCabe. Westport, CT: Greenwood Press.

Heck, R.S. 1973. "Students, Teachers, and Librarians." *Illinois Libraries* 55 (January): 31-34.

Hegarty, K. 1971. "School-Housed Public Library." *Virginia Librarian* 18 (Summer): 11-13.

Hendley, M. 1991. "Community Cooperation in Reference Service Via a Librarian's Liaison Committee." *The Reference Librarian* 33: 191-205.

Henington, D.M. 1986. "Cooperation in Serving Students." In *The Urban Public Library Makes Connections for Better Service*, edited by A. Ladenson. Chicago: Urban Libraries Council.

Hewitt, V.D. 1975. "Utilizing Public and Special Libraries to Service Post-Secondary Education." Pp. 288-297 in *New Dimensions for Academic Library Service*, edited by E.J. Josey. Metuchen, NJ: Scarecrow Press.

Heyns, B. 1978. *Summer Learning and the Effects of Schooling*. NY: Academic Press.

Hiebring, D. 1970. "School/Public Library Cooperation in Illinois." *Illinois Libraries* 52 (April): 351-355.

"High School Annuals Offer a Glimpse Into the Past." 1988-1989. *Texas Libraries* 49 (Winter): 108.

Hill, J. 1992. "Is Anybody Out There?" *Colorado Libraries* 18 (March): 26-27.

Hirsch, S.D. 1973. "Public Library Service in Porirua Schools." *New Zealand Libraries* 36 (December): 400-405.

Hollifield, S., and W. Lawrence. 1986. "Literary Resource Seminars for Public School Teachers: One Library's Experience." *South Carolina Librarian* 30 (Fall): 27-31.

Holloway, C. 1983. "Teaching the Research Paper at the Public Library." *Community College Review* 11 (Summer): 27-31.

Holton, J.E. 1990. "Document Delivery Services in a Special Library: How to Get What You Haven't Got!" *Colorado Libraries* 16 (December): 36-37.

"Home Grown Research." 1975. *American Libraries* 6 (February): 88-89.

"Homework Help Wins Kudos in Georgia and New York." 1983. *Library Journal* 108 (November 1): 2010.

"Homework: LA Response to DES." 1985. *Library Association Record* 87 (September): 333.

Horn, A. 1987. "Children and Books: Norwegian Public and School Libraries in Co-operation." *Scandinavian Public Library Quarterly* 20 (2): 22-27.

Hornbeck, J.W. 1983. "Academic Library's Experience with Fee-Based Services." *Drexel Library Quarterly* 19 (Fall): 23-36.

Horncastle, D.R. 1973. "Public Library Within a School: Can It Work?" *APLA Bulletin* 37 (Winter): 106-107.

Horowitz, R.G. de. 1979. "School Library and NATIS in Developing Countries: the Need for Integration." *IFLA Journal* 5 (1): 22-29.

Howes, M. 1986. "Evaluation of the Effect of a Public Library Summer Reading Program on Children's Reading Scores Between First and Second Grade." *Illinois Libraries* 68 (September): 444-450.

Hules, D.A. 1982. "Reciprocal Borrowing Between Academic and Public Libraries." *The Sourdough* 19 (July): 12.

Huntoon, E. 1979. "Effective School Visits-a Guide." *School Library Journal* 25 (April): 33.

Hyland, A.M. 1983. "Why Can't I Find Verbs in the Card Catalog?" Pp. 30-46 in *Educating the Public Library User*. Chicago: American Library Association.

"Industry and Academe Cooperate." 1973 *American Libraries* 4 (April): 192.

"Interim Report of the Select Committee on the Utilization of Educational Facilities: School and Public Libraries." 1973. *Ontario Library Review* 57 (September): 192-193.

"Interlibrary Cooperative Project." 1977. *New Jersey Libraries* 10 (April): 12-13.

"Iowa Takes Team Approach to School/Library Co-operation." 1982. *Library Journal* 107 (March 15): 593.

Izard, A.R. 1974. "Disturbing Your Universe." *Elementary English* 51 (March): 399-401.

Jaffe, L.L. 1985/1986. "Collection Development and Resource Sharing in the Combined School/Public Library." *Collection Management* 7 (Fall/Winter): 205-215.

———. 1982. *Combined School/Public Library in Pennsylvania*. Thesis (PhD), University of Pittsburgh.

Johnson, J.S. 1980. "Public Library: A College for Every Community." *Kentucky Library Association Bulletin* 44 (Spring): 14-16.

Johnson, W.W. 1977. "Public Library/School Cooperation." *California School Libraries* 48 (Winter): 2-5.

Joint Committee of the National Education Association and the American Library Association. 1941. *School and Public Libraries Working Together in School Library Service*. Washington, DC: National Education Association.

"A Joint Venture in Rural Library Development: School and Public Library Service in a Single Community Location." 1993. *Illinois Libraries* 75 (4): 230-239.

Jones, A.C. 1977. "Dual Purpose Libraries: Some Experiences in England." *The School Librarian* 25 (December): 311-318.

Jones, A. 1989. "Small Library-Big Service." *Colorado Libraries* 15 (September): 21-22.

Josephine, H.B., and M. Reneker. 1989. "In Defense of FIRST [Fee-Based Information and Research Team] and Freedom of Access to Information." *College & Research Libraries News* 5 (May): 377-379.

Judd, B., and B. Scheele. 1984. "Community Use of Public Academic Libraries in New York State: a SUNY/CUNY Survey." *The Bookmark* 42 (Winter): 126-134.

Junkin, E. 1975. "Dream Come True." *American Libraries* 27 (November): 10-11.

Karp, H. 1990-1991. "Synagogue, School, and Center Libraries and the Public Library." *Judaica Librarianship* 5 (Spring-Winter): 159-160.

Katz, L. 1978. "Public Library Newsletters for Teachers." *Unabashed Librarian* 27: 17.

Kauppinen, J. 1987. "Libraries, Schools and the Young." *Scandinavian Public Library Quarterly* 20 (2): 4-6.

Kemp, B.E., M.M. Nofsinger, and A.M. Spitzer. 1986. "Building a Bridge: Articulation Programs for Bibliographic Instruction." *College & Research Libraries* 47 (September): 470-474.

Kennedy, D.J., and L.J. Wilson. 1986. "Developing a Partnership in Library Instruction." *College & Research Libraries News* 5 (May): 321-322.

Kerns, B.F. 1991. "Providing the Library Advantage to Disadvantaged Students." *Arkansas Libraries*

Kinney, E.M. 1988. "Thirty Minutes and Counting: a Bibliographic Instruction Program." *Illinois Libraries* 70 (January): 36-37.

Kinsey, S., and S. Honig-Bear. 1994. "Joint-use Libraries: More Bang for Your Bucks." *Wilson Library Bulletin* 69 (November): 37-39.

Kitchens, J.A. 1973a. "Merger Without Jeopardy: an Overview of the Olney Project." Pp. 12-128 in *Conference on Total Community Library Service, Washington, DC Total Community Library Service*, edited by G. Garrison. Chicago, American Library Association.

———. 1973b. "Public Libraries and School Libraries: Is There a Better Way?" *Texas Libraries* 35 (Spring): 17-22.

———. 1980. "Some Libraries Do Everything Well! An Example of School/Public Library Cooperation." *Top of the News* 36 (Summer): 357-362.

Kitchens, J.A., and J. Bodart. 1979. "Community Library Alive and Well in Olney, Texas." *Texas Libraries* 41 (Winter): 162-166.

Koldenius, M., and Nilsan, E. 1992. "Integrated Libraries." *Scandinavian Public Library Quarterly* 25 (1): 7-11.

Kreigh, H.L. 1980. "Students-Scapegoats of the Public Library?" *Indiana Media Journal* 2 (Spring): 25-28.

Kuhn, L. 1977. "On Public Library/School Library Cooperation." *Ohio Library Association Bulletin* 47 (October): 21-24.

LaBrake, L. 1991. "Planning a Joint-Use Library." Pp. 147-154 in *The Fifth Off Campus Library Services Conference Proceedings*, edited by C.J. Jacob. Albuquerque, NM. October 30-November 1 1991. Mt. Pleasant, MI: Central Michigan University.

Lagerbloom, M.K. 1980. "Yesterday's Children are Beautiful: Merrill Brings Students and Senior Citizens Together." *Wisconsin Library Bulletin* 76 (March/April): 76-77.

Lambert, B. 1985. "Right from the Start." *Illinois Libraries* 67 (January): 31-32.

Landwirth, T.K., M.L. Wilson, and J. Dorsch. 1988. "Reference Activity and the External User: Confluence of Community Needs at a Medical School Branch

Library [University of Illinois at Chicago Library of the Health Sciences; Paper Presented at the 87th Annual Meeting of the Medical Library Association, Portland, Oregon, 1987]." *Bulletin of the Medical Library Association* 76 (July): 205-212.

LaRue, J., and S. LaRue. 1991. "Is Anybody Home? Home Schooling and the Library." *Wilson Library Bulletin* 66 (September): 32-37.

Latham, S. 1991. *Library Services for Off-Campus and Distance Education: an Annotated Bibliography.* Canadian Library Association; American Library Association.

Laughlin, M. 1990. "The Media Specialist and Public Librarian as Partners." Pp. 97-101 in *Public Relations for School Library Media Centers.* Littleton, CO: Libraries Unlimited.

"Learning Center Opens in P.L. Branch: St. Louis Public Library and Local Community College Share Resources." 1994. *Library Journal* 119 (May 1): 20.

Leavy, M.D., and E.E. Moore. 1988. "I & R in an Academic Library." *The Reference Librarian* 21: 109-119.

LeClercq, A. 1986. "The Academic Library/High School Library Connection: Needs Assessment and Proposed Model." *The Journal of Academic Librarianship* 12 (2): 12-18.

_____. 1989. "High School Library Access to an Academic Library." Pp. 11-17 in Library Instruction Conference [16th: 1988: Bowling Green State University] *Reaching and Teaching Diverse Library User Groups.* Ann Arbor, MI: Pierian Press.

Legg, J. 1970. "Coordinating Library Services within a Community." *American Libraries* 1 (May): 457.

Leitle, K. 1985. "The Northside Junior High Review; a Public Library and the Public Schools Working Together." *Show-Me Libraries* 36 (August): 32-34.

Lemerande, C.M., and A.A. Sturzl. 1983. "Combined School/Public Library in Laona, Wisconsin." *Wisconsin Library Bulletin* 78 (Fall): 94-96.

"Lenape Regional High School District Media Centers Participate in Federally Funded Library Project." 1977. *School Media Quarterly* 5 (Summer): 243-244.

Lesh, N., and R.H. Geeman. 1987. "Research for a Strong Tomorrow." *The Sourdough* 24 (Winter): 10.

"Librarian Tells of the Tyndale Turmoil." 1976. *Library Association Record* 78 (February): 56.

"Library Co-op Splits in Pennsylvania: Colleges Part Company, Dissolving Joint Library After 20 Years." 1993. *Library Journal* 118 (October 15): 14.

"Library Keeps Tabs on Old Clippings." 1972. *Kansas Library Bulletin* 41 (1): 6.

Lindauer, D. 1975. "Regional Coordination: A Modest Proposal." *The Bookmark* 34 (May): 135-137.

"Linking Into the Future." 1989. *The School Librarian's Workshop* 9 (June): 2-3.

Little, P.L., and J.K. Gilliland. 1977a. "OASES [Open Access Satellite Education Services]: Public Library/Community College Partnerships." *Community and Junior College Journal* 48 (October): 14-15.

_____. 1977b. "Public Library and a Community College Start Open Access Satellite Education Services, Known as...OASES in Oklahoma." *Library Journal* 102 (July): 1458-1461.

"Long Overdue Partnership." 1973. *American Libraries* 4 (May): 266-267.

Louie, R.L. 1985. "Los Angeles Chinatown Branch: a Working Model for a Library/ School Joint Venture." *Illinois Libraries* 67 (January): 25-30.

MacWilliams, P. 1976. "Library Shelters Youth Center: Highland Falls Alternative Learning Center Changes Kids." *Wisconsin Library Bulletin* 72 (May): 111-112.

Madden, S.B. 1991. "Learning at Home: Public Library Service to Homeschoolers." *School Library Journal* 37 (July): 23-25.

Mahony, A.P. 1991. "Westchester Librarians Study Multiculturalism." *School Library Journal* 37 (November): 14.

Major, J.A. 1990. "Library Service for Small Business: an Exploratory Study." *RQ* 30 (Fall): 27-31.

Mallette, P. 1981. "Special Education Classes in the Public Library." *Emergency Librarian* 9 (November/ December): 6-8.

Maminski, D. 1993. "Up Close and Personal: Middle School Students Read and Meet Young Adult Authors." *Wilson Library Bulletin* 68 (1): 35-37.

_____. 1982. "Youth Helping Youth." *Voice of Youth Advocates* 5 (December): 18-20.

_____. 1990. "Youth Helping Youth." In *YOYA Reader*, edited by D.J. Broderick. Metuchen, NJ: Scarecrow Press.

Mancall, J., and M.C. Drott. 1983. *Measuring Student Information Use: A Guide for School Library Media Specialists.* Littleton, CO: Libraries Unlimited.

Mansbridge, J. 1991. "Kangaroo and Beaver: Similar Physical Settings but Different Results." *PNLA Quarterly* 55 (Winter): 13-14.

Marchand, J., and C.E. DeVinney. 1972. "School-Public Library Cooperation in Macomb County." *Michigan Librarian* 38 (Autumn): 6-7.

Markey, P.S., and M.K. Moore. 1983. "Year-Round Reading Program: an Experimental Alternative." *Top of the News* 39 (Winter): 155-161.

Marshall, J.G. 1982. "McMaster University Health Sciences Library and Hamilton Public Library, Hamilton, Ohio." Pp. 154-171 in *Developing Consumer Health Information Services.* NY: Bowker.

Martins, D. "U. Document Supply for Industrial Users." 1988. *IATUL Quarterly* 2 (September): 171-179.

Marvin, S. 1988. "ExeLS: Executive Library Services." *The Reference Librarian* 22: 145-160.

Mashinic, A. 1984. "Acres Homes Branch Tutorial Center." *Texas Libraries* 45 (Summer): 70-71.

Maxwell, C.Y., and E.C. Reinheimer. 1988. "Librarian and Information Broker: the Challenge of Cooperation." *The Reference Librarian* 22: 105-112.

McAndrew, G.L. 1989. "Improving Urban Schools: How to Make Winners Out of Losers." Pp. 127-135 in *Urban Library Management Institute [1988: University of Wisconsin-Milwaukee]. Trends in Urban Library Management,* edited by M. Aman and D.J. Sager. Metuchen, NJ: Scarecrow Press.

McCombs, J. 1991. "Deta's Recitation Contest." *The Sourdough* 28 (Summer): 6-7.

McCormick, E. 1986. "'Seussamania' in Geisel's Hometown: Springfield (Mass.) Library Branches and Schools Pair Off to Celebrate." *American Libraries* 17 (June): 485.

McDonald, E. 1985. "University/Industry Partnerships: Premonitions for Academic Libraries." *The Journal of Academic Librarianship* 11 (3): 82-87.

McFadden, W.C. 1977. "Cooperation Between Public Libraries and Schools." *Wyoming Library Roundup* 33 (September): 22-23.

McNamara, J.R., and D.E. Williams. 1992. "High School Students and Libraries in Public Universities." Pp. 55-65 in *Academic Libraries in Urban and Metropolitan Areas*, edited by G.B. McCabe. Westport, CT: Greenwood Press.

McShane, V. 1975. "Best of Two Worlds: A Public Librarian Working with Schools." *California School Libraries* 46 (Spring): 6-10.

McWilliam, D., and J.B. Fatzer. 1988. "The Problem Assignment and the Public Library." *RQ* 27 (Spring): 333-336.

Messineo, N. 1991. "'ASSC' and You Shall Receive: Community Partnerships in California." *School Library Journal* 37 (July): 19-22.

Middleton, G., and J.N. Scott. 1976. "Wendell Smith Library: A Cooperative Venture in Chicago." *Illinois Libraries* 58 (September): 553-554.

Miller, D.W. 1976. "Coquitlam: An Excerpt from the Report, 'A Public Library Service for Coquitlam'." *BCLA Reporter* 20 (June): 3-8.

Miller, J.H. 1991. "New Library Serves School and Community." *New Jersey Libraries* 24 (Fall): 26-29.

Miller, R.E., and R.E. Russell. 1987. "High School Students and the College Library: Problems and Possibilities." *Southeastern Librarian* 37 (Summer): 36-38.

Miller, V. 1971. "Attorney General's Opinion on School District Petition to be Excluded From the Regional System." *Kansas Library Bulletin* 40 (3): 10.

"Minneapolis Brings COM to Area High Schools." 1980. *Library Journal* 105 (November 15): 2370.

"Minnesota County Library to Back up Grad Center." 1976. *Library Journal* 101 (June 15): 1366.

Minnesota Department of Education. 1966. *Policy Statement Regarding Public Library Services in School Buildings*. Hennepin, MN: Department of Education.

Minnesota Educational Media Organization and Minnesota Library Association. 1980. "Public Library/School Media Center Relationships." *Minnesota Libraries* (Summer): 594-598.

"Missouri Public Libraries Can Charge Schools AV Fees." 1974. *Library Journal* 99 (October 1): 2427.

Mitson, R. 1982. "After the Dream? A Look At How One 'Ideal'."*Audiovisual Librarian* 8 (Spring): 72-74.

Mittelman, M. 1975. "New York Public Library Services to the CUNY Community." *LACUNY Journal* 4 (Fall): 33-36.

Moon, M. 1970. "Which Way Cooperation!" *Illinois Libraries* 52 (April): 331-334.

Morley, D.G., and T. Wooten. 1993. "Public Libraries and the Home-schooling Program." *North Carolina Libraries* 51 (Spring): 38-42.

Morris, R. 1973. "Keeping the Independent Student Independent." *American Libraries* 4 (July): 421-423.

Mynatt, S. 1981. "School and Public Libraries: Combination or Cooperation?" *Tennessee Librarian* 33 (Winter): 23-26.

National Commission on Excellence in Education. 1983. *A Nation at Risk.* Washington, DC: US Department of Education.

————. 1984. *Alliance for Excellence.* Washington, DC: US Department of Education.

National Commission on Library and Information Science. 1980. *Final Report of the 1978 White House Conference on libraries and Information Services.* Washington, DC: National Commission on Library and Information Science.

————. 1975. *Toward a National Program for Library and Information Services: Goals for Action.* Washington, DC: US Government Printing Office.

National Education Association. 1899. *Report of the Committee on the Relations of Public Libraries to Public Schools.* Washington, DC: National Education Association.

"N.C. Homework Hotline Attracts ≡ in its Third Year." 1982. *Library Journal* 107 (December 15): 2300.

Nelson, K.R. 1972. "From the State Librarian: Community Libraries." *Vermont Libraries* 2 (October): 170-171.

Nelson, O., and A. Wagnitz. 1980. "Cooperation Games: It's Your Move." *Ohio Media Spectrum* 32 (3): 66-69.

Nettlefold, M.B. 1976. "No Time for Artificial Divisions." *Library Association Record* 78 (April): 166.

"New Consortium to Run Independent Study Project." 1976. *Library Journal* 101 (May 1): 1069.

"New Co-op Library to Serve 21 Conn. Communities." 1973. *Library Journal* 98 (May 15): 1626.

"New York Public Library Receives Grant for Library School Initiative." 1992. *Public Libraries* 31 (March/April): 71.

Nicholson, H. 1992. "Uncomfortable Bedfellows: Enterprise and Academic Libraries." *Journal of Library and Information Science* 24 (March): 9-13.

Nickel, M.L. 1970. "The Seven C's of School-Public Library Relations." *Illinois Libraries* 52 (April): 325-326.

Nimon, M. 1978. "Adelakle, South Australia: a Mother's Reading-Discussion Group." *School Media Quarterly* 7 (Fall): 70-71.

Nofsinger, M.M. 1989. "Library Use Skills for College-Bound High School Students: A Survey." *Reference Librarian* 24: 35-56.

Nopenger, M.M. 1989. "Library Use Skills for College-Bound High School Students: A Survey." *The Reference Librarian* 24: 35-56.

"North Dakota Standards for Community Library Service From School Media Centers." 1972. *North Dakota Library Notes* 3 (August): 123-128.

————. 1973. *North Dakota Library Notes* 4 (August): 33-38.

————. 1976. *North Dakota Library Notes* 7 (February): 87-92.

"Northwestern Organizes NQUERY." 1988. *Wilson Library Bulletin* 62 (June): 6-7.

"North Point (MD) Library Stores College Collection; Joliet Junior College (IL) Opens Library to the Public." 1972. *Library Journal* 97 (April 1): 1231.

Nosek, J.T., and G. Yaverbaum. 1991. "Overcoming Obstacles to University and Industry Synergy in Information System Education: Lessons from Action Research." *Education for Information* 9 (March): 3-19.

Nylin, D.W. 1970. "Extinction, Peaceful coexistence, or Purposeful Cooperation." *Illinois Libraries* 52 (April): 358-362.

O'Connell, M.J., and K.A. Thurner. 1982. "Cooperation for Improving Services." *Media Spectrum* 9 (3): 14.

"Ohio Public Library to Share Resources with Franklin University." 1989. *Library Journal* 114 (March 1): 15.

O'Keefe, R.L. 1975. "University Library Services to the Industrial and Research Communities." Pp. 46-57 in *Library Lectures, Numbers Twenty-One through Twenty-Eight.* Baton Rouge, LA: Louisiana State University Library.

Oliver, E. 1979. "Purcell's New Experiment." *Oklahoma Librarian* 29 (April): 13-15.

Olivera, A. 1974. "Heresies: Close All Public Libraries and Devote the Time and Energy Spent in Running Them To School and University Libraries." *Australian Library Journal* 23 (December): 414.

Olson, R. 1994a. "LAPL May Host High-Tech High School." *American Libraries* 25 (5) (May): 386.

Olson, R. 1994b. "Young Adults Read Year 'Round in Reading." *American Libraries* 25 (6): 579-580.

Olsson, L.T. 1991. "The School-Library Connection in Gotland." *Scandinavian Public Library Quarterly* 24 (2): 5-8.

O'Keefe, R.L. 1975. "University Library Services to the Industrial and Research Communities." Pp. 46-57 in Louisiana State University, Baton Rouge. Graduate School of Library Science. *Library Lectures, Numbers Twenty-One Through Twenty-Eight.* Baton Rouge, LA: Louisiana State University Library.

O'Neal, K. 1976. "The School/Public Library Summer Reading Program Successful." *School Media Quarterly* (Winter):

Ontario Ministry of Colleges and Universities. Provincial Library Service. "Brief to the Select Committee on the Utilization of Educational Facilities." 1973. *Ontario Library Review* 57 (March): 15-17.

Opatow, D. 1976. "Implementation of a School/Public Library Cooperative." *Pennsylvania Library Association Bulletin* 31 (March): 33-34.

"Open University Course Held at Maryland Library." 1973. *Library Journal* 98 (January 15): 114.

Pammett, M. 1973. "Competition or Co-operation?" *Moccasin Telegraph* 16 (November): 20.

"Pa. Public Library Director also School Library Head." 1973. *Library Journal* 98 (February 15): 590.

Paramore, P.J. 1992. *Developing a Model Public Library Orientation Program for Senior High School Students.* Thesis (MLS) Texas Women's University.

Paton, W.B. 1971. "Changing Patterns in School and Public Libraries: Address Given to the Fourth National Weekend Course of the School Library Association." *SLA News* 105 (September): 337-344.

Pautz, M.R. 1972. "Library Support for Business and Industry." *Southeastern Librarian* 22 (Spring): 16-21.

Persell, J.H. 1980. "Cobb County—A Study in Synergism." *The Georgia Librarian* 17 (May): 10-11.

Peterson, J. 1973. "Public Library Service to Education in Denmark." *Scandinavian Public Library Quarterly* 6 (2): 34-38.

Petrino, P. 1972. "Pursuit of Self-Realization: Implications for Public Libraries." *Connecticut Libraries* 14 (Fall): 7-11.

Petty, M.C. 1976. "Library Cooperation." *Illinois Libraries* 58 (September): 551-553.

Pettem, D. 1978. "Problems in School and Public Library Resource Sharing." *Canadian Library Journal* 35 (October): 361-363.

"Philadelphia Student Library Project." 1973. *Catholic Library World* 45 (July): 41-42.

Pierce, M.A. 1991. "Out of This World: Science Fiction Booktalks for the Adolescent as Public Library Sponsored Programs in the Schools." *Voice of Youth Advocates* 14 (August): 148-158.

Piersa, B. 1981. "Sharing Facilities in East Hartford." *Connecticut Libraries* (Spring): 25-27.

"Pioneer Urban Program Reports from Marquette." 1973. *Library Journal* 98 (February 1): 377.

Piternick, A.B. 1979. "Problems of Resource Sharing with the Community: A Case Study." *The Journal of Academic Librarianship* 5 (3): 153-158.

Piternick, A.B., and D.N. McInnes. 1975. "Sharing Resources: Outside Use of Academic Libraries in British Columbia." *Canadian Library Journal* 32 (August): 299-304.

Power, C., and L.M. Keenan. 1991. "The New Partnership: the Role of the Public Library in Extended Campus Service Programs." *Library Trends* 39 (Spring): 441-453.

Prince, W.W., and W.N. Nelson. 1985. "Public Access to Academic Libraries." *Tennessee Librarian* 37 (Winter): 25-28.

Process, S. 1983. "Cooperating for Automated Circulation in Spokane County." *Library Journal* 108 (June 15): 1226-1227.

Proseus, L.S. 1989. "Elementary Students, Reading Achievements, and the Public Library." *North Carolina Libraries* 47 (Summer): 111-114.

"Public and School Libraries Merge in Tanana, Alaska." 1973. *Library Journal* 98 (February 1): 375.

"Public Libraries Become University Campus in N.Y." 1976. *American Libraries* 7 (October): 563.

Public Library Association. 1979. *The Public Library Mission Statement*. Chicago: American Library Association.

————. 1964. *Standards for Children's Services in Public Libraries*. Chicago: American Library Association.

Public Library Association. Committee on Standards for Work with Young Adults in Public Libraries. 1960. *Young Adult Services in the Public Library*. Chicago: American Library Association.

"Public Library-Community College Cooperation." 1977. *PLA Newsletter* 16 (Fall): 17.

"Public Library Use by Teachers Surveyed." 1977. *Library Journal* 102 (June 1): 1234.

"Public/School Libraries Increasing in Colorado." 1985. *Library Journal* 110 (September 1): 122.

Pukk, E. 1991. "Libraries Around Australia: The Mannum High School Community Library." *Australian Library Journal* 40 (August): 251-255.

"Pupil I.D. Form." 1990. *Unabashed Librarian* 76: 1.

Quinn, K.C. 1979. "Public and School Libraries-a Case Against Combination." *Public Libraries* 18 (Winter): 107-108.

Rader, B.A. 1990. "Humanities Programming in Public Libraries: the Connecticut Perspective." *Public Libraries* 29 (November/December): 242-248.

Raedeke, A., and M. Meyers. 1982. "Public Library and a University Team up to Offer a Unique Program." Pp. 19-21 in *Library Resource Sharing*. Minnesota Library Association.

Ralston, Y., and A.L. Oldenburg. 1992. "Joint-Use Library Services at Distant Campuses: Building Cooperation Between a Community College and a University." Pp. 143-156 in *Academic Libraries in Urban and Metropolitan Areas*, edited by G.B. McCabe. Westport, CT: Greenwood Press.

Ramachandran, R. 1974. "Community/School Library Concept in Hawaii." *Unesco Bulletin for Libraries* 28 (July): 200-205.

Ray, S.G.B. 1991. "Initiatives." *The School Librarian* 39 (November): 137.

Razzano, B.W. 1983. "Public Library/School Library Cooperation: Applications for Reference Service." *Reference Librarian* 7/8 (Spring/Summer): 123-128.

Reading, B. 1992. "School/Public Library Cooperation." *Show-Me Libraries* 44 (1): 45-47.

"Reading Emphasis Year: A Decatur, Ill. Project." 1976. *School Library Journal* 23 (November): 14.

Reckenback, F.W. 1977. "Visits with Principals and Teachers Brings Results." *Ohio Library Association Bulletin* 47 (October): 30-33.

Reid, R. H. 1976. "Place of the University Library in the State." *Arkansas Libraries* 33 (4): 10-13.

Reilley, G.K. 1978. "Development of a Circulation Policy for Public Patrons of an Academic Library." *Southeastern Librarian* 28 (Summer): 88-91.

Richards, B.G., and R.P. Widdicombe. 1985. "Fee-Based Information Services to Industry." Pp. 59-64 in International Association of the Technological University Libraries. Meeting (11th: 1985: Oxford, England). *The Future of Information Resources for Science and Technology and the Role of Libraries*. Oxford, England: IATUL.

Richards, D. 1991. "Starting a Fee-Based Service in a Rural Area." *The Bottom Line* 5 (Spring): 14-17.

Rinzenberg, M., and R. Currie. 1988. "Read It! Literacy: Child/Parent/School/Library." *Illinois Libraries* 70 (January): 34-35.

Ristau, H. 1990. "Suggestions for Public Library and School Library Cooperation." *Illinois Libraries* 72 (February): 185-187.

Robbers, S. 1991. "Libraries and Homeschoolers." *Unabashed Librarian* 80:18.

"Rocky Road to School-Public Cooperation." 1973. *American Libraries* 4 (November): 594.

Roeder, J. 1983. "School/Public Library Cooperation: a View From the 'School Yard'." *Illinois Libraries* 65 (September): 452-454.

Rogers, M. 1992. "Library Searching Powers Attract Private Firms: Librarians Become Business Community Resource." *Library Journal* 117 (April 1): 36.

Rollock, B.T. 1978. "Public Library-School Cooperation: the New York Public Library's George Bruce Branch Media Center." *The Bookmark* 37 (Summer): 131-135.

Rovenger, J. 1986. "School/Library Cooperation: West Chester Finds a Way." *School Library Journal* 32 (May): 33-36.

Rowbottom, T. 1982. "Knitting Up in Knowsley." *Library Association Record* 84 (April): 140.

Royal, S.W. 1986. "The Public/School Library Connection." *Arkansas Libraries* 43 (September): 27-30.

Russell, R.E. 1979. "Services for Whom: a Search for Identity." *Tennessee Librarian* 31 (Fall): 36-40.

————. 1992. "External User Access to Academic Libraries in Urban/ Metropolitan Areas." Pp. 27-32 in *Academic Libraries in Urban and Metropolitan Areas*, edited by G.B. McCabe. Westport, CT: Greenwood Press.

Sager, D.J. 1992. "Professional Views: the Best Intentions; the Role of the Public Library in the Improvement of Public Education." *Public Libraries* 31 (January/February): 11-17.

Savage, D.A. 1988. "Town and Gown Re-examined: the Role of the Small University Library in the Community." *Canadian Library Journal* 45 (October): 291-295.

Sayre, S. 1976. "Shoshone-Bannock Library and Media Center." *Idaho Librarian* 28 (April): 64-65.

Scarpellino, A. 1979. "School-Public Library Cooperation: Some Practical Approaches." *Unabashed Librarian* 32: 29-30.

"School and Public Libraries Cooperate in David City Plan." 1979. *Nebraska Library Association Quarterly* 10 (Winter): 17.

"School and Public Libraries Cooperate in a Grant to Provide Computer-Assisted Instruction." 1982. *School Library Media Quarterly* 10 (Summer): 300-301.

"School/Library Book Exchange Brings Booming Circulation." 1980. *Library Journal* 105 (January 15): 144-145.

"School/Library Co-op Get Focus in Oklahoma." 1979a. *Library Journal* 104 (October 1): 2032.

"School/Library Co-op Growing in Rhode Island." 1980. *Library Journal* 105 (November 1): 2257-2258.

"School/Library Co-op Works in Massachusetts." 1977. *Library Journal* 102 (June 15): 1335-1336.

"School Library Cooperation: Broader Involvement Urged." 1974a. *Library Journal* 99 (November 15): 2926.

"School-Library Cooperation Can Misfire, Says Librarian." 1973. *Library Journal* 98 (May 15): 1626.

"School Library Cooperation in Colorado and Alabama." 1975a. *Library Journal* 100 (December 15): 2285.

"School Library Cooperation in Minnesota and Pennsylvania." 1975b. *Library Journal* 100 (October 15): 1881-1882.

"School/Library Cooperation in Rural America Eyed." 1979b. *Library Journal* 104 (December 15): 2611-2612.

"School Library Cooperation: New Buildings, Projects." 1978. *Library Journal* 103 (February 15): 422.

"School-Library Cooperation: New Mergers Reported." 1974b. *Library Journal* 99 (July): 1753.

"School-Public Co-Op: Signs of Progress." 1974. *Library Journal* 99 (January 15): 90.

"School/Public Library Co-op Spearheaded in N.Y." 1979. *Library Journal* 104 (October 1): 2032.

"School/Public Library Cooperation." 1981. *Connecticut Libraries* 23 (Spring): 25-28.

Schwartz, S. 1976. "Information Services to Industry: the Role of the Technological University Library." *Journal of Documentation* 32 (March): 1-16.

"Seattle Juvenile Center: School/Public Library." 1972. *Library Journal* 97 (May 15): 1857.

Shannon, D.M. 1991. "Cooperation Between School and Public Libraries: A Study of one North Carolina County." *North Carolina Libraries* 49 (Summer): 67-70.

Shapiro, L. 1975. *Serving Youth.* New York: Bowker.

Shaw, M. 1990. "Top Valley: a Joint-Use Success Story." *The School Librarian* 38 (May): 51-52

Sheen, B.D. 1974. "Community-School Libraries." *Australian Library Journal* 23 (October): 311-313.

"Sheldon Jackson College-Sitka Community College Advisory Consortium Committee to Bring Increased Educational Services to the Community of Sitka." 1972. *PNLA Quarterly* 36 (April): 34.

Shirk, J. 1978. "Public Librarians Look at Community Education: What is the Role?" *School Media Quarterly* 7 (Fall): 19-24.

Shockey, A. 1978. "School and Public Library Cooperation: a Call to Action." *Catholic Library World* 49 (May): 438-440.

Shoup, J., and S. Tadin. 1979. "Bridging the Gap." *School Library Journal* 26 (November): 53.

Shuman, B.A. 1983. "College/Library Cooperation: The Queensboro Hill Project." Pp. 151-160 in *New Directions for Young Adult Services.* New York: Bowker.

Sigala, S.C. 1990. "Everybody Wins: Public Programs in the Museum Library." *Art Documentation* 9 (Winter): 187-189.

Simon, M.J. 1992. "Forging New Organizational and Communications Structures: the College Library-School Library Partnership." *Library Administration and Management* 6 (Winter): 36-40.

Simons, L.K., and E.D. Garten. 1992. "Urban University Library Services to Business and Industry." Pp. 45-53 in *Academic Libraries in Urban and Metropolitan Areas,* edited by G.B. McCabe. Westport, CT: Greenwood Press.

Simpson, D.J. 1973. "Open University and United Kingdom Public Libraries." *Library Association Record* 75 (September): 173-175.

Sliney, M. 1988. "One-Man Band in Education: Some Management Considerations." *Library Association Record* 90 (April): 223-224.

Smith, D.F., L. Fowler, and A. Teasley. 1988. "Homework Help: Problem-Solving Through Communications." *North Carolina Libraries* 46 (Spring): 33-37.

Solberg, K.J. 1974. "Boxes of Books or Open Doors: Intertype Library Cooperation Grows in La Crosse." *Wisconsin Library Bulletin* 70 (January): 30.

Soltow, M.J. 1976. "University Industrial Relations Libraries: an Overview." *Special Libraries* 67 (April): 195-201.

Sones, C.M. 1981. "School-Public Library Co-operation Adds Strengths and Resources." *Canadian Library Journal* 38 (April): 85-90.

Sorensen, B. 1987. "How Public and School Libraries Collaborate in Denmark." *Scandinavian Public Library Quarterly* 20 (2): 19-21.

Soules, A. 1979. "Off-Campus Library Services: Those In-between Years." Pp. 568-576 in *New Horizons for Academic Libraries*, edited by R.D. Stueart and R.D. Johnson. London: Saur Verlag.

Spinella, G.M., and J.A. Hicks. 1988. "Cooperative Bibliographic Instruction: a Program Between Wilmot Junior High School and Deerfield Public Library." *Illinois Librarian* 70 (December): 656-659.

Stenstrom, R.H. 1978. *Cooperation Between Types of Libraries: 1940-1968.* Metuchen, NJ: Scarecrow Press.

Sterling, B.J. 1980. "Public Librarian in the Vocational High Schools." *The Bookmark* 38 (Summer): 428-430.

Stephens, A.K., and K.D. Wright. 1990. "Planning Multitype Services in a Rural Environment." *Rural Libraries* 10 (2): 25-44.

Stone, M. 1980. "School Libraries and Networking." *Show-Me Libraries* 32 (December): 23-24.

"Students Start Library in California Work Program." 1974. *Library Journal* 99 (February 15): 442.

Stump, F. 1982. "School and Public Libraries Co-Operated to Help Non Readers." *West Virginia Libraries* 35 (Spring): 33-34.

"Suffolk County, N.Y., Surveys School-Public Library Co-Op." *Library Journal* 98 (April 15): 1333.

Sullivan, P. 1974. "Science in a Shoebox." *Unabashed Librarian* 12 (Summer): 10.

_____. 1984. "Libraries and the Learning Society: Relationships and Linkages Among Libraries." Pp. 110-145 in *Libraries and the Learning Society.* American Library Association.

_____. 1970. "Problem: To Find the Problem." *Illinois Libraries* 52 (April): 327-330.

_____. 1979. "Library Cooperation to Serve Youth." Pp. 113-118 in *Libraries and Young Adults*. Littleton, CO: Libraries Unlimited.

Sundquist, R. 1976. "Information Service to Finnish Industry and to Helsinki University of Technology." Pp. 35-41 in International Association of Technological University Libraries Conference, 1975, Zurich. *IATUL: University Libraries as Information Centers.* Loughborough, England: University of Technology Library.

Sunseri, L. 1994. "School Media Matters: The Best of Both Worlds." *Wilson Library Bulletin* 68 (June): 72-74.

Sutton, R. 1987. "'My Teacher Says'." *Unabashed Librarian* 65: 9-10.

Swarm, C. 1975. "Role of School Libraries in a Continuing Education Program." *Adult Leadership* 24 (November): 105-106.

Tameem, J.A. 1988. "School/Public Library Cooperation." *Aslib Proceedings* 40 (March): 87-99.

Taylor, J. 1989. "School Library Media Specialists and Public Librarians: Together at Last, Maybe." *Nebraska Library Association Quarterly* 20 (Winter): 18-19.

Teahan, S., and M. Huska. 1990. "Personal Views of Joint School/Public Library Operations." *Emergency Librarian* 18 (November/December):14-16.

Telford, G. 1974. "School-Library Co-Operation." *BCLA Report* 18 (June): 10-12.

Tell, B.V. 1972. "Selective Dissemination of Information (SDI) in a Technological University Library." *Unesco Bulletin for Libraries* 26 (November): 301-306.

Terland, I., and H. Terland. 1979. "Friends, Foes, or Partners: a City Library Watches an Academic Library Grow." *Scandinavian Public Library Quarterly* 12 (2): 73-79.

Tevis, R. 1979. "Library Cooperation in Granite City: the Public Library and the High Schools, 1975-1977." *Illinois Libraries* 61 (January): 6-9.

"Texas School/Library Merger: a Progress Report." 1974. *Library Journal* 99 (May 1): 1261-1262.

"Thirteen-Plus Programs." 1973. Pp. 94-131 in *Getting People to Read*, edited by C.B. Smith and L.C. Fay. NY: Dell.

Thompson, R.K.H., and G.T. Rhodes. 1986. "Recruitment: a Role for the Academic Library? Creating a Good Impression for Visiting High School Students." *College & Research Libraries News* 9 (October): 575-577.

Tilles, K. 1992. "Cooperation: Private Academic and High School Libraries." Pp. 67-72 in *Academic Libraries in Urban and Metropolitan Areas*, edited by G.B. McCabe. Westport, CT: Greenwood Press.

"Timberland Regional in Washington Lauded for School Cooperation." 1979. *Library Journal* 104 (June 15): 1301.

Tolliver, D.L. 1976. "Citizens May Use Any Tax-Supported Library?" *Wisconsin Library Bulletin* 72 (November): 253-254.

"Toronto Libraries Cooperate: Joint Services Studied." 1972. *Library Journal* 97 (January 15): 238.

Toyne, D. 1987. "The Community Role of Academic Art Libraries." *Art Libraries Journal* 12 (3): 35-38.

Trait, H. 1977. "School Community libraries in Australia." *New Zealand Libraries* 40 (October): 56-61.

Treweek, B.J. 1977. "Reaction to Access Project." *Wisconsin Library Bulletin* 73 (March): 93.

Tuccillo, D. 1986. "First Step on the Bridge: Preparing a YA Spring Booktalking Program for 6th Graders." *Emergency Librarian* 14 (November/December): 9-10.

"Two Ohio Systems Share One Branch." 1994. *Library Journal* 119 (October 15): 15.

Tyson, C. 1989. "Coalition-Building: Maybe Tomorrow? Maybe Today!" Pp. 41-53 in *Managers and Missionaries*. Urbana-Champaign, IL: University of Illinois. Graduate School of Library and Information Science.

"UC-Santa Cruz Committed to Community Service." 1985. *Library Journal* 110 (July): 14.

Unger, C.P. 1975. *School-Housed Public Library, Revisited*. Thesis (MA) University of Chicago.

"Unique Story Hour at Three Lakes." 1977. *Wisconsin Library Bulletin* 73 (November): 272-273.

"University Library and Public Library Linked." 1979. *College & Research Libraries News* 6 (June): 195.

"University of Tennessee Library at Knoxville is Offering Extended Services to Off Campus Patrons." 1972. *Tennessee Librarian* 24 (Winter): 34.

"Utah Broadens School Service: Staff Sharing in Illinois." 1976. *Library Journal* 101 (May 15): 1173.

"Va. School and Library Merger Challenged in Court Suit." 1973. *Library Journal* 98 (July): 2031.

Van Orsdel, D.E. 1975. "Cooperation With Results: Ramsey County Libraries/ Media Centers Serve All." *Wisconsin Library Bulletin* 71 (May): 113-114.

Van Puleo, N. 1989. "School/College Cooperation: Building BI Bridges in Ohio." Pp. 29-33 in *Library Instruction Conference [16th: 1988: Bowling Green State University] Reaching and Teaching Diverse Library User Groups*. Ann Arbor, MI: Pierian Press.

Varley, R.D. 1973. "Sweetwater County National Library Week." *Wyoming Library Roundup* 28 (June): 13-14.

Venett, A.J. 1981. "Technology Transfer for Industry and Business Through the University Library." *Special Libraries* 72 (January): 44-50.

Venkateswarlu, T. 1980. "Usage of University Libraries by Non-Academic Community in Canada and the United States of America." *Herald of Library Science* 19 (January-April): 3-7.

Vernerder, G. 1988. "Publication of a Literary Magazine: A Cooperative Project Involving the Public Library and Local Schools." *Illinois Libraries* 70 (January): 68-73.

Vincent, I. 1983. "Nice But Peripheral; Some Australian Teacher Librarians' Attitudes to Cooperation Between School and Public Libraries." *Public Library Quarterly* 4 (Summer): 39-53.

Vonko, L. 1971. "Metropolitan Library Reaches Out." *Illinois Libraries* 53 (September): 462-466.

Vulturo, R. 1985. "Kansas City Public Library's Branch Study." *Show-Me Libraries* 36 (April): 5-12.

Wallace, J. 1983. "Park Mains: An Experiment in Joint-Usage." *SLA News* 174 (March/April): 5-6.

Wallace, M.G. 1990. "Viewing Problems as Challenges." *Voice of Youth Advocates* 13 (August): 147-148.

"Waniassa College/Community Center, Canberra." 1977. *Australian Library Journal* 26 (May 20): 127-129.

Warncke, R.E. 1973. "Total Community Library Service: the Impossible Dream?" *Utah Libraries* 16 (Spring): 12-18.

Waters, R.L., and A. Mashinic. 1983. "Buildings [Combined Services in a Community Education Center]." *Texas Library Journal* 59 (Fall): 80-81.

Webber, S.A.E. 1989. "Priced Business Information Services From the Public Sector: Will They Succeed?." *IFLA Journal* 16 (2): 220-230.

Weech, T.L. 1979. "School and Public Library Cooperation-What We Would Like To Do." *Public Libraries* 18 (Summer): 33-34.

Weenstein, F.R., and W.L. Thwing. 1989. "Components of Cooperation: Schools and Public Libraries Link for Enhanced Services and Information Access for Youth." *Indiana Libraries* 8 (2): 90-95.

Weir, D.J. 1975. "Counterpoint: Should School and Public Libraries be Combined?" *Connecticut Libraries* 17 (1): 13-14.

Weiss, K. 1980. "Work Together...Share the Wealth!" *Illinois Libraries* 62 (December): 914-916.

Welborn, L. 1992. "The Cooperative Spirit: A Challenge." *Colorado Libraries* 18 (June): 47-48.

Wheeler, R. 1985. "Information Dissemination Service: Service for the Community From an Academic Health Sciences Library." *The Bookmark* 44 (Fall): 27-32.

"Where Will All the Children Go?" 1971. *American Libraries* 2 (January): 56-61; 2(June): 601-603.

White, R.M. 1963. *The School-Housed Library: A Survey.* Public Library Reporter No. 11. Chicago: American Library Association.

Whitelock, A.T. 1975. "Them and Us." *Wyoming Library Roundup* 30 (December): 6.

Whitney, G., and D. Burgess. 1974. "Nix on a Mix: Problems of a School/Public Library." *Virginia Librarian* 20 (October): 14-15.

Will, M.C. 1970. "Chicago's Children and the Chicago Public Library." *Illinois Libraries* 52(April): 348-350.

Williams, M. 1970. "The Challenges of Tomorrow." *Illinois Libraries* 52 (April): 335-338.

Williams, W.H. 1975. "County and School Libraries Have an Obligation to Cooperate: An Editorial." *Idaho Librarian* 27 (April): 76.

Willis, D.G. 1980. "Seattle Public Library and Local University Join in $140,000 Community Information Experiment." *American Libraries* 11 (November): 624.

Winslow, T. 1979. "Homework Helpers." *New Jersey Libraries* 12 (September): 16-17.

Wintersteen, T. 1980. "Kuskokwin Consortium Library." *The Sourdough* 17 (September/October): 1.

Wisconsin. Department of Public Instruction. Division for Library Services. 1976. "Public Library and School Library: Organizational Relationships and Interlibrary Cooperation." *Wisconsin Library Bulletin* 72 (May): 131-134.

"Wisconsin Drafts New Statement on School/Library Co-Op." 1976. *Library Journal* 101 (September 1): 1681.

Wiseman, J.A. 1975. "Community Use of University Libraries." *Canadian Library Journal* 32 (October): 373-376.

Wolford, J. 1975. "Cooperation Means Action." *Ohio Library Association Bulletin* 45 (July): 34.

Woolard, W.L. 1978. "Study of the School/Public Library Concept: Summary, Conclusions, and Recommendations." *Illinois Libraries* 60 (March): 281-289.

_____. 1980a. *Combined School/Public Libraries: A Survey with Conclusions and Recommendations*. Metuchen, NJ: Scarecrow Press.

_____. 1980b. "Combined School/Public Libraries in the United States." *Rural Libraries* 1 (Spring): 61-78.

Woolls, E.B. 1974. "Cooperation and Communication, a Study." *Focus on Indiana Libraries* 28 (Spring): 16-17.

_____. 1985/1986. "The Use of School Libraries and Public Libraries and the Relationship to Collection Development." *Collection Management* 7 (Fall/Winter): 173-181.

Wroblewski, M. 1987. "Teacher's Aide Totes." *School Library Journal* 33 (August): 44.

Wyjesinghe, M.N. 1988. "Provision of Library Resources for Open University Students in Sri Lanka." *Library Acquisitions* 12 (3-4): 297-302.

York, M.C. 1992. "Local History in the Classroom: the Public Library/School Partnership." *Wilson Library Bulletin* 67 (October): 44-47.

Young, A. 1972. "Cooperation: Try it, You'll Like It." *Illinois Libraries* 54 (May): 380-383.

Young, D.D. 1979. "School/Public Library Cooperation." *Public Libraries* 18 (Winter): 104-105.

_____. 1985. "Workout Book: Getting in Shape to Cooperate." *Public Libraries* 24 (Summer): 71-73.

Zavortink, D. 1987. "Cooperation= $avings." *The Sourdough* 24 (Winter): 11.

Zipsie, J. 1977. "Happy Bookers: Public Library-School Library Cooperation in Baraboo." *Wisconsin Library Bulletin* 73 (November): 274.

Zizis, C. 1977. "Summertime Sharing: Baraboo Schools Find it Successful and Easy." *Wisconsin Library Bulletin* 73 (March): 62.

ABOUT THE CONTRIBUTORS

Onadell Bly is Assistant Professor of Bibliography and Systems Coordinator for the University Libraries at the University of Akron in Ohio. She holds an MSLS from Kent State University and has worked in academic libraries since 1968, first in reference, then in acquisitions, and finally in library systems beginning in 1983.

Erik de Bruijn is Assistant University Librarian for Human Resources and Staff Development at the University of British Columbia. His responsibilities include human resource management and administration, staff training and development, and labor relations. His current research interests are focused on effective human resource utilization, the impact of technological change on librarians and library support staff, and organizational structure. He has been involved in library human resource management for more than 20 years.

Geri R. Bunker is Head, Library Systems Operations for the University of Washington Libraries in Seattle. She is currently serving as Interim Associate Director of Libraries for Technical Services. She has also recently served as team-teacher for the Intercollegiate Athletics section of the Uwired information technology project. This program piloted a collaborative effort among the computing and communications organization, the libraries, the office of undergraduate dducation and the UW Huskies men's and women's basketball teams. Geri received her Master's degree in Library and Information Studies from the University of California at Berkeley. And worked previously in computing at both Texas A&M University and at UC Berkeley.

Robert R. Burkhardt is the Director of the Library at Athens State College in Athens, Alabama. He received the Ph.D. in Librarianship at the University of Alabama in 1995. He devotes a part of his work week to staffing reference services, using both electronic and traditional resources.

Margaret Friesen is the half-time Staff Training and Development (STD) Coordinator at the University of British Columbia Library. She has planned, programmed, and facilitated STD activities for over 25 years for annual workshops of member libraries of the B.C. Post Secondary Interlibrary Loan Network and for annual conferences of provincial, national, and international professional associations. Her current research interests include adult education, STD planning, job evaluation systems, and project management.

Michael W. Galbraith is Professor of Adult Education in the Department of Educational Leadership at Florida Atlantic University. His areas of scholarship and research include facilitation of adult learning, methods and techniques of adult learning, community-based adult education, critical issues, and mentoring. He is the author of more than 100 books, chapters, and journal articles. In addition, he serves as editor in chief for the national book series titled *Professional Practices in Adult Education and Human Resource Development.*

Linda Marie Golian is the Serials Department Head and Associate Professor at Florida Atlantic University Library in Boca Raton, where she is also a doctoral student in the Educational Leadership Department. Her areas of specialization in library management and education include serials/acquisitions, microforms, service to older patrons, family literacy, and the utilization of volunteers.

Barbara H. Horgan is Associate Vice-President for Information Services at Seattle University where she is responsible for administrative and academic computing, user services, instructional media, networking, and telecommunications as well as support for technology initiatives in the main library and law library. She has over 15 years of experience in management and information technology in health care, state government, and higher education. She began her academic career working for the library at Georgia

Institute of Technology and has also worked for the University of Delaware, Clayton State College in Georgia, and the University of Massachusetts at Dartmouth. She serves on the board of directors of the regional network, NorthWestNet, and CAUSE, the association for managing and using information resources in higher education.

Rashelle S. Karp is a Professor at the Clarion University Department of Library Science. She has worked as a children's librarian, a special librarian, a cataloger, and the Rhode Island state librarian for the blind. Her special interests include collection development, library services to special groups, and special libraries.

Marilyn Lary has been the Director of the Library at North Georgia College since July 1996. She received her MSLS from the University of North Carolina at Chapel Hill and her Ph.D. in Library Science from Florida State. Prior to moving to North Georgia, she held administrative posts at Dalton College, Hillsborough Community College, and the Sumter Campus of the University of South Carolina, and taught library science at Michigan, South Florida, Radford, and East Carolina.

James W. Marcum is Director of Library Services and Senior Lecturer in History at the University of Texas, Permian Basin in Odessa. Formerly library director at Centenary College of Louisiana in Shreveport, he holds an MSLS from the University of North Texas and a Ph.D. from the University of North Carolina . His background includes 15 years in college teaching, primarily at Oklahoma Baptist University, and 10 years in business.

INDEX

J A I P R E S S

Advances in Library Automation and Networking

Edited by **Joe A. Hewitt,** *Associate Provost for University Libraries, University of North Carolina, Chapel Hill*

The purpose of this series is to present a broad spectrum of in-depth, analytical articles on the technical, organizational, and policy aspects of library automation and networking. The series will include detailed examinations and evaluations of particular computer applications in libraries, status surveys, and perspective papers on the implications of various computing and networking technologies for library services and management. The emphasis will be on the information and policy frameworks needed for librarians and administrators to make informed decisions related to developing or acquiring automated systems and network services with special attention to maximizing the positive effects of these technologies on library organization.

Volume 5, 1994, 282 pp. $73.25
ISBN 1-55938-510-3

Edited by **Joe Hewitt**, *Associate Provost for University Libraries, University of North* Carolina, *Chapel Hill* and **Charles Bailey, Jr.** *Assistant Director for Systems, University of Houston.*

CONTENTS: Introduction, *Joe A. Hewitt.* Next-Generation Online Public Access Catalogs: Redefining Territory and Roles, *Carolyn O. Frost.* Full-Text Retrieval: Systems and Files, *Carol Tenopir.* What Can The Internet Do for Libraries, *Mark H. Kibbey and Geri R. Bunker.* Electronic Document Delivery: An Overview with a Report on Experimental Agriculture Projects, *John Ulmschneider and Tracy M. Casorso.* Campus-Wide Information Systems, *Judy Hallman.* Use of a General Concept Paper as RFP for a Library System Procurement, *Mona Couts, Charles Gilreath, Joe Hewitt, and John Ulmschneider.* Research on the Distributed Electronic Library, *Denise A. Troll.* Notes on the Contributors.

Also Available:
Volumes 1-4 (1987-1991) $73.25 each

Advances in Serials Management

Edited by **Marcia Tuttle,** *Head Serials Department, University of North Carolina, Chapel Hill* and **Karen D. Darling,** *Head Serials Department, University of Oregon*

Change has always been characteristic of serials, and now the nature and speed of that change have altered with the development of electronic technology. Inflation, research in preservation methods, and changes in publishers' practices and vendors' reservice all make their mark on serials librarianship. *Advances in Serials Management* will present essays on current issues in the topics, emphasizing response to change and clear communication among those who work with serials as producers, processors and users.

Volume 5, 1995, 138 pp. $73.25
ISBN 1-55938-511-1

CONTENTS: Scholarly Publishing: Today and Tomorrow, *Nancy L. Eaton, Cynthia Dobson, and William K. Black.* A Prehistory of Electronic Journals: The EIES and Blend Projects, *Bernard Naylor and Marilyn Geller.* Serial Linking Notes and MARC 760-787 Fields in OPAC Displays, *Joe Altimus.* Government Publications as Serials: Serials as Government Publications, *Charles A. Seavey.* Integrating Depository Documents Serials into Regular Serials Receiving and Cataloging Routines at the University of Oregon Library, *Karen D. Darling.* Publisher/Vendor Relations, *Mary Devlin and Ronald Akie.* List/Servs Within the Pantheon of Written Materials, *Sharon H. Domier.*

Also Available:
Volumes 1-4 (1986-1991) $73.25 each

JAI PRESS INC.
55 Old Post Road No. 2 - P.O. Box 1678
Greenwich, Connecticut 06836-1678
Tel: (203) 661- 7602   Fax: (203) 661-0792

J
A
I

P
R
E
S
S

J
A
I
P
R
E
S
S

Advances in Collection Development and Resource Management

Edited by **Thomas W. Leonhardt**, *Director*
Bizzell Memorial Library, University of Oklahoma

Volume 1, 1995, 185 pp. $73.25
ISBN 1-55938-213-9 .

CONTENTS: Introduction, *Thomas W. Leonhardt.* Duplication and Overlap Among Library Collections: A Chronological Review of the Literature, *Sue O. Medina.* Weeding Academic Libraries: Theory Into Practice, *Mary Bushing and Elaine Peterson.* Major Microform Sets: The Alabama Experience, *Sue O. Medina, T. Harmon Straiton, and Celia Schmitz.* Statewide Cooperation in Alabama: Improving Academic Library Resources, *Sue O. Medina and William C. Highfill.* Resource Sharing Ideals and Realities: The Case of Australia's Distributed National Collection, *Margaret Henty.* Censorship in Academe: The Necessity for Vigilance, *A. Bruce Strauch.* Computer and Information System Warranties: Cave at Emptor, *J. Michael Alfor and A. Bruce Strauch.* Education for Acquisitions, *William Fisher.*

JAI PRESS INC.

55 Old Post Road No. 2 - P.O. Box 1678
Greenwich, Connecticut 06836-1678
Tel: (203) 661- 7602   Fax: (203) 661-0792